I0883421

DAWN OF DEMOCRACY IN THE EASTERN HIMALAYAN KINGDOMS

This book traces the beginnings of democracy in the three Himalayan kingdoms of Sikkim, Nepal and Bhutan. Charting the mobilizations and political experimentations that took place in the former buffer states under monarchies to establish democratic regimes, this book investigates their varying degrees of success and offers a critical commentary on the consequent socio-political histories of this region.

The volume sheds light on the nuances of their different geopolitical contexts of the three Himalayan states while tracing the social origins of the movements. It also undertakes a close analysis of the political participation and leadership involved to understand their achievements and limitations.

A comprehensive analysis of a hitherto unexplored chapter in South Asian history, it will be of an immense interest to scholars and researchers of international relations, modern history, sociology and social anthropology, politics, South Asian studies, area studies, especially Nepal and Himalayan studies, as well as policy makers and government think tanks.

Awadhesh C. Sinha has been a professor of Social Sciences at Gujarat Vidyapeeth, Ahmedabad, Indian Institutes of Technology, Kanpur and Delhi, India. He has also served as the Dean, School of Social Sciences, North Eastern Hill University, Shillong and as a former ICSSR National Fellow at Nehru Memorial Museum and Library, Teen Murti House, New Delhi.

NEPAL AND HIMALAYAN STUDIES

This series brings the larger Nepal and the Himalayan region to the centre stage of academic analysis and explores critical questions that confront the region, ranging from society, culture and politics to economy and ecology. The books in this series examine key themes concerning religion, ethnicity, language, identity, history, tradition, community, polity and democracy, as well as emerging issues regarding environment and development of this unique region.

NEPALI DIASPORA IN A GLOBALISED ERA
Edited by Tanka B. Subba and A. C. Sinha

THE HIMALAYAS AND INDIA-CHINA RELATIONS
Devendra Nath Panigrahi

DEMOCRATISATION IN THE HIMALAYAS
Interests, Conflicts and Negotiations
Edited by Vibha Arora and N. Jayaram

SEX WORK IN NEPAL
The Making and Unmaking of a Category
Lisa Caviglia

STATE, SOCIETY AND HEALTH IN NEPAL
Madhusudan Subedi

CONFLICT, EDUCATION AND PEOPLE'S WAR IN NEPAL
Sanjeev Rai

GODDESSES OF KATHMANDU VALLEY
Grace, Rage, Knowledge
Second Edition
Arun Gupto

DAWN OF DEMOCRACY IN THE EASTERN HIMALAYAN KINGDOMS
The 20th Century
Awadhesh C. Sinha

For more information about this series, please visit www.routledge.com/Nepal-and-Himalayan-Studies/book-series/NHS

DAWN OF DEMOCRACY IN THE EASTERN HIMALAYAN KINGDOMS

The 20th Century

Awadhesh C. Sinha

Routledge
Taylor & Francis Group
LONDON AND NEW YORK

First published 2019 by Routledge

2 Park Square, Milton Park, Abingdon, Oxon, OX14 4RN
605 Third Avenue, New York, NY 10017

Routledge is an imprint of the Taylor & Francis Group, an informa business

First issued in paperback 2020

British Library Cataloguing-in-Publication Data
A catalogue record for this book is available from the British Library

Library of Congress Cataloging-in-Publication Data
A catalog record has been requested for this book

ISBN: 978-1-138-55040-7 (hbk)
ISBN: 978-0-367-73301-8 (pbk)

Typeset in Sabon
by Apex CoVantage, LLC

TO ARAV

CONTENTS

PREFACE

I have been wondering for some years why the democratic history of Sikkim has not been written as yet and why the history of democratic struggle of India has missed its chapter on Sikkim. I shared my misgivings with octogenarian political animal Chandra Das Rai some years back in one of my visits to Gangtok. And prompt came his response: "Why don't you do it?" Then I chanced to discuss the issue with the indomitable scholar of the region, Dr Kumar Pradhan at Siliguri, and he gave me great encouragement and hints on where to look for the source materials. It made me to think: was I qualified to do the justice to the theme? I expressed my doubts to him and he responded that I could try at least, as nobody had thought of doing so. I made a note of it and began working on the theme on my own. I recall vividly how various activists in the 1960s and early 1970s used to fondly relate their acts in the events of the 1940s, when placid Sikkim was stirred with the speeches of Tashi Tshering, Dimik Singh Lepcha, C. D. Rai and others; how the palace was gheraoed by the SSC volunteers; how its vice president, Namgyal Tshering, snatched the keys of the jeep from the Maharaj Kumar, forcing him to turn back to the palace; and, ultimately, how the short lived 'popular' government was formed and dismissed. There were persons still alive who had participated in the movement, who had listened to the impassioned fiery speeches and who had dreamt of abolition of various types of slave labour imposed by the Kazis and the *thikadars*.

Similarly, much later, I learnt how the Nepali Congress was founded in Calcutta; procured arms from Kashmir, Hyderabad and Burma; and launched its guerrilla war in Nepal Terai in October 1950 and how the Delhi Agreement was hammered out, leading to formation of an interim government between the Ranas and Nepali Congress. Incidentally, my maternal uncle's village in the Champaran district of Bihar was on the gateway to Nepal and they could still relate the events of the armed revolution being fought in the adjoining Terai and Tharuhat. And much later, I read biographies of B. P. Koirala and his elder brother, M. P. Koirala, confirming the details of those eventful moments from 1950 to 1960. I also chanced to meet briefly Panishwar Nath Renu, publicly in-charge of Mukti Vahini, who had given me an idea how the volunteers of Nepali Congress had fought the war of liberation in eastern Terai of Nepal. I revisited the eventful days of 1950s when the Bhutan State Congress came into being, launched its Satyagraha and reached its pinnacle. As I had superannuated from my service in the university, my limited resources were not adequate enough to undertake such an assignment, necessitating visits to archives and knowledgeable respondents. Thus, I waited for the right moment to come my way.

An opportunity arrived when the Indian Council of Social Science Research (ICSSR) in New Delhi awarded me with a National Fellowship in 2012, and I collected a variety of related archival data and visited knowledgeable activists who were witness to those eventful historical landmark dates. The present manuscript is a byproduct of my National Fellowship report on the Federation of the Himalayan Kingdoms and Greater Nepal conducted at Nehru Memorial Museum and Library (NMML), New Delhi, in 2012–14. However, the materials presented here are not parts of the report submitted to the patrons. And in fact, it turned out to be an independent work in its own right.

A number of individuals and institutions came forward to help me in my study in a variety ways; it is impossible to mention them individually and I record my sense of appreciation to all of them. However, it will be unbecoming of me not to mention some of my main benefactors. First all, I value ICSSR New Delhi for the award of the National Fellowship for the study and its generous sponsorship to my previous studies since 1971, which created a lifelong interest in me for things Himalayan. Second, the Nehru Memorial Museum and Library, New Delhi, its director and the staff were gracious enough to provide me with the most congenial locale for the study by affiliating me with NMML. Third, in Sikkim, something of a second home, nonagenarian C. D. Rai has been a living reference point for my work and for that, I shall ever be obliged to him. Furthermore, Nandu Thapa, former member of the Lok Sabha, Prem Das Rai, worthy son of C. D. Rai and member of the Lok Sabha, the scion of the legendary Kashi Raj Pradhan, Advocate Bhaskar Raj Pradhan, my old associate Ash Bahadur Subba, the Vice Chancellor T. B. Subba and his colleagues in Sikkim University provided instant support and academic ambience in

Gangtok for dialogue and discussions, for which I shall ever be grateful to them.

I value and depend on the decades' long academic collaboration and dispassionate criticism of Prof. Tanka Bahadur Subba, anthropologist from North Eastern Hill University, Shillong. Fourth, colleagues such as Prof. B. P. Misra at the Centre for Himalayan Study, professor of Nepali, Ghanshayam Nepal, North Bengal University, Darjeeling, noted historian the late Dr Kumar Pradhan, Siliguri, Dr Rajendra Dhakal and Advocate Anmol Prasad, Kalimpong, were spontaneous source of support to me. Next, from Bhutan, I was fortunate enough to draw on insightful details from late Paras Mani Pradhan and his Phuntshilong-based son, Indra Mani Pradhan, and the author activist, Dr D.N.S. Dhakal. Fifth, in Kathmandu, distinguished scholar and bibliophile late Shri Kamal Mani Dixit of Madan Puraskar fame and his family provided me home, Shamik Mishra, Director, Madan Puraskar Pustakalaya for source material support and Drs Shriram Sharma and Deepak Thapa of Social Science Baha for their hospitality during my field study. Professors Prayagraj Sharma and Lok Raj Baral, columnist C. K. Lal, sociologist Udhab Pyakurel and others were of great assistance in my research in a variety of ways and I do appreciate their invaluable assistance in my work. I have re-read the text of the manuscript with all seriousness once more in the light of the reports of the reviewers given to me by the publisher, and needless to say I have immensely benefited by their valuable comments. However, I hasten to add that I stand responsible for errors, misjudgements and any unintended lapse on my part and offer my instant sincere apology for that. And lastly, nearer home, Krishna, my better half, on whom I unavoidably depend and instantly make all sorts of demands, provided me with most congenial and amiable home to work on vexing issues on hand. And lastly, from my publisher's side, I am extremely fortunate to have an editor in Kate Fornadel, who patiently chiselled ideas even from my uneven expression. I thank her and the team involved in the production of the book.

A. C. Sinha
Vasantkunj, New Delhi
June 28, 2017

1

INTRODUCTION

The eastern Himalayan kingdoms of Nepal, Sikkim and Bhutan were ruled by the feudal oligarchy on the name of religion prior to the advent of the British in India. The three kingdoms unavoidably were linked with the district of Darjeeling of the Bengal Presidency in British India. Darjeeling, thinly inhabited by the Bhutia and Lepcha communities, was originally a Sikkimese territory, which soon became a predominantly Nepali-speaking district. Soon it became known for its thriving tea plantations invariably owned by the British entrepreneurs. It was secured by the British from the Sikkimpati Maharaja in 1835 and developed as a health resort for the convalescent Europeans. The Christian missionaries joined the administration with a number of evangelical, educational and service-oriented institutions within decades. Within a few years, urban centres of Darjeeling, Kalimpong and Kurseong turned out to be known hill resorts in India with a variety of amenities for the tourists. Its significance further increased by the British efforts to open the trans-Himalayan trade to Tibet and then to China by laying down roads and railways.

Impoverished labour, skilled artisans, the ambitious traders and all types of fortune seekers turned to Darjeeling by the end of the 19th century. Within no time, the blue coat Nepalis began improvising their tongue, variously known as Khas Kura, Gorkhali or Nepali, as the link language among the bulk of the migrants. It may be remembered that prior to the British takeover, the Darjeeling hills and Sikkim, west of the river Teesta, were parts of the kingdom of Nepal for about four decades. Similarly, parts of the foothills and the present Kalimpong sub-division of the district were taken over by Bhutan from Sikkim. Thus, Darjeeling was the focal point where Nepalese, Sikkimese and Bhutanese intermixed under the benign gaze of the British. Within no time, it turned out to be the ethnic melting pot for the region where labour, traders, missionaries and scions of regional ruling families rubbed shoulders through the medium of Nepali.

Darjeeling as the cultural hub of eastern Himalayan kingdoms

Darjeeling emerged as the cultural hub of the Nepalese of India, Nepal, Sikkim and Bhutan by the end of the 19th century. The Darjeeling Government School was started in 1892 by merging the old Government Middle School and the Bhutia Boarding School. Prior to that, Padri Ganga Prasad Pradhan had already published his pioneering works on Nepali grammar and vocabulary. The Nepali speakers and their sympathizers petitioned to the provincial government to grant Nepali as one of the native languages for the entrance examination of the Calcutta University, which was accepted in 1918. By then, one of the pioneers of the Nepali language movement, Parasmani Pradhan, was editing a Nepali journal, *Chandrika*, with a view to providing the forum for the authors and standardizing diction, spelling and grammatical forms in the language. Very soon, a triumvirate of Suryavikram Gyavali, Dharanidhar Sharma Koirala and Parasmani Pradhan – with the acronym of SUDHAPA created from the names of the three scholars – emerged as the driving force behind the development, spread and acceptance of Nepali as the most significant language in region. Apart from that, they began publications in Nepali, staging Nepali drama in the public, opening up the public libraries and canvassing for Nepali candidates in various vocations.

This was also the time when an important political forum of Nepalis in India, the All India Gorkha League (AIGL), was established in Dehradun by Thakur Chandan Singh, an ex-soldier with connections with the Ranas of Nepal, but soon it shifted to Darjeeling. The AIGL was basically a pro-Rana, pro-British and Hindu forum whose functionaries invariably attended the sessions of the Hindu Mahasabha. The League was active among the ex-soldiers in most of the cantonments towns with the Gurkha soldiers. However, its decline set in by the 1930s and it became inactive by 1940. It was revived by another ex-soldier, Damber Singh Gurung, in 1943 with a demand for a separate autonomous administrative unit for the loyal Gurkhas in Darjeeling (Subba, 1992). In view of Matrika Prasad Koirala, AIGL "was inspired by the White Missionaries and the White (British) tea planters of Darjeeling. This organization was avowedly pro-Rana and was very critical of the nationalist movement in Nepal and its leaders" (Koirala, 2008: 97).

By then, though the Second World War was being fought on various fronts, the nationalist Indians had taken their struggle against the British colonial rulers to a crescendo. The political atmosphere in the region was clouded with uncertainty. The Communist Party of India (CPI), which had a sizeable following in Darjeeling and tea plantations around, passed resolution for creation of Gorkhasthan, consisting of Nepal, parts of Sikkim, Darjeeling, southern Bhutan and north Bengal as a homeland of the Gorkhali-speaking peoples. Incidentally, by then Darjeeling had emerged as a cosmopolitan region with Nepalese, Sikkimese, Bhutanese, tea tribes and a sizeable multilingual plainsman. Two more points need to be added to the above: Darjeeling had also seen the growth of a strong creative literary movement in Nepali language and a vigorous left-oriented trade union movement affecting almost every walk of organized labour in Darjeeling. These developments strongly influenced the placid political atmosphere of the three Himalayan kingdoms leading to formation of political parties with serious consequences. In terms of the sequence of events, the democratic movement started in Sikkim among the three kingdoms, which was followed by Nepal and then Bhutan. We shall follow the same sequence in terms of our presentation.

The broad issues to be examined

In what ways did the Nepali cultural renaissance in Darjeeling influence the three eastern Himalayan kingdoms of Nepal, Sikkim and Bhutan? Will it not be desirable to understand the reasons for a hundred-year-old demand of regional autonomy raised by the Nepalese remaining unfulfilled? As the politically more experienced and organizationally more mature operatives, in what ways did they influence the political events and democratic movements in Nepal, Sikkim and Bhutan? Has the failure of AIGL in its central objective to secure Darjeeling as an autonomous political entity in India influenced the course of political movements in the three Himalayan kingdoms for the Nepali-speaking peoples?

Democratic movement in the Namgyal principality of Sikkim

Sikkim was a Buddhist principality ruled by a Bhutia king since 1642. It had an archaic feudal-cum-theocratic political structure, which was invariably belaboured by Bhutan from the east and Nepal from the west. The scenario changed after the British colonial power emerged on the Indian horizon after the Anglo-Nepalese War of 1813–15. The British not only settled the present boundary of Nepal but in 1817 they also gave back to Sikkim their territories in the hills and adjoining plains secured from Nepal. Within the next five decades, they created the district of Darjeeling in the Bengal Presidency by taking territories from Sikkim, Bhutan and Nepal and fixing the boundaries of these kingdoms. They stationed a resident political officer in Gangtok, the capital of Sikkim, since 1889, and ruled it indirectly through the ruler and his autocratic courtiers, the Kazis. These feudal lords ran the administration, had their own police and jails and exploited the tenets through a series of impress labour. It was a ruthless system in which subjects were mercilessly assaulted by the landlords with a view to creating a reign of terror and compliance to their wild demands.

Suppressed commoners got together at various localities to organize themselves in the social welfare bodies with a hidden political agenda, as any political activity was ruthlessly suppressed. Once Indian independence was declared, they boldly unfurled the flag of resistance to the feudal accesses by organizing a public meeting at the capital to criticize the state of affairs and form the first political party among the three Himalayan kingdoms on December 7, 1947: the Sikkim State Congress (SSC). That was the day the Sikkimese heard political speeches being made on their soil for the first time. Till then nobody in the principality knew how to address a public meeting, how to draft a political resolution and how to conduct a public meeting with mass attendance. SSC was a multi-ethnic political outfit with three significant demands to the Maharaja: (1) formation of a popular government, (2) abolition of *zamindari*, and (3) merger of Sikkim with India. The State Congress reached the Maharaja with its resolution, which remained unanswered; they resorted to squatting around the palace (Dharana), and the Maharaja ran away to the political officer to take shelter against his own people.

All through these years, politically conscious volunteers from Darjeeling and other neighbouring states in India, Nepal and Bhutan took part in the democratic upsurge in Sikkim. So much so that apart from others, even B. P. Koirala attended the Rangpo session and Girija Prasad Koirala was at the Malli session of SSC on behalf of their Nepali National Congress. At last, a popular government was formed with three representatives of State Congress and two representatives of the Maharaja in April 1949 without defining the contours of the functioning of the so-called popular government. The two palace nominees in the cabinet, it appears, were only to expose that the State Congress leaders were inexperienced in administration and arrogant in their behaviour. Popular expectations were very high from them, but they were unable to accomplish much because of the deliberate hurdles created by the palace and the administration. In the process, chaos was being created by unruly and drunken behaviour of the Congress volunteers in the capital town of the state. Consequently, the political officer dismissed the popular government in the name of the Government of India on May 29, 1949 (Basnet, 1974; Sinha, 1975).

The Maharajkumar Palden Thondup Namgyal, who looked after administration on behalf of His Highness, answered the Congress resolution by organizing a parallel outfit, Sikkim National Party (SNP), as an 'antithesis' of the Sikkim State Congress. By the mid-20th century, Sikkim had two-thirds of its population of Nepali extraction and the rest of the Sikkimese consisted of the indigenous Lepcha tribesmen and Bhutia immigrants from Tibet, a community to which the ruler belonged. The Maharaja refused to accept about a hundred year old Nepali immigrant residents as the Sikkim subjects of Sikkim. And he insisted that as the immigrants were brought by the British, they were the responsibility of the Indian Union, as being the successor to the British power. In that situation, at last, a compromise was hammered out at the instance of the Government of India, in which two-thirds of Nepalis had to have an equal representation in the State Council with one-third Lepcha-Bhutia combined. This formula came to be known as the 'parity system', in which two artificial ethnic blocks were envisaged. The parity formula was agreed for political representation of the people in the administration, which was soon extended to every walk of public life of the principality. The Nepalese had struggled for a democratic system in Sikkim, but they got a communal representation, which naturally they resented. However, they lost sight of the fact that at least they were recognized as the Sikkimese subjects at the teeth of opposition from the obstinate Maharajkumar, the proxy ruler of the land.

The Durbar was determined to show that SSC was out and out an immigrant Nepali party and the leaders of Lepcha and Bhutia communities among them were discredited troubleshooters without political support of their community. With a view to prove the above, the Maharajkumar used all his resources to see that Congress could win on the reserved Nepali seats only and Sikkim National Party candidates won on the Lepcha-Bhutia reserved seats by defeating inexperienced and loudmouthed congressional leaders in the election for the State Council. Two hand-picked state councillors were appointed as the executive councillors in 1953, who miserably failed to continue in the trust of the masses. The next general election held in 1958 was more chaotic, and by then the political atmosphere of the state was getting dirty by labelling charges of corruption on most of the councillors. By then, though the Sikkim National Party continued to be run by the Maharajkumar, the Sikkim State Congress got reduced to a Newar Party, as its affairs were controlled by Kashiraj Pradhan, a Newar and his relatives. Fed up with the antics of sectional politics, old stalwarts such as former president and one of the main founders of SSC, Kazi Lhendup Dorji, resigned from its active membership and formed a parallel political forum, the Sikkim National Congress, which pushed SSC to the political margin within the state. This new outfit attracted a large number of former political activists such as Sonam Tshering and C. D. Rai, from both the old political parties. The SSC continued for another decade, but for all intents and purposes, it was politically a dead horse (Sinha, 2008).

The issues to be examined

Why did a politically pioneering political forum such as the Sikkim State Congress, with clear objectives, multi-ethnic leadership and mass political support, fail to negotiate a transition from politics of agitation to redressal of the popular demands of the masses? Was it really a multi-ethnic political party? If so, why did the supporters of the Lepcha and Bhutia communities desert it on the eve of electoral politics? What was the social base of the party in the state, and why and how did it permit itself to be reduced to a Nepali party, a charge flung on it by the crown prince and others? Does it mean that the democratic movement launched by the SSC went in vain? Why is it that nobody has cared to write the social history of the SSC as an integral part of the Indian democratic movement?

Ranacracy, Nepali Congress and the Nepalese Revolution of 1950 and its role in the 1950s

Rana Jung Bahadur, the founder of Ranacracy, and his family created for themselves a new class, completely cut off and isolated from society. M. P. Koirala, the commoner to be the prime minister, informs that

> they would not even marry into a commoner's family. Their mode of language, behaviour and bearance had completely changed; and bore the stamp of audacious arrogance. They always spoke about themselves in the royal plural and expected the people in general to treat them as such. The people on the

> other hand knew very well that they were usurpers of power at the expense of the real royalty, which was the dynasty of the Shahs. They married their sons to the daughters of the royal house and their daughters too to the royal princes or else or to the scions of the princely states in India. Thus, they completely lost touch with the common man in Nepal from among whom they themselves came, and alienated the common fellow brethren . . . Power made them blind.
>
> (Koirala, 2008: 29)

The Ranas were themselves divided on a variety of sub-groups and to add to the confusion, they were classified in three categories (A, B and C) and accordingly they controlled the offices in the state at different levels. Many of disinherited Ranas resided in India with their considerable ill-gotten wealth and were invariably engaged in conspiring against the reigning Ranas. And further they saw to it that any chance of opposition to their omission and commission was ruthlessly suppressed. One such sufferer was Krishna Prasad Uppadhyay (Koirala), father of three future prime ministers of Nepal: M. P., B. P. and G. P. Koirala.

Soon after the Second World War, the Nepalese residing in India, many of whom had participated in the Indian democratic movement, made efforts to organize themselves politically with a view to effecting political change in Nepal. For example, there was a political forum functioning from Patna known as the Nepal Democratic Congress (NDC), and there was another one at Banaras known as the Nepali National Congress (NNC), almost with the same objectives. However, none of them operated from within Nepal, as the Ranas could not permit any political activities. In such a situation, the functionaries of both the Congresses realized the need for a collective struggle and for that they decided to merge the two outfits into one and work together under a collective leadership. With that objective in mind, the two sides met and hammered out a common strategy for their merger and action. Thus writes the first president of the newly created political forum, M. P. Koirala:

> Finally it was decided that I shall be the president of the newly merged parties, while the flag of the NDC would be adopted for the new emerging party. And the mouth-piece paper *Nepal Pukar* would remain the same name as it had of the NDC. The executive would be so nominated that it would give adequate representation to both the wings. The main points of negotiations having been agreed to, it was decided to give everything a final and formal shape. The Working Committees of

> both the parties ratified the proposal and a joint statement of appeal by presidents of both the parties was issued. The two parties announced a date to meet in a national convention in Calcutta.
>
> (Koirala, 2008: 108)

About 200 delegates of the two parties met on April 8, 1950, in Tiger Cinema, Chawringhee, Calcutta, and by and large approved the above proposals and thus founded the new political party of Nepal, the Nepali Congress (Koirala, 2001: 97).

The Nepali Congress (NC) raised a Nepal Liberation Army (Mukti-Vahini) and decided to launch a guerrilla war against the Rana establishment in October 1950. The entire country was divided into three command zones (eastern, central and western) and regional commanders were appointed under General Shubarna Shamsher, the commander in chief. The armed attack was mounted from the eastern Terai at Biratnagar, which was followed in the middle at Birganj and Bhairwa in the western Terai. Many demobilized soldiers of the Second World War vantage joined the Liberation Army on their own. Volunteers came from adjoining Bihar and West Bengal for providing logistics to the voluntary Liberation Army: Kuldeep Jha, Bhola Chatterjee, Narnarayan Singh, Phenkan Chaudhury, Dasrath Chaudhury, Madhusudan Singh, Bhola Mandal, Surya Mishra, Phanishwar Nath Renu and Tarapada Babu. Some of them, like Kuldeep Jha and Tarapada Babu, expired in action (Renu, 1977).

This heroic struggle in one of the most backward regions was not in vain; within three months they would liberate almost one-third of Nepal from the Rana regime. However, it was reported that King Tribhuwan had taken shelter in the Indian embassy in Kathmandu on November 7, 1950, and asked for political asylum in India, which was granted. The king was evacuated from Kathmandu to New Delhi, and the desperate Rana prime minister crowned his four-year-old grandson, Gyanendra, as the legitimate king of Nepal by deposing the rightful king in self-exile. However, the king, popular leaders and the Rana prime minister were forced by the circumstances to negotiate for an agreed formula to end the impasse. Thus the Delhi Agreement was signed on February 17, 1951, and the king returned to his capital with honour. Naturally, the negotiation and Tripartite Agreement were resented by the common members of the Nepali Congress and its mukti-bahini, who had taken to arms against the Rana autocracy. And naturally, they felt let down with the very idea of compromise and working with the autocratic Ranas.

As per the terms of the Tripartite Delhi Agreement, a cabinet of five members each from the Nepali Congress and the Ranas was formed under the Rana prime minister, Mohan Shamsher as the prime minister. B. P. Koirala from the NC was appointed as the home minister and leader of his group in the cabinet. This experiment of taking everybody together did not work to the expectation of anybody and very soon the prime minister had to resign. That led to a series of democratic experiments and cabinet formation without a constitution and set rules and procedures. Though the Ranas had formally lost the power, democratic political parties suffered from internal attrition and factionalism. In the process, the king emerged as the strongest institution in the country within a few years. He could call upon anybody to form his cabinet and most of such worthies proved their inadequacy within a few months. At the top of it, the popular King Tribhuwan developed a serious illness and expired in Switzerland after months of treatment. Crown Prince Mahendra, who was antithetical to his father in his political approach, was sworn in as the next king of Nepal in 1955.

King Mahendra did not hide for long his ambition to reign and rule simultaneously over his kingdom as the Hindu king, an incarnate of the Lord Vishnu. He invited various political operators to form the government, which could last for some months. At last, he ordered a general election in May 1959 on an ill-prepared constitution, in which the Nepali Congress led by B. P. Koirala was victorious with a comfortable majority in the National Assembly. He was invited by the king to form his cabinet, which he did, and he began functioning assured of his majority in the house. The popular prime minister perhaps forgot that Nepal had a very limited tradition of democratic functioning and the political culture was still attuned to the feudal court culture in its overall orientation, which rubbed the king the wrong way. The clash of intent and purpose between the two was bound to happen. And thus, on December 15, 1960, the king dissolved parliament, imprisoned the prime minister and most of his ministers, banned the political parties and took the administration into his own hands. And for the next three decades, it was the king, Mahendra, and his son, Birendra, who ruled Nepal in the name of the Panchayati Raj.

Issues involved

Did the Tripartite Delhi Agreement evolve among the contracting parties or was it thrust upon the unwilling partners? Was there an alternative available to them which could have been explored? Was the democratic attrition among political parties in general and the

Nepali Congress in particular inevitable, or was it because of the clash between styles and personalities of the two senior Koirala brothers? Was the social and organizational base of the Nepali Congress strong enough to sustain the liberation struggle at its own? The Nepali Congress liberation struggle had attracted instant support from neighbouring Bihar, Bengal, Sikkim and possibly the Bhutan Duars. There are enough instances to support the view that the Nepali Congress tried to reach Darjeeling, Sikkim and Bhutan in their democratic movements. Why did it fail to cash in such an instant support in its hours of crisis? Why was the Nepali Congress not readily available to stand by the beleaguered fraternal bodies from its eastern frontiers among its brethren when they badly needed their counsel and support?

Bhutan State Congress, its democratic movement and aftermath

The All India Gorkha League and the Ranas of Nepal saw the Bhutanese Nepalese (Lhatshampas, the 'southerners' in Zongkha), settled in Bhutan Duars, as their special preserves. It was possible because of the fact that there was no effective control over the Nepalese settled Southern Bhutan Duars from Bhutanese authorities, where the Nepalese had been going and coming at their will. There were individual Nepalese from the Duars who tried to raise some mild voice in the favour of their suppressed brethren, which led to harsh treatment inflicted on them in the early 1940s (Dhakal and Strawn, 1994; Hutt, 2003). It is claimed that Bhutan State Congress (BSC) was established at Patgaon in the Goalpara district of Assam in 1952. It petitioned to the king of Bhutan on the plight of the Bhutanese Nepalese and demanded clear administrative arrangements and equality with the Dukpas, the dominant ethnic group, in treatment by the state in terms of taxation (Rose, 1977; Sinha, 1991). As their petition remained unanswered, they decided to resort to civil disobedience with a clear charter of demands such as formation of popular government, abolition of zamindari and merger of Bhutan with India. With these demands, they launched their march to Sarbhog in southern Central Bhutan from Goalpara with about a hundred volunteers drawn from Nepalese in Bhutan, Assam, Nepal, Sikkim and Darjeeling.

Both sides were unprepared for this eventuality, as this agitation was the first of its kind in the history of Bhutan. Volunteers did not know what to do and expect from the administration and the Bhutanese militia had never experienced handling such a crowd in their memory.

Before somebody could reach to the authorities with the charter of demands, the nervous J. B. Pradhan, the commissioner of Southern Bhutan, the man on the spot, ordered to open fire. The crowd ran back to the Indian Territory on the sound of guns. Naturally, a few of them reportedly died and some were injured in the firing. The entire civic agitation ended in a fiasco for the leaders of the BSC. They did not know what to do next, as there was no regular administrative structure in the region, nor was there a fast and reliable way to reach the king at his 'capital' with the grievances in the absence of communication. The young king appeared on the scene after many weeks and took some decisions. But the Bhutanese administration lodged a protest to the Government of India that the Indian Territory was being used for anti-Bhutan activities by the non-Bhutanese Nepalese, who had created disaffection among the loyal Bhutanese subjects. Naturally, the Government of India took corrective measures and warned the BSC activists not to do anything against Bhutan from India. The leadership of BSC, especially its president, Dal Bahadur Gurung, kept on filing claimed 'resolutions' of the party to various visiting authorities and kept on writing in the journals for years. The last anyone heard of him in 1958, when he gave a petition to Pt Nehru at Gangtok, when the latter was on a state visit to Bhutan.

Issues involved to be pursued

What was the social support base of the Bhutan State Congress? What were the sources which inspired the BSC programmes and its organizational affairs? Why did it not reach its political activities inside Bhutan before and after the 1954 agitation? What impact did it make to the politics of Bhutan as the first organized political party in the country or the region at large?

Common denominators

Did the lack of opportunity to participate in the political process in the three archaic kingdoms prior to August 15, 1947, the landmark date of Indian independence, affect the outcome of the democratic struggles in the three kingdoms?

How did the rudimentary middle class and newly educated persons in special positions react to the democratic participation in the state of affairs against the feudal-colonial dispensation?

What were the inspirations behind the charter of demands made by SSC and BSC and the Mukti-Bahini in Nepal?

- Why did the anti-feudal democratic struggles in Sikkim, Nepal and Bhutan not receive similar support from the Indian political class after Indian independence, as they had received earlier?
- Why could the Nepali Congress functionaries, who had tried to reach their eastern brethren of Sikkim and Bhutan in their struggles, not sustain their momentum in 1950s when such support was urgently needed?
- What were the factors responsible for the re-emergence of the rulers much stronger in the 1950s after the democratic movements in the princely states?

It is significant that the dawn of democracy in the region that was initiated by the AIGL in Darjeeling in 1940s effectively came to an end in 1960 with the arrest of the democratically elected prime minister of Nepal, B. P. Koirala, and proscription of the Nepali Congress. The democratic movement, which had been revived in 1943 by D. S. Gurung of AIGL, met a setback when the State Re-organization Commission, empowered to recommend creation of new political units by the Indian Union, rejected AIGL's demand for creation of a linguistic state of Gorkhaland in Darjeeling. Next in sequence, the Sikkim State Congress, launched in December 1947 and despite getting its members elected to the Sikkimese Nepalis seats for the State Council elections in 1953 and 1958, lost its sheen once it became a party to the notorious parity system. The dramatic rise in 1950 and fall in 1960 of the Nepali Congress cast a question mark on the course of democratic movement in the eastern Himalayan region. Lastly, the Bhutan State Congress appeared to be in a hurry to catch up with its western sister feudatories in the democracy and met with a sad demise, as perhaps it had not done its homework properly to reach the dominant community of the state, the Dukpas in Bhutan. Neither was Bhutan, universally illiterate in modern administration, ready for such a political step, as she still lived in the mediaeval age. The dawn and fall of democratic movements in the eastern Himalayan principalities within an eventful span of about two decades was a significant development. These setbacks to the cause of democracy continue to haunt the travail of participative democracy in the eastern Himalayan states and it will be worthwhile to draw appropriate lessons for the future. On the other hand, the rulers in the eastern Himalayan kingdoms emerged much stronger than before after the first phase of democratic experiments in their domains. The study has been largely based on the secondary data from various sources. However, various sources of information were tapped and still surviving individual activists and knowledgeable individuals were interviewed for the purpose.

Bibliography

Basnet, L. B., 1974, *Sikkim: A Political History*, S. Chand, New Delhi.
Dhakal, DNS and C. Strawn, 1994, *Bhutan: A Movement in Exile*, Nirala, New Delhi.
Duff, A., 2015, *Sikkim: Requiem for a Himalayan Kingdom*, Random House India, Gurgaon.
Hutt, M., 2003, *Unbecoming Citizens*, Oxford University Press, New Delhi.
Koirala, B. P., 2001, *Atmabrittanta: Late Life Recollections*, Himal Books, Kathmandu.
Koirala, M. P., 2008, *A Role in a Revolution*, Jagdamba Prakashan, Patan.
Renu, P. N., 1977, *Nepali Kranti Katha* (in Nepali: Story of the Nepalese Revolution in Hindi), Rajkamal Prakashan, New Delhi.
Rose, L. E., 1977, *The Politics of Bhutan*, Cornell University Press, New Haven.
Sinha, A. C., 1975, *Politics of Sikkim*, Thomson Press, Faridabad.
Sinha, A. C., 1991, *Bhutan: Ethnic Identity and National Dilemma*, Reliance Publishing House, New Delhi.
Sinha, A. C., 2008, *Sikkim: Feudal and Democratic*, Indus, New Delhi.
Subba, T. B., 1992, *Ethnicity, State and Development: A Study of the Gorkhaland Movement in Darjeeling*, Har-Anand, New Delhi.
Tshering, T., 1960, "A Few Facts About Sikkim", *Mankind*, New Delhi.

2

EASTERN HIMALAYAN KINGDOMS

Nepal, Sikkim and Bhutan

The geographers identify the Great Himalayan arc from the Pamir knot in the west to the Namcha Barwa peak in the east, where the mighty Brahmaputra takes a southward turn from the eastern Tibetan plateau to the Indian plains. The ancient land of modern Nepal is located in the centre of the Himalayan arc and its eastern boundary joins with that of the old Namgyal principality of Sikkim, which is the western neighbour of lHo-mon, or the mediaeval Lamaist Church State of Bhutan. These three states happened to be the dynastic principalities under the benign gaze of the British colonial Empire from the second half of the 19th century. It so happened that the British colonial administration evolved a strategy to guard its Indian colonial possession against the alleged covetous designs of competing Russian, French and Chinese empires. It is also a fact that all three non-British competing empires were also busy in pushing their imperial domains towards the Himalayan region, which the British considered their backyard. This concern for guarding its Indian imperial possession against the designs of the competing powers has been termed by the scholars as imperial 'Great Game'. The British secured the Himalayas by creating a network of internal and external buffer states from the west, north and east of India. For illustration, Afghanistan, Tibet and Thailand were created as the external buffer states between British India and her western, northern and eastern neighbouring imperial states, so far as the British were concerned. Similarly, a chain of internal buffer states were created right from Baluchistan on the Iranian border in the west to Bhutan in the east. While closer non-British relations among the external buffer states were politically, diplomatically and even militarily opposed by the British Indian establishment, internal buffer states were deliberately kept underdeveloped so that the land army of the potential aggressors could not easily cross over to the Indian plains. The British consciously created Nepal, Sikkim and Bhutan as internal buffer states and maintained them as such till they remained rulers in India. Not only that, they left an advisory note for the successor states to maintain them as buffers between themselves and their northern neighbours with serious consequences for their peoples in the changed geopolitical situation in the mid-20th century. Before we come to that, it will be worthwhile to briefly survey the historical travail of the three kingdoms.

The garrison[1] state of Gorkha

Unlike other two eastern Himalayan kingdoms of Sikkim and Bhutan, Nepal was territorially a big country and ethnically a complex land. There were Khush, Magars and Gurungs in the west; Tharus in the south-west; Newars in the Kathmandu Valley; Maithils and other occupational and peasant communities in the south and south-east; Kirats in the east and a variety of Bodhi (Buddhist) communities in the north in the lap of the high Himalayas. The topography permitted existence of numerous small and big polities, especially in the west and middle of the country, which used to forge occasional alliances of convenience. For example, there were about four and a half dozen principalities in present-day Nepal in the 17th century in four bunches: Baisis (24 principalities), Chaubisis (22 principalities), and three units of Mallas in the Kathmandu Valley and three Sen principalities in the east. Though Palpa among the Chaubisis and Jumla among the Baisis with about 24,000 households (roofs) each were the largest two principalities, there were other very small units among them such as Gajur with only 140 households.

Gorkha, a small principality in the Chaubisi, was founded in 1559 by an adventurous and quarrelling brother of the Lamjung ruler Narahari Shah, Drabya Shah; thus the two states continued to fight for their supremacy for years to come. It was of a middling size with 12,000 roofs with limited agricultural output and still less scope for trade. The rulers of most of these principalities claimed the Kshatriya (ruling caste in the fourfold division among the Hindus world) status, once they got their regimes stabilized. They ordered genealogies prepared by their faithful and sycophant Brahmin courtiers or bards, who linked them to the known Kshatriya ruling dynasties of Chittorgarh and Kanauj in India. However, the scholars believe that most of them were possibly Magar or Khash or Khus chieftains, who got their status as ruler sanskritized with a view to claiming legitimacy as sanctified Hindu rulers.

It appears that 10 successive rulers of Gorkharajya struggled hard for the next two centuries from its inception with its neighbours, especially with its adversary, Lamjung. It could manage to survive as a distinct unit in spite of its limited resources, when Prithvi Narayan Shah (b. 1722, r. 1742–5) came to power. Prior to that, it was one of his predecessors, Rama Shah (1609–36), who had extended the frontiers of Gorkha kingdom through wars and marital ties. More significantly he organized the administrative structure and social system of the state by assigning various positions to his loyal warrior courtiers in perpetuity. For example, Pandes, Pants, Aryals, Khanals, Rana Magars and Bohras came to be known as Chhathar (six nobles). Similarly posts of chamberlain (Kapardar), policing (Dandagimana), treasurer (Khajanchi), ecclesiastical head (Dharamadikari), and cook (Bhagche) were created and duly assigned to individual families. He introduced maintenance of forests and grazing grounds; regulated irrigation system; and divided the subjects in four *vernas* and 36 castes (Vaidya, 1993: 81–2).

Prithvi's father, Narbhupal Shah (r. 1716–42) mounted an attack on the Kathmandu Valley and tried to snatch Nuwakot from the Malla rulers of the valley, but the Mallas got united and drove the Gorkhas away. He sought support from Kantipur and Lalitpur against the Malla king of Bhaktapur and attacked the valley once more, but he was beaten back again. Narbhupal lost some of his ablest armed commanders in this battle, and others such as Jayant Rana defected to his adversaries because of intense intrigue and counter-intrigue in the court. All these led to such a pressure on him that he lost his mental balance and died soon thereafter.

Having succeeded to the throne of Gorkha, 20-year-old Prithvi Narayan came under the guidance of his stepmother, Chandraprabha, who trained him in statecraft and administration. He impatiently attacked Nuwakot as if to avenge his father's defeat, but lost badly. That made him to think aloud on the strength and weakness of his kingdom. He evolved the strategy of alliance with potential adversaries and mounted a determined, consistent and aggressive pressure on the potential zones of expansion. And for that he raised a dedicated loyal force, armed them adequately with new supplies, fed them well and evolved provision of food on the war fronts and gave ranks and jagirs to his commanders, who stood by him for their lives. He was determined to take over Kathmandu Valley against the backdrop of his father's failure to do so. And for that he minutely studied the strategic location of the valley and found that it had plenty of fertile and well-irrigated land and income from trans-border trade with Tibet. He stealthily took over Nuwakot and cut off the valley from its access to trade and profitable coin transaction with Tibet in 1744 and he had patience to wait for the next two and half a decades while sitting on Nuwakot looking for opportune moment to take over the valley. That opportune moment came on November 12, 1769, when one of Bhatgaon rulers, Ranajit Malla's lieutenants waved his *pagari* (head gear) from a window of the palace as token of surrender. At last Bhatgaon had fallen to the Gorkha king; the conquest of the Kathmandu Valley was complete and capital of Gorkha principality was shifted from Gorkha to Kathmandu.

Prithvi Narayan was an extraordinary state-builder who inspired his subjects; he gave hope and courage to his commanders and generated confidence and faith among his functionaries, who took pride to carry out his wishes without caring for the risks involved. Hamilton rightly found him as "a man of insatiable ambition, sound judgement, great courage, and ceaseless activity. Kind and liberal, especially in promises to his friends and dependants, he was regardless of faith to strangers, and of humanity to his enemies" (Hamilton, 1971: 245). His victory came after the long years of wait in which he grew old and weary; he lost many of his tested commanders on various war fronts and expeditions and many of their children turned out young to be dependent on him. His consistent and resolute determination to establish 'great Gorkharajya' was something like a pole star which guided his followers to wage ceaseless wars, raids, attacks and expeditions against the adversaries. Prithvi Narayan was a great visionary in the sense that while he went out of his way to mount attacks and defeat his relatively weaker targets in the hills, he scrupulously avoided confronting the emerging British power in India on his southern frontiers and was even willing to pay rent for the fertile Terai land to the British overlords, a Mughal tradition of acknowledging its sovereignty by paying a token tribute.

He had thought over the handicap of limited resources of Gorkha, which made him to realize the significance of fertile land in the Terai, the foothills of the Himalayas. Thus, he made efforts to acquire them through various devices. With a view to securing an added advantage in the east, he used Brahmins and Chhetris as his pioneer agents, who would be advised to establish themselves at strategic points, and when the call came they worked as scouts in favour of the Gorkhas. He managed to run over Makwanpur, Chaudandi and Vijaypur by 1774 and extended his domain to the Morang plains in the Sikkim foothills. In this way, his domain was extended up to the Jungta Falcatta duars of Bhutan and cutting Sikkim from its access to south to Morang in the Indian plains. In fact, Prithvi Narayan was in touch with the former Deb Raja bZhidar (r. 1768–71) of Bhutan for forging an alliance with a view to keeping the British away from the eastern Himalayan principalities. However, the scheme could not materialize, as bZhidar was defeated by the British in his Koch Behar expedition, which led to his removal from the political scene of Bhutan. However, Prithvi's three and half decades of ceaseless campaigns led to the creation of a huge Gorkharajya from Gorkha in the middle of Nepal to Limbuan and Khambuan adjoining Sikkim. He had already established his headquarters at the cultural heart of the land at Kathmandu, ensured the economic strength of the domain by integrating fertile southern and eastern plains and located his allies at strategic points in the east with a view to thwarting potential threats to the regime.

In view of Ludwig Stiller, in a society such as Gorkha, where life, wealth and prestige were intimately bound up in land, ownership of the land had been the ultimate expression of power. In a way,

> the land was life; the land was security; the land was wealth and prestige. And the land was raja's. The raja, therefore, controlled life; he controlled security; he controlled wealth and prestige. And therefore, he controlled his people . . . Ultimate ownership of the land was vested in the crown. The peasant was not a serf bound by any particular locality, but remained free to migrate or not, to till the soil or not. However, if the peasant opted to till the soil- and to an agricultural society this option was obvious one- his rights to the land he farmed were limited to tenancy rights, contingent on his regular payment of taxes. The land itself remained property of the crown. Furthermore, just as the peasant was not obliged to remain on the land, so the raja was under no obligation to keep him on the land, but could evict him at will. Thus, the peasant's tenure was as much dependent on his obedience to the raja as it was on his payment of taxes . . . the raja could call upon the labour of his peasants to build up his defences and help work his lands. This compulsory, unpaid labour, or *jhara*, played an important role in the day to day conduct of the business of the kingdom. But it was a source of added strength in the time of war.
>
> (Stiller, 1973: 48–9)

Prithvi Narayan Shah had conceived his state as resting on two strong pillars: a contented peasantry and a loyal army. He had commanded his courtiers to keep the lifestyle of the court simple and to see that the taxation system was fairly administered. Salaries of the court officials were kept low and they were awarded for good and superior work in terms of honour rather than wealth. Taxes were collected by the officials directly and not on a contract basis. The king himself was to see that the full justice was administered to the peasants and bribery was to be strictly punished. Soldiers were to be provided with lands, exempt from major taxes, so that they could fight on the war-front without anxieties for the welfare of their families. The king did not only demand his soldiers to be courageous and skilful in the war, but also to possess absolute loyalty to the crown. The successful commanders were awarded *jagirs* from the vanquished territories, which provided extra incentive to the leaders on the war fronts. However, it was a feudal and oligarchic state, in which the king was the most significant pivot; he was assisted by the Chautariyas, the collateral kinsmen of four Kazis, four Sardars, two secretaries or Kharidars, the chamberlain and the treasurer, who were invariably drawn from the *tharghar*. Apart from that, there were leading Brahmin families, which not only provided with the scriptural guidance and legitimacy to the royal/regents' omissions and commissions, but also provided spectacularly successful commanders to the Gorkha army. The army and tharghar always stood by the crown and it was up to the king to command, control and lead the way to the strongest institution of the state, the army.

In spite of the personal likes or otherwise, the kings used effectively and profitably the practice of *pajani*, the annual administrative review to take stock and streamline the entire state administration. Stiller notes that by judicious use of this power, the king could call into question the performance of any functionary of the state from the highest nobles to the ordinary soldiers; remove and punish those who failed to deliver the result; and reward with posting, promotion and jagir (fief) to the performers. The normal tax on the land was 50 percent of the produce on the agriculture and the rulers disfavoured collecting anything beyond that by the state apparatus. Moreover, whenever the losing ruler of an adversary state agreed to accept the Gorkha over lordship, that state was provided with all the laxities such as continuation of their earlier revenue administration and tribute payment to the Gorkha as per old convention. But the enemy states opposed to the Gorkha advances were to be harshly dealt with, involving mutilation of persons, burning and looting of settlements and heavy capitation on the populace. And at that stage, there could be little distinction between the military and the civil administrations: and only then, the real picture of the garrison state of Gorkha emerges. It was a state in which it was the militia or the armed forces called the shots.

From Prithvi Narayan's death in January 1775 to Jung Bahadur Rana's ascent to power in 1846, four kings of the Shah dynasty were enthroned in seven decades. While Prithvi Narayan's son, Pratap Sinha Shah, came to power at the age of 23 years and remained on the throne for about three years before dying of smallpox, three of his consecutive successors were enthroned at three, one and a half and two years of age, respectively. In fact, they never ruled the state by themselves. Their reigns were spent in infancy, immaturity and ever-impending danger of usurpation of the throne by strong regents or warlords. The Gorkha court was a happy hunting ground of intrigue and factionalism on the part of the ambitious courtiers and warlords. There were invariably two strong claimants to the regency and two strong factions of the warlords all those years. The practice of polygamy and keeping concubines by the royalty made it possible for the infant kings' grandmothers, mothers and fathers' brothers and other closer kinsmen to stake their claims to be the natural claimants to the regency. Incidentally that was also the period when successful resolution of war by a commander enhanced legitimacy of his claim to wield power in the state. Thus, the strong Gorkha army went beyond the control of the infant kings and influence of the warlords such as Bahadur Shah, Damodar Pande and Amar Singh Thapa and their successive followers grew stronger. The regents were dependent on two factions of courtiers, either Pandes or Thapas, for their armed support in the game of their survival. Ascendency of one faction to power meant physical elimination, confiscation of the properties and banishment of the members of the other faction. With a view to achieving a spectacular feat and consolidation of their hold on the regime, the regents egged on loyal warlords to wage wars on the neighbouring states. Thus, the Gorkha state was at war all the time with some or other neighbours at the cost of the civil administration.

The Gorkhas preferred to call their kingdom Gorkharajya and their king the Gorkhadhipati. Gorkha was the nucleus of Gorkharajya and there is no evidence to suggest that Prithvi Narayan had an image of a unified state beyond larger Gorkha. The expansion of Gorkharajya resulted unwittingly in unification of the territories conquered by him to what is known as Nepal now. For this expansion, the Gorkha ruler adopted various moral and immoral ways. To Prithvi Narayan, the end justified the means. So he adopted all sorts of means: moral or immoral, right or wrong, human or inhuman. Most ferocious atrocities were committed. As per the classical Kautilyan provision of the statecraft, four methods were adopted to achieve the central objective, the expansion of the Gorkha state. First, armed and military activities including harsh atrocities were resorted to cow the adversaries. Second, economic blockades were imposed, as in the case of the Malla rulers of Kathmandu Valley from 1744 to 1764. Third, agents were sent to win over and divide the adversaries. And lastly, promise of security of life and property of the government functionaries of the enemy states were made and honoured, in case they stealthily supported the Gorkha ruler. One point needs to be noted, that Prithvi Narayan had no intention of integrating various states into one or unifying Nepal; rather his intention was to expand the Gorkha kingdom as much as possible at the cost of the weaker and more vulnerable states. Since the eastern neighbours of Gorkhas were weaker, he moved towards the east, while his efforts in the west were miserable failures. In the middle of the 18th century, when a great churning was going on all around Gorkha, Prithvi Narayan emerged as an effective expansionist and greater Gorkharajya came into existence (Vaidya, 1993: 139–40).

With a view to securing legitimacy unavailable to his competitors in Nepal, Prithvi Narayan sought a mythical recognition of his regime in the hills from the then titular Mogul emperor of India, Shah Alam II in 1772. A *firman* (proclamation) was said to have been issued conferring the title of "Bahadur – Shamsher Jung, Zamindar Amir and Sardar of Gorkha" with Pancha Hazari (Five Thousand Army) and Char Hazara Swarka Jagira (the Chief of Four thousand cavalry; Vaidya, 1993: 204–5). And thus, the Gorkha rulers began writing 'Shah' with their nomenclature indicative of nobility and in course of time, adopted various Persian/Urdu terms for various functionaries in the state such as Kazi, Khazanchi, Subba, Dewan and so forth. Prithvi Narayan's vision is expressed clearly in his Dibya Updesh, in which he spoke to his heirs, nobles and military generals. True, such a vision was not a collective one to begin with. It was more like the personal ambition of one man, but he wanted to pass it on and entrust it to a wider group of people in his state (Sharma, 1997: 477). Thus, he addressed his descendants, noblemen and army commanders in his Dibya Updesh: "But if anyone is alert, this will be true (asal) Hindustan of four jats, greater and lesser, with the thirty-six classes [jats: castes?]. Do not leave your ancient religion. Don't forsake the salt of the king" (Pfaff-Czarnecka, 1997: 419).

Early in his life as the Gorkhadhipati, he undertook a journey to Banaras, the holy city of the Hindus, and offered death rites to his departed father. It is another matter that he also used the occasion to buy arms and cultivate new allies. The model of his state was that of the rule of the mythical Hindu divine kings, who were above the common law. Brahmins were the preceptors, lawgivers and the royal advisors on statecraft and rules of socio-religious conducts. They were above the common law applicable to other subjects and could not be awarded capital punishment even if they committed heinous crimes. The Kshatriya, the warriors and defenders of the domain, were his main support base throughout all the campaigns to wage wars against the adversaries or for punishing the internal dissenters. All through his three decades of rule in the little state of Gorkha, Prithvi Narayan either fought wars on battle fronts, laid siege to beleaguered adversaries or chased his enemies through most devious means to victory. The Gorkha state was nothing but a standing army from 1742 to his end and even beyond. It was an institution under the most competent Gorkha commanders, who always clamoured for war, and they could acquire everything of worth in their lives on the battlefields by waging wars.

The popular saying in common parlance of the Hindu world is that of *desa* (country), *kala* (time or the period of time), *calan* (practice or the tradition) and *vyahar* (behaviour or the conduct) as the key concern of an effective ruler. It is expected that a king, more so the righteous one, will keep in mind the terrain of the country, the time in which he rules, the customs naturally followed by the subjects and the practices or behaviour unique to the social segments of the various sets of people for an effective rule. As per Prayag Raj Sharma,

> a Hindu state must have four recognized ingredients to it . . . These comprise: (a) *rajan*, meaning a sovereign king or ruler in whom all the power of the state resides; (b) *rajya*, or *rastra*, which describes the territorial extent of such a state within a defined boundary; (c) *praja*, which refers to the subjects of such a state; and finally, (d) *stithi*, referring to an established social order in the state. This last, in a broad conceptual sense, relates to an order ranging from the abstract notion of a cosmic to moral, social and more pragmatically, a legal order . . . Every reigning Hindu king of some ambition at all times of history has seen himself in the role of giving the best social order of his time to his people. In his Dibyopadesa, Prithwinarayan Shah refers to such an order as a task unfulfilled by him.
> (Sharma, 2004: xviii)

It is a fact that Prithvi Narayan spent almost all his 53 years in warfare, though he modelled himself as an ideal Hindudhipati (lord of the Hindus) and tried to establish Gorkha as an ideal Hindu kingdom, but his death at a relatively young age possibly prevented him to create an ideal Hindu state from the point of civil administration.

Andras Hofer notes that the

> era following King Prithwi Narayan Shah's death in 1775 was marked by an overall political instability. The weakening of power of the royal house, an economic crisis, frequent changes in key political positions and the lacking legal continuity from its internal problems. Military expansion was too rapid to follow political expansion and the establishment of an administration to follow. As the newly formed state was not founded on a homogenous ethno-cultural basis, it lacked the loyalty of its subjects . . . In order to protect the truncated state from the British menace, a security screen against the outside world was as imperative as an internal consolidation of the country . . . The *Maluki Ain* (the Nepalese civil code imposed in 1854 by Rana Jung Bahadur) demarcated the country's society against the foreign societies and cultures by defining it as a specifically Nepalese "national" caste hierarchy. Its homogenous legislation aimed at creating a homogenously constituted society.
> (Hofer, 2004: 2)

As a builder of the future Gorkha nationhood, Prithvi Narayan tried to consolidate the various communities into a hierarchical Hindu caste model. Granting for the sake of argument that he belonged to the Kshatriya caste, he took Magars, Gurungs, Brahmins and professional artisan castes such as the Kami, Damai and Saraki in the Gorkha army as integral parts from the very beginning. No doubt, the first three were assigned commanding roles to lead the forces, but the artisan castes had equally significant assigned roles, for which they were handsomely rewarded for their meritorious service. Perhaps he did not give much weight to the fighting prowess of the Newars even after being duly established at Kathmandu Valley. He did realize the significance of the martial qualities of the Kirats and did not hesitate to integrate Limbus and Rais on his eastward march to the Sikkim frontier. Similarly, he was aware of the significance of fertile land in the Terai in the southern Himalayan foothills, which could easily produce sufficient food for the agriculturally impoverished Gorkhas. And for that, apart from waging wars on his southern adversaries and defeating them, he did not sit on prestige and was agreeable to paying rent as if he was a subordinate tenant to the British in India. In fact, such pragmatic actions keep him apart as a visionary from his contemporary rulers in South Asia. In the ultimate analysis, what resulted in continuation of the Gorkharajya in spite of an aggressive and hostile endeavour on the part of the British Indian empire? And for such a sterling achievement on the part of the Gorkhas, due credit must be given to Prithvi Narayan Shah, who created a myth, a halo, a desire and a hunger for things Gorkha, and to live and die for that. After his departure from the Gorkha scene in 1775, his descendants continued to rule for another seven decades, surrendering their authority to Rana Jung Bahadur in 1846, who created the notorious Ranacracy, a national curse, which ended in 1951.

The Lamaist kingdoms of Sikkim and Bhutan

There are two cardinal principles of polity formation in the Lamaist world: prophecy by the holy men, invariably on the name of the Padam Sambhava or the universal Guru Rimpoche, believed to have predicted events of the future happenings; and hiding of the holy texts (*gter-ma*) of the noted ascetics on difficult mountainous abodes or water bodies to be discovered by the right type of 'text discoverers' at the appointed time. The prophecies may originate through some or other legends; recited over time, again by holy men and laypersons so repeatedly that they come to be accepted as something like preordained truth or as if they were historical events containing real-life human actors and events (Aris, 1979: 156–65; Mullard, 2011: 9–12). Similarly, *gter-ma* had to be discovered at a preordained occasion or time by the predicted personnel in an appropriate manner to maintain its sanctity. Any violation on these prescriptions might lead to disastrous results and calamity to the wrong text discoverer. Apart from these main sources of traditional legitimacy, there are other ways of myth making of events, individuals and location. It goes without saying that the eastern Himalayan region was visited by the Tibetan herdsmen on their grazing expedition right from first millennium of the Christian era. An illustrious Tibetan king, Srong-tsen Gampo, established an extensive kingdom, stretching beyond Tibet to China and Nepal. It is said that Buddhism was introduced in Tibet during that time, but it soon got perverted to tantric and *bon* forms of the faith. Guru Padam Sambhava was invited by some mythical rulers of the region, who impressed upon his hosts with his religiosity, ascetic feats, and occult powers that he soon turned out to be an extraordinary person and ultimately the guardian deity of a number of peoples in the region. The type of Buddhism he preached came to be known as Nyingmapa, the red hat (because of the colour of the head gear of their holy men) or mythical-shamanistic-tantric form of Buddhism, which was similar to that of the indigenous faith of Bonism in the region.

Fed up with the alleged perversion,

> about the middle of the 14th century, a great reformer, known as Tsong-ka-pa, was born and he revived the religion in a purer form, introducing laws of discipline, insisting on celibacy of the priesthood, forbidding the consumption of alcoholic liquor, and restricting the proliferation of lesser gods and devils in the Tibetan religion and the worship the magic loving people gave to them.
>
> (Patterson, 1963: 224)

This new form of reformist Tibetan Buddhism came to be known as Geylugpa, or the yellow hat (based on the colour of the head gear of their monks), symbolizing the office of incarnation of the god-king, the Dalai Lama, whose 14th incarnation is in office in exile in India since 1959. However, from the 14th century onwards, the proponents of this new faith took over the central administration of Tibet and waged something like a militant holy war on the various forms of Nyingmapa followers, who by then had established a series of religious orders inclusive of the monastic pattern of dynastic succession. In the course of time, the proponents of the Geylugpa established a strong theocratic state, which drove the followers of older faith to new destinations with a view to establishing new regimes of their choice. Though the Geylugpa authorities, over time, would deal with the various Nyingmapa polities politically and diplomatically, they were hostile to them to begin with.

Formation of the Namgyal theocratic[2] dynastic principality

It is claimed that the Guru Rimpoche had set apart Sikkim (Denjong: land of rice) from the mundane world and created it as 'a hidden blessed land' (*sbas yul*). This theocratic model of state draws upon the Tibetan idea of invitation of a king to rule and the Indic model of Dharamraja (the Chho+ rgyal) and Chakravartin (whose wheel of reign moves in all the four directions). Interestingly, kingship in the Tibetan tradition was seen as contractual between the king and ministers and not as prize sought for; rather it has to be seen as a burden, shouldered at the request of others in order to benefit 'poor subjects'. It has to be seen as a social contract between the king and his subjects; failure on the part of the king could result in regicide or rebellion. In words of Saul Mullard,

> The appearance of these themes in 17th century sources have to be understood as legitimatizing agents of the newly formed state and monarchy and not as a reflection of political reality; as the political reality of formation in 17th century Sikkim, however, was far complex and was brought about, not by religious invitations to the first Sikkimese Chos-rgyal, but by conquest, alliance formation, and the subjugation of the population under the figure of the Chos-rgyal. The reason they appear in later historical narratives is to characterize the formation of the Sikkimese State as the fruition of divine prophecy.
>
> (Mullard, 2011: 27)

The official history of the former ruling family of Sikkim, the Namgyals, runs as the following. A prince, who happened to be a descendant of King Indrabodhi of Himachal Pradesh in India, is known to have founded the Mynak kingdom towards the ninth century of the Christian era (in eastern Tibet). Twenty-five generations later, in the first half of the 15th century, a scion of the Mynak house went on pilgrimage westwards with his five sons to Sakya, to his guru, who was building his abode. Many persons failed to erect a pillar, which one of his sons was able to erect alone, earning title of Khaye Bumsa (one with strength of 10,000 persons). So pleased was the hierarch that he offered his daughter in marriage to Khaye Bumsa, who happily got settled in the nearby Chumbi Valley, which later became the nucleus of the later kingdom of Sikkim (Unknown, 1963: 1). It is claimed that the issueless Khaye Bumsa contracted blood brotherhood with the regional powerful Lepcha chief, Thokengtek, which proved profitable for the immigrants, as one of his descendants, Phuntsog, a peasant patriarch from Gangtok, was consecrated as the first Bhotia king of Denjong in the course of time.

It is claimed that three Nyingmapa lama missionaries travelled from three directions to the Himalayan region in search of a holy land to establish their respective kingdoms in the aftermath of Geylugpa supremacy in Tibet. They debated among themselves on the respective merits of their individual claims to Denjong. Lhatsun Chhenpo is credited to have said:

> In the prophecy of the Guru Rimpoche (Padamsambhava) it is written that four noble brothers shall meet in Sikkim to arrange for its government. We are three of those come from the north, west and south. Towards the east, it is written, there is at this epoch a man named Phuntsog, a descendant of brave

> ancestors of Kham in Eastern Tibet. According, therefore, to prophecy of the Guru, we should invite him.

Two messengers were then dispatched to search for this man, Phuntsog. Going towards extreme east, near Gangtok, they met a man churning milk and asked him his name. He, without replying, invited them to sit down and gave them milk to drink. After they were refreshed, he said his name was Phuntsog. He was then conducted to the lamas, who crowned him by placing a holy water vase on his head and anointed him with water, and exhorted him to rule the country religiously, giving him Lhatsun's own surname of Namgye (Namgyal) and the title of the Chho-rgyal, or religious king (Patterson, 1963: 226) at Yoksom in western Sikkim.

Since then, Lhatsun Namkha Jigme turned out to be the guardian saint of the new regime. It is claimed again that the newly appointed king selected 12 of his Bhotia elders from among (or soldiers?) as his *kalongs* (councillors or advisors) and another bunch of 12 Lepcha chiefs as *dZongpens* (regional administrators) and they were advised to intermarry among themselves laying the foundation of the Sikkimese aristocracy, Kazihood. It is also claimed that the borders of the state were extended from Dibdala (?) in the north to Naxalbari and Titalia in the south, and Walung and then following the course of river Arun in the west to Thangla in the north-east. However, in spite of the best scheming of the Bhotia grandiose, there appears to have been armed clashes and violence on the occasion. Possibly from the Lepchas, the ninth descendant of Phuntsog Namgyal recorded thus:

> So he (Phuntsog Namgyal) started forth with (from Gangtok) with his entire retinue of followers, officers and household establishment . . . as the party happened to be riding on ponies and some of the retainers had matchlock guns, which they went on firing along the road, the simple natives, who had never seen a pony nor fire arms, said to others: "the entire party rode on huge hogs, and some of them bore sticks, which when pointed towards you, produced great sound"
>
> (Namgyal and Dolma, 1908)

It is difficult to believe that they were just celebratory or ceremonial displays. Possibly, there were either violent oppositions or some latent opposition was forestalled with display of mounted armed forces from Lepchas and Limbu communities.

Phuntsog's ancestor, Khaye Bumsa, had already contracted ritual brotherhood. Incidentally, the pre-Namgyal Sikkim was inhabited by Rong (Lepcha) and Tshong (Yakhthumba). The ninth Namgyal ruler Thutub and his consort wrote: "Hearing that in the interior of Sikkim, there was a great Lepcha patriarch and wizard, called The-Kong-Tek, who was reputed to be the incarnation of the Guru Rimpoche, he (Khaye Bumsa) after due consultations with his lamas and divinations, all of which promised success, resolved to pay a visit to the great Lepcha wizard, and started with 16 followers, carrying various kinds of silk etc. . . . they came upon The-Kong Tek and his wife, Nyo-Kong Ngol, who were clearing a patch of jungle for the purpose of cultivation. Gyad (Khaye) dBum asked them where The-Kong-Tek and Nyo-Kong-Ngol lived, not being aware that they were the identical persons. Both said they do not know. On asking again, the couple said, 'Let your party stay here, while we go to find them'. So saying, they went away and did not return. After waiting some time, the party saw that they had been given the slip, now they tracked them to the bamboo house. Entering inside they discovered the old gentleman on a raised throne of bamboo. He had washed off the dust and ashes, which had covered his face during his work of clearing jungles. He had donned on his feather cap and his garland of teeth and claws of wild beast, interspersed with various cowries and shells. He sat with a dignified mien, while his wife was busily engaged in getting food and drink ready. When the strangers entered, a wide bamboo mat was spread on the ground, where they sat and instantly were served with tea (?) and wine. Khaye Bumsa, seeing that this was The-Kong-Tek, offered him presents, which he had brought for him, asked for the boon of a son, which the wizard promised him. This was at Ringchom. And sure enough as soon as they returned to Chumbi, in the proper time, Jomo Guru showed the sign of conception, and birth of a son, which event was followed by two more issues. He thought that in the time to go to celebrate the thanks giving by puja, of local deities of Sikkim. So came down via Cho-la and had arrived at the cave . . . There they were met by The-Kong-Tek and Nye-Kong-Ngol, who had come upbringing various fruits from Sikkim, upon the same errant: viz. to see Khaye dBumsa and to celebrate the thanks giving by a puja . . . As eternal friendship was made between Khaye Bumsa and The-Kong-Tek, they agreed by this that all the males should be considered to be related to the sons and all the females of the daughters. The friendship was cemented by a ceremony at which several animals, both domestic and wild, were sacrificed and all the local deities were invoked to bear witness to this solemn contract of friendship, binding the Lepchas and Bhutias in an inseparable bond. They sat together on the raw hides of the animals, entwined the entails around their persons, and put their feet together in a vessel filled with blood, thus, smearing the blood troth to each other. The invoking all the local spirits, asked them to stand witness to this solemn contract, invoking blessings on those, who observed these faithfully, and curses on those who broke this eternal hereditary and national contract between the two" (Namgyal and Dolma, 1908). There was nothing unusual about this act of the Bhotia patriarch. Amalendu Guha informs that once the Ahoms, the Thai migrants to Assam, were settled down in Upper Assam and realized the significance of ploughing the paddy fields and scrapping the land surface to dead level, they too incorporated Maran and Barahis in their political structure. Not only were those, but a few of the tribal chiefs and headmen were also admitted into even the respectable Ahom clans. And the rest were transformed into peasants doing militia duty like the Ahoms (Guha, 1987: 170).

It appears that Phuntsog, the Bhotia prince, had managed to buy a level of peace with the local notables from the Lepchas, autochthons of the land. But there was another community which still had reservation on the new dispensation and they were the Limbus, though some of them were won over by the Lamas and were persuaded to join the new faith and earn a new nomenclature: Tshongs. The Namgyal establishment invariably talked about an ethnic commonwealth of communities, as the original inhabitants of Sikkim. It appears that there was sufficient dissention among the various communities of Sikkim in middle of Phuntsog's rule and he was forced to call for an ethnic conclave in 1663, in which an agreement known as Lho-mon-tshong Gsum was signed:

> Henceforth confirming to the command of his majesty [?], the humble (12) ministers and leaders of Lho, Mon and Gtsong have met here with the desire for unification and solidarity and hereby make the statement that there shall not be separate governments of Lho, Mon and Gtsong. During the previous Mon Pa war (13) people from all the different ethnic groups intentionally rebelled and this has been remembered. Henceforth with from this year (1663) take hold (of this order) and in accordance with orders of the Lord the Chos-rgyal laid down the affirmation and grasps the solution and so the humble and dedicated minister Dag shar (affixed his) seal.
>
> (Mullard, 2011: 142–3)

The point to be noted is that though some of the members of the nobility and the aristocracy would marry with Limbus, in the course of time no Limbu was elevated to the status of the aristocracy, Kazihood. Even the maternal uncle of one of Namgyal kings was murdered by the mechanizations of the Bhotia courtiers. It appears that unlike the Lepchas, the Limbus, in spite of their various contributions such as the very nomenclature of Sikkim, were not completely assimilated within the Namgyal state structure even after Sikkim's claim on the Limbuan as part of their domain.

Though there is not much mention of the two other lamas, after coronation of Phuntsog, but Lhatsun Lama remained in Sikkim to guide the king in the theocratic statecraft. He established the famous Pemiyangtse (Pemiyangchi) monastery and laid the tradition that the chief abbot of the said monastery would be entitled to crown the Namgyal kings. Then a series of monasteries was established and the king was commanded to rule as per tenets of the religion, thus justifying the nomenclature, Chos-rgyal, the religious king or the Dharamraja. The Kalons and Jongpens were left to mind their estates and contribute to the upkeep of the kings. Moreover, they were commanded to maintain two establishments each: one in their respective estates and another one at the king's court. However, at the kings' court, the capital was bereft of attributes of a township: there was no town, no market, and no commerce or industry. There was no standing state army; rather, whenever the contingency arose, ethnic groups raised their forces to fight against adversaries. The kings were invariably weak and were manipulated by their strong armed courtiers. Out of a total of a dozen of Namgyal rulers from 1642 to 1975, there were half a dozen of them, who ascended the throne either from birth or up to 14 years of age, making them vulnerable to manipulation by others. The Namgyal rulers remained obliged all along to the monastic order for their smooth reign in such a situation. The Bhotia highlanders avoided residing in the hot, humid and wild Morung foothills below the Dorji-liang hills in the south, leaving it vulnerable to rulers from the Gangetic plains in the south, Bhutan in the east and Nepal from west in course of time.

The entire divine and mythical narrative of the founding of the Namgyal dynastic rule in Sikkim suggests a series of legitimatizing criteria. First, Phuntsog Namgyal was a descendant of an Indian Kshatriyan king and a Tibetan king of antiquity. Thus, his ancestors were claimed to have ruled over Himachal Pradesh in India and Kham in Tibet. In this way, he was not an ordinary mortal; rather he was something like larger than life. Second, the Namgyal dynasty was established in Denzong, which could be verified by visiting the coronation site, the stone slab at Yoksom, other historical landmarks and the original monastery at Pemiyangtse, established by venerable Lhatsun Gampo. And third, stories of contracted blood brotherhood between the Lepchas and the Bhotias chiefs and the ethnic alliance of Lho-Mon-Gtsong are repeated time and again to hammer out the Lepcha-Bhotias' ethnic antiquity vis-à-vis the immigrant ethnic Nepalis of Sikkim. The appearance of these themes in 17th-century sources has to be understood as legitimatizing agents of the newly formed state and monarchy and not as a reflection of political reality of state formation in 17th-century Sikkim. However, it was far more complex and it was brought about, not by religious invitations to the first Chos-rgyal, but by conquest, alliance formation, and subjugation of the population under the figure of the Chos rgyal. The reason they appear in the later historical narratives is to characterize the formation of the Sikkimese state as the fruition of divine policy (Mullard, 2011: 27).

The church state[3] of Bhutan

Oxford historian Michael Aris writes on the nature of the Bhutanese theocracy:

> until the establishment of monarchy, the (secular) interests never became fully identified with a particular group or class, and the spiritual principles underlying the theocratic ideology remained the accepted norm. The doctrine of the "dual system" of religious and secular law had first developed in the second half of 13th century at the time, when Kublai Khan and Phags-pa Lama were trying to work out the ideal political balance in their relationship. When it was adopted in Bhutan, the concept came to imply the total subservience of the state to religion. This is evident throughout the legal code. The "dual system" never helped to define the political relationship between secular and ecclesiastic authorities as it is said in Tibet, where many of the civil officials had their monastic counterparts, the pairs working together on an equal basis. In Bhutan the situation appears to be quite different; lay officials had to assume a semi monastic character before reaching high positions. In particular, if a layman happened to become the sde-srid, he was usually required to take the vows of the minor order and receive a new name.
>
> (Aris, 1979: 262)

Like Lhatsun Namgyal Lama (1597–1654) in the case of Sikkim, his Bhutanese contemporary and counterpart, Nawang Namgyal Zhabdrung (1594–1651) of the Brug school of the Nyingmapa sect of Lamaism, was driven away from southern Tibet with the emergence of an aggressive Geylugpa hierarchy. But unlike Lhatsun, Nawang Namgyal Zhabdrung had succeeded his grandfather as the 18th prince abbot of the monastic seat at Ra-lung in 1606. He appears to have picked up succession and theological disputes in Tibet and thus was forced to exile himself to lHo-Mon (Bhutan) in 1616. By then, a number of Brugpa followers and the adherents of other Nyingmapa sects, sympathetic to Zhabdrung, had already established themselves in an appreciable number in western Bhutan, so much so that even Zhabdrung's father was already settled among them. However, he had to encounter a series of Tibetan invasions even in Bhutan, which he successfully warded off with his leadership, strategic planning, and manoeuvring the competing sects in to his fold. He managed to secure a number of regional monasteries, raised a series of *rDzongs* (forts) on strategic defensive locations and established his theocratic regime on a sound footing. He felt confident enough to take a local theocrat's daughter as his consort and his only son was born in 1631 in Bhutan. The Geylugpa *sDe srid* mounted attacks on his regime from 1644 to 1649, but were soundly beaten back. He then concentrated on internal administration of his domain, put the monastic order on a sound footing, organized revenue administration and introduced laws in lawless land of the communities used to transhumance. With these achievements came the recognition from the neighbouring countries such as Cooch Behar, Nepal, and other smaller monastic establishments. In 1651 he felt confident enough to leave his regime in the hands of his trusted ally, Tamdin Brugpa, as the sDe srid (Deb Raja) and took Samadhi (retreat), in which state he continued up to 1707, when it was made public and in the absence of a legal successor, efforts were made to discover his incarnations to the head the Brugpa theocracy.

In a complicated theocratic manner Zhabdrung's successors were identified in three forms: his spirit, his speech and his body. Possibly this ingenious device was initiated to accommodate conflicting claims to the most significant offices of the regime. However, there were occasions when it took time to discover an incarnation. The incarnations had to be identified in the form of infants to be ordained properly in intricacies of the august office in the care of the qualified persons of monastic order. In the process, the incarnate infant sovereign was a captive of his secular deputy functionary, the sDe srid, of the time. In fact, it was the sDe srids, who ran the Brugpa theocratic system on the name of the incarnated Zhabdrungs. From the year 1724, when the first official Zhabdrung's incarnation was 'discovered' to the demise of the last, incarnation in the year 1903, during 180 years, there were only five such persons, recognized as the Zhabdrung, with an average reign of 36 years. But this average was rarely achieved: the incarnate sovereigns invariably came to their ends quite young in their lives. It was not always easy to discover the incarnations quickly as the process was intricate and time-consuming. At times, those who were responsible to discover the incarnations had their reasons to delay the process. And there were occasions, when there was more than one such incarnate persons claiming to the office of Zhabdrung, as it happened in 1740s (Sinha, 1998: 107–8).

In spite of the strife, conflict, uncertainty and ubiquitous civil wars, the institution of the sDe srid had a fantastic continuity in Bhutan. From 1751, when the Zhabdrung went in to Samadhi and handed over the secular affairs of the state to his trusted ally to 1905, when the term of the last incumbent came to an end, there were 55 sDe srids with an average rule of 4.62 years (Sinha, 2004: 74). There were 13 sDe srids who remained in their office for longer than their normal three-year terms and these defended the state against foreign invasions, extended the state boundaries, fought wars, signed treaties and developed a system of theocratic oligarchy, which continued up to the first decade of the 20th century. However, there were five occasions, when there were two recognized sDe srids ruling from two different rDzongs. Many of the incumbents came to position, quite late in life, close to retirement or death, when their physical faculty was no match to the statecraft and ongoing political intrigue. In such a situation, it is not surprising that half a dozen of them were killed in harness and another dozen were forcibly removed from office. By the second part of the 19th century, the last 15 sDe srids were simply the puppets in the hands of the regional governors, the Penlops (Aris, 1979: pt. 3, ch. 3).

The Brugpa church state had some uniqueness which kept it apart from its Sikkimese counterpart. It was a theocracy and remained so for more than two and half centuries formally. And in spite of the advent of monarchy, in a way it continues to be so even today, as the present monarch is supposed to be the fifth dynastic representative in the line of the sDe srid. The king's coronation begins at Punakhas rDzong, when the ceremonial scarf from the Zhabdrung's remains is offered to the person of the impending king. So in a way, the Brug *rGyalpo* (king of Bhutan) represents two offices in one: the secular one (sDe srid) and the theocratic one (Zhabdrung). Unlike Sikkim, Bhutan had basically been an almost mono-ethnic country with a variety of the Lamaist faiths, and most of them got incorporated in the dominant faith of the land, the Nyingma Brugpa, in the course of time. Like their Sikkimese Bhotia counterparts, even Brugpa highlanders did not settle in the hot, humid and wild Duars by tradition, but they had led numerous raids in the plains beyond the duars for capturing slaves and looting variety of consumer goods and cattle. And thus, Bhutan maintained its territorial integrity intact in spite of hostile and aggressive designs of the British.

Not only that; one of the sDe srids extended Bhutanese domain to eastern Sikkim and even clashed with the Tibetan authorities with a view to controlling Gangtok area in Sikkim. The then sDe srid, dZhidar (1768–71), who was incidentally the 16th such functionary, overran Koch Behar in the plains leading to the British intervention and subsequent mediation by the then Panchen Lama of Tibet on behalf of Bhutan. This ambitious sDe srid had sought an alliance with the emerging Gorkha King Prithvi Narayan Shah with a view to joining hands to stop British penetration in the eastern Himalayan region. However, he did succeed to some extent as his domain in the foothills east of river Teesta was adjacent to that of the Gorkhas in Sikkim Morang for a while. It is an interesting contrast with Sikkim, where dynastic kings never emerged strongly in the state affairs and invariably worked in the shadow of their theocratic and feudal courtiers. On the other hand, the Bhutanese theocratic functionaries exhibited a strong strategic, diplomatic and administrative acumen in their dealings in the affairs of the state. One may pay a high compliment to the contributions of these Dukpa theocrats, as the basic administrative units in Bhutan till today continue to be the old rDzong system initiated by the Zhabdrung. In the process, the ancient system of church state gave birth to the Bhutanese political culture, which uniquely continues its traditions and incorporates many an alien elements after modifying them in their ethos. This is not for nothing; of late the Bhutanese political system has emerged as one of the most vibrant traditional polities of 21st century in this part of the world.

The Himalayan kingdoms in the beginning of the 20th century

Some significant points emerge from the preceding narratives. First, the Tibetan immigrants to the eastern Himalayan region transplanted pre-Gyelugpa polities in Sikkim and Bhutan in the second quarter of the 17th century of the Christian era, which were already absorbed in the new faith with the emergence of an aggressive Gyelugpa theocracy in Tibet. Second, the immigrants maintained themselves in their new homes in the same old Tibetan style of life socially, economically, culturally and religiously. But in spite of the topographical similarity, unlike Tibet the new land had not only a hot, humid and malarial climate, but it was also inhabited by some of local/regional communities with unfamiliar social and cultural traditions, which required serious consideration on the part of the aggressive immigrants. Moreover, the Tibetan immigrants, familiar with the dry mountain climate of Tibet, realized soon that they must adapt not only to the regional climatic conditions but also to the fast-growing wildlife and vegetation. Third, as they were not used to living in tropical southern slopes of their domain, they avoided settling down in the eastern Himalayan foothills, locally known as morang and duars; this was their biggest undoing, which cost them dearly over time. Fourth, the founders of the three Himalayan kingdoms were great charismatic leaders who fought wars to expand their domains, vanquished their adversaries with their suitable strategies and laid the foundations of states which survived for centuries in a hostile environment. While the founder of the garrison state of Gorkha consolidated a mighty Gorkharajya in a matter of decades, his two eastern counterparts from Sikkim and Bhutan created new theocracies in the eastern Himalayas, which were not known to have such centralized polities in the past. Fifth, all three of them used religion to legitimatize their rules: Prithvi Narayan intended to establish 'asal Hindustan' (the real [unadulterated 'pure' form] of Hinduism) in Gorkharajya; Phuntsog Namgyal wished to established Nyingmapa in Sikkim and Nawang Namgyal Zhabdrung laid the foundation of Brugpa polity in Bhutan.

Sixth, it is significant to remember that the Gorkha state maintained its nature of being a garrison state, as the southern Terai region was seen as an area of expansion to be invaded as personal fiefs of the de jure rulers. For example, one of the reasons of the Anglo-Nepalese War (1813–15) was the Gorkha encroachment on Terai areas of Awadh Nabobs. Even when Rana Jung Bahadur, the prime minister, was gifted with the western Terai areas between the Rapti and Mahakali (Sarda) rivers by the British as a reward for his armed assistance to the belaboured British during the Sepoy mutiny in 1858, he transferred them to the prime minister's office. The same practice continued even after his demise in 1877, when his successor prime ministers appended Kaski and Lamjung estates to the office of the prime minister. The fertile Terai provided much required foodstuffs for their armed forces as well as the cash revenue to the incumbents. On the other hand, the Namgyal theocratic dynasty and Dukpa church states did not depend on their regional officers such as Kazis to manage the southern Morung and Duars, from where neither the cash revenue nor foodstuffs were sent to the roadless, interior capitals of the overlords (Bell, 1903, 1904). Lastly, the demographic features of expanding Gorkharajya could not be contained within its limits, while the socio-cultural rationale of fecundity and the pastoral economic style of life among the Lamaists in two eastern states did not encourage them to descend to the hot, humid and forested lower Himalayan foothills, the Morang of Sikkim and Duars of Bhutan were left as the potential source of revenue, which were normally avoided by the highlanders to settle down. Here the Gorkhas' ingenuity in weaving their ethnic diversity into a single Gorkharajkiya identity must be acknowledged, which provides its own dynamism on the eastern Himalayan foothills. Thus, starting with Prithvi Narayan's invasion of Vijaynagar in 1768, ethnic Gorkhas were settled in Nepal Terai, the former Maithil region, Sikkim Morung and Bhutan Duars, and in less than 200 years with far reaching consequences for three states.

The 19th century proved to be catalytic for three polities. One by one, first it was Nepal, which lost the war to the British colonial masters, the newly emerged Indian rulers in 1815. Then it was the turn of Sikkim in 1861, when it was decisively brought within the British imperial domain. And lastly, it was Bhutan, which lost the Anglo-Bhutan war with the British in 1864. These wars resulted in the British control over the entire Himalayan foothills from Dehradun in the western Terai to the Brahmaputra Valley in Assam in the east. But this vast region did not remain an empty space; the thriving ethnic Nepalese and Medhesis came in a big way to fill the ethnic vacuum, causing headache to the three states from which they are yet to recover. Of course, there were many factors pushing the immigrants out from Nepal and similarly there were factors pulling the people to immigrate to the alleged land of opportunity in the British India. These processes resulted in a massive human movement from Nepal, first to Darjeeling, then to Sikkim and simultaneously to Assam and lastly to Bhutan Duars. This massive human migration is still on and the three states of India, Nepal and Bhutan are struggling to live with it. It is not that we forget about Sikkim, Darjeeling and Bhutan (they will emerge in the discussion at the end of the presentation and frequently in between), but the next chapters will concentrate on the various aspects of the Nepalese scenario leading to the phenomena of Greater Nepal all through the eastern Himalayan foothills.

Notes

1 Garrison: troops stationed in a fort or fortified place; a fortified place with troops, guns, etc.; a military post or station.

2 Theocracy: it is based on a Greek word, *theokratia*. Literally, it means rule of station by God or gods, hence the government by priests claiming to rule with divine authority, a country governed in this way or a group of clerics with political power (*Webster's New World Dictionary*, Macmillan Company, London, 1962). Theocracy is the 'rule by God' and refers to a type of government in which God or gods are thought to have sovereignty or to any state so governed. The concept has widely been applied to such varied cases as theocratic Egypt, ancient Israel, medieval Christendom, Calvinism, Islam and Tibetan Buddhism.

> Theocracy has not been rigorously defined concept in either social science or history of religions, although the term is used in historical writings. Theocracy designates a certain kind of placement of the ultimate source of state authority, regardless of form of government. The term theocracy may be usefully given, with examples relevant to each meaning: hierarchy or rule of religious functionaries; royal theocracy, or rule by sacred kings; general theocracy, or rule in a more general sense by a divine will or law; eschatological theocracy, or rule by divine.
>
> (*The Encyclopaedia of Religion*, Vol. 14, Macmillan Company, London, 1987, p. 427)

3 Church: it is a building set apart or consecrated for public worship, especially one for the Christian worship; public worship; religious service; the ecclesiastical government of a particular religious group' or its power, as opposed to secular government (*Webster's New World Dictionary*, Macmillan Company, London, 1962, p. 262). *The Encyclopaedia of Religion* provides a historical perspective to church state:

> Between 1050 and 1150, a large part of clergy throughout western Christendom united under the bishop of Rome to form an independent polity, separate from secular authority . . . This was papal revolution, which claimed that emperors and kings had no authority over the church; that the bishop of Rome alone had authority to ordain, discipline, depose and reinstate bishops; that only the pope had authority to 'enact' new laws according to the needs of the time. In the twelfth century, the Roman Catholic Church established itself as a unified, hierarchical, autonomous, political-legal entity. The Church also asserted its own independent property rights in the vast ecclesiastical holdings that constituted nearly one-third of the land holdings of Western Europe. Thus dual authority of governance was introduced; both secular and ecclesiastical authorities ruled in the same territories and over the same people with overlapping jurisdictions. The secular state raised armies, dealt with violence, taxed, regulated commerce, and

governed property relations, and in doing so it inevitably exercised large power not only over laity, but also over clergy. The ecclesiastical state not only governed most aspects of the life of the clergy, but also controlled the religious, family, moral, and ideological aspects of the life of the laity.

(*The Encyclopaedia of Religion*, Vol. 3, Macmillan Company, London, 1987, pp. 489–91)

Bibliography

Aris, M., 1979, *Bhutan: The Early History of a Himalayan Kingdom*, Vikas Publishing House, New Delhi.

Bell, C. A., 1903, *Settlement Report on Kalimpong*, to the Deputy Commissioner, Darjeeling, India Office Library (IOL), MSS: EUR: F. 80/Se-2.

Bell, C. A., 1904, *Confidential Report*, Office of the Political Officer, Gangtok.

Guha, A., 1987, "The Ahom Political System: An Enquiry Into State Formation in Medieval Assam: 1228–1800" in *Tribal Polities and State Systems in Pre-Colonial Eastern and North-Eastern India*, edited by S. C. Sinha, K. P. Bagchi, Calcutta.

Hamilton, F., 1971, *An Account of the Kingdom of Nepal*, reprint, Vol 10, Series 1. Bibliotheca Himalayica, New Delhi.

Hofer, A., 2004, *The Caste Hierarchy and the State in Nepal: A Study of the Maluki Ain of 1854*, Himal Books, Lalitpur, Nepal.

Mullard, S., 2011, *Opening the Hidden Land: State Formation and Construction of Sikkimese History*, Brill, Leiden and London.

Namgyal, T. and Y. Dolma, 1908, *History of Sikkim*, MSS.

Patterson, G. N., 1963, *Peking Versus Delhi*, Faber & Faber, London.

Pfaff-Czarnecka, J., 1997, "Vestiges and Visions: Cultural Change in the Process of Nation-Building in Nepal" in *Nationalism and Ethnicity in a Hindu Kingdom: The Politics of Culture in Contemporary Nepal*, edited by D. A. Gellner et al., Harwood Academic, Amsterdam, The Netherlands.

Pradhan, K., 1991, *The Gorkha Conquests: The Process and Consequences of the Unification of Nepal, With Particular Reference to Eastern Nepal*, Oxford University Press, Calcutta.

Sharma, P. R., 1997, "Nation-Building, Multi-Ethnicity and the Hindu State" in *Nationalism and Ethnicity in a Hindu Kingdom: The Politics of Culture in Contemporary Nepal*, edited by D. A. Gellner, et al., Harwood Academic, Amsterdam, The Netherlands.

Sharma, P. R., 2004, "Introduction" in Hofer, A., *The Caste Hierarchy and the State in Nepal: A Study of the Maluki Ain of 1854*, Himal Books, Lalitpur, Nepal.

Sinha, A. C., 1987, "Frontier Feudalism and State Formation in Sikkim" in *Tribal Polities and State Systems in Pre-Colonial Eastern and North Eastern India*, edited by S. Sinha, K. P. Bagchi, Calcutta.

Sinha, A. C., 1998, *Bhutan: Ethnic Identity and National Dilemma*, Reliance Publishing House, New Delhi, 2nd Edition.

Sinha, A. C., 2004, *Himalayan Kingdom Bhutan: Tradition, Transition and Transformation*, Indus, New Delhi, 2nd Edition.

Stiller, L. F., 1973, *The Rise of the House of Gorkha: A Study in the Unification of Nepal: 1768–1816*, Manjushri Publishing House, New Delhi.

Unknown, 1963, *Sikkim: A Concise Chronicle*, Published by Royal Wedding Committee and Printed by Sikkim Durbar Press, Gangtok.

Vaidya, T. R., 1993, *Prithvinarayan Shah: The Founder of Modern Nepal*, Anmol, New Delhi.

3

DREAM OF A DEMOCRACY IN THE EASTERN HIMALAYAN KINGDOMS

The Himalayas have been a unique entity for humans in the South Asian land mass for time immemorial. They have shaped the psyche and the character of the people and determine the vegetation, wildlife and the pattern of life of living things. The Himalayas range from the Arabian Sea to the Bay of Bengal, and all across the northern belt of the land they arrest the northern icy winds from crossing to the south and similarly stops the moisture-laden monsoon winds by their lofty ranges causing the heavy downpours of rainfall in the region. Thus, the region is known for its fertile land and plentiful of agricultural products to sustain its teeming inhabitants. Naturally, this land has attracted humans for ages, and in the course of time hordes of invaders mounted attacks on the settled populace of the region. It had one of the most ancient human civilizations, evidence of the earliest urban centres and organization of the society into states. With a view to understand various aspects of the regional socio-political aspects, it is imperative to uncover the broad contours of its geographical features and historical events, which led to the formation and development of states in the eastern Himalayan region.

Geographical background

With a view to understanding the unique status of the eastern Himalayan kingdoms, it is imperative to understand their geographical locale and the historical evolution of three polities. First, we propose to provide brief description of Himalayan geography; second, we turn to the brief historical sketch of the three kingdoms. The Himalayas, the abode of snow, stands guard in the north of India spread from west to east in about 5,500 kilometres and walls of Indian land mass from snow blizzards of Central Asia. Its massive ranges extend its western arm from Gwador on the Arabian Sea to the Mizo-Arakan ranges bordering

Bangladesh, India and Myanmar in the east. Of this, the western wing from Baluchistan to trans-Indus syntactical bend at Nanga Parbat in Kashmir is 1,500 kilometres. The eastern wing from Namcha Barwa on Arunachal border in the north-east to the Chittagong Hills on the Bay of Bengal is about 1,000 kilometres; and in between the central Himalayan arc from Nanga Parbat to Namcha Barwa is about 2,500 kilometres (Bose, 1972: 11). Though its width varies from areas to areas, the great Himalayan arc between the Indus and the Brahmaputra bends has an average width of about 200 kilometres.

The massive Himalayan land mass with its glorious snowy vista, its web of holy and life-giving rivers, its rare breed of herbal and wild vegetation, and its variety of birds, beasts and other life forms has stirred the Indian psyche for ages. And the Indians had their reasons to consider it holy, the abode of the gods, mystics, sages and source of the divinity. Various classical and modern poets composed their immortal lyrical classics in Sanskrit and modern languages on it. It was vaguely considered as the natural boundary of the South Asian land mass, though in reality there had been passes through which adventurous beings had been travelling across throughout the ages. There are dozens of mountain peaks which are counted among the highest in the world. It is higher, wider and drier in the west and lower, trimmer, and more rain-soaked in the east; accordingly the snow line is higher in the eastern Himalayas compared to its western wing. Its eastern corner in India has the distinction of being the region with the highest rainfall in the world, where rare animals such as rhinoceros are found and commercial crops such as Assam and Darjeeling tea are grown. Similarly, there are at least four river systems: Indus, Ganges, Brahmaputra and Irrawaddy, which originate in the Himalayas and provide life support system to their inhabitants to about a dozen of countries in South and Southeast Asia.

The Himalayan region is normally divided into three parallel zones from north to south on the basis of physiography. These are the greater Himalayas or the high mountains; the inner Himalayas or the *pahar*; and the foothills, variously referred as *terai* in the west in Nepal, *morang* in the middle in former Sikkimese territory and present Siliguri sub-division of Darjeeling district and the Duars, ceded by the Dukpa Kingdom to the British India. While the great Himalayas are snowbound year round, it is the home of the some of the highest mountain peaks in the world such as Everest (29,028 ft), Kanchenjunga (28,146 ft), Nanda Devi (26,645 ft), Kamet (25,447 ft), Namcha Barwa (25,445 ft), Chomo-lHari (23,997 ft) and others. There is little permanent settlement in the virtual snow desert except the occasional huts of the transhumance herdsmen. However, it abounds in a variety of rhododendrons and alpine coniferous forests. Moreover, the region is a haven for adventure-seeking mountaineers. It is interesting to note that the snow line is lower in the west (at 14,000 feet above sea level) than in the eastern Himalayas.

The inner Himalayas have various considerable valleys interposed between the mountain ranges full of deciduous forests. In between, there are extensive valleys such as Kashmir, Kathmandu, Pokhra, Paro, Thimphu, Bhumthang, Tongsa and so forth, known for their old settlements such as Kashmiri Pandits and the Newars of Kathmandu Valley. Rivers are fast, meandering and unfordable. There are alpine and tropical forests which have invariably been denuded for cultivation. Though bulk of the residents is peasant; rather they are marginal farmer, who subsist their economy by grazing cattle, goats and sheep. This is the region where petty principalities were established, taking advantage of difficult mountainous terrain in the mediaeval period by adventurous and enterprising personalities. There were about four dozen such principalities in western Nepal alone prior to the creation of Gorkharajya by Prithvi Narayan Shah, unifier of the modern Nepal. Similarly, Namgyal dynastic rule and the Dukpa theocracy were established in Sikkim and Bhutan in the first half of the 17th century. Some of them, such as Kathmandu Valley, Gangtok in Sikkim, and Kalimpong in Darjeeling were ideally suited for trans-border trade across the Himalayan passes between India and Tibet.

The foothills of the Himalayan region are low mountainous ranges running from west to east parallel to the inner Himalayas consisting mainly of boulders, moraine and sandy soil on which evergreen tropical forest abounds. It is known as 'negative zone' because of its unhealthy climate for human settlement. It was avoided by the highlanders like the Bhutias of Sikkim and Dukpas of Bhutan. Moreover, the region abounds in ferocious wild animals, and the climate is hot, humid and malarial (Karan, 1963: 11; Sinha, 1987: 337). The region was thinner in the western sector and wider in the eastern. In the past there were no permanent human settlements except some wild tribes such as Tharus, Koch, Mech, Toto and so forth which had developed immunity against the climatic harshness. Hill tribes such as the Gorkhas, Bhotias, Dukpas, Nyishis, Adis and the like used to raid the Gangetic and Brahmaputra plains below the foothills with a view to enslaving the plainsmen for working in the inner Himalayan fields. Terai in Nepal were known as the hunting grounds of the wild animals for the pleasure of the royalty. It is a fact that the terai region was avoided by peoples from the hills and the plains alike, but it was also considered as the potential source of wealth such as precious timber, wild animals, and agricultural land after clearing the forests.

The British empire carved out an effective Indian imperial boundary in the north, which took them about 75 years from the Anglo-Nepalese War, 1813–14 to 1888, when Sikkim was finally turned into the British Indian protectorate. This was made possible for them to bring the Himalayan foothills right from Muree on the Anglo-Afghan border to Sadiya in the north-eastern corner of India, in Assam. With establishment of effective administration, the foothills were cleared of the jungle first in the Nepal terai by the land-hungry peasants from the Gangetic plains (Gaige, 1975). There was a growing demand for the timber of the sal tree to be used as railway sleepers in colonial India. There were two significant developments affecting the Himalayan foothills in the first part of the 19th century. First, the British felt the need for creating health resorts in the cool and rarefied mountainous environment of the Himalayas, which were to be linked with the transport network of the empire for the convenience of the colonial rulers. And that is how Muree, Dalhousie, Shimla, Dehradun, Mussoorie, Nainital, Ranikhet, Darjeeling, Kalimpong, Shillong and so forth were developed as the summer hill stations on easy communication networks with the plains. Second, by the middle of the 19th century, it was realized that the eastern Duars were ideal landscape for cultivation of a newly discovered commercially miracle crop: tea. Thus, there was a mad rush from Lakhimpur in Assam in the east to Kangra in Punjab in the west for acquiring the malarial lands on long-time contract as the wasteland and clearing of the forests for laying down tea gardens. In this background, it is to be noted that the third quarter of the 19th century saw the introduction of forest reservation in India with a view to ensuring supply of timber for commercial and industrial purposes. In the process, some of the precious forests of the region were saved from the planters' axe and were treated as the 'reserved forests' as the state property.

The Himalayan ranges determined the possible extent of expansion of the three political systems in the eastern Himalayas: an orthodox (Sanatani) Hindu Kingdom in Nepal, a Bhutia principality of Sikkim in the middle and a Dukpa theocracy of Bhutan in the east. Though they made occasional sorties across the Himalayas to the foothills, their southward expansion in the 'negative land' of the Himalayan foothills was no more rewarding from material points of view. Three Himalayan kingdoms came in conflict with the Koch kings in the east, the Subedars of Rajshahi, Dinajpur and Purnia in the middle and the Nabobs of Awadh in the west over the Himalayan foothills. The highlanders avoided the hot, humid, wild and malarial foothills and would immediately withdraw to the hills after a short encounter in the foothills as reprisal raids. These foothills were rich in wild game and natural resources and provided easy cash revenue as levy on rivers and taxes on some of the riverside land and various forest products. The hill kingdoms found it convenient to effectively engage with the local rulers to the southern plains in the beginning, but soon they realized that they had to confront a more sophisticated, determined and organized enemy in the form of the British from the mid-18th century onwards. Furthermore, they found that their new southern adversary, the British, were more determined to pursue a policy of trade across the Himalayas at any cost.

History in the background

There is limited evidence to believe that there were extensive centralized political systems in Nepal, Sikkim and Bhutan prior to the 15th century for a variety of reasons. The topographically undulating region was thinly populated by isolated nomadic bands with primitive technology, which could not produce enough surplus for maintenance of an elaborate state structure. Even the limited flat lands in the valleys could not develop intensive agriculture in the harsh, cold climatic conditions. The rugged mountainous passes could not facilitate trade in the goods across the Himalayas in an appreciable way. In such a trying condition, ascetics, fugitives, adventurers, fortune seekers, exiles and the like found shelter in the region as a safe sanctuary against their adversaries. Possibly, many of them perished in the hostile environment, leaving behind occasional folk literature as a vague reminder of their presence in the region. However, a few of them might turned out to be lucky ones, "who came to the region as the victim prince in exile from elsewhere" alone, without an admiring crowd and the followers, who excelled their competitors in bravery, chivalry, swordsmanship, archery and winning hands of the local chieftain's daughters after gruelling trials. Naturally, such fugitive princes could establish kingdoms in the hills and win over local indifferent communities after displaying extraordinary skills in hunting, wrestling, controlling a ferocious wild creature and the like. The story of the founding of Namgyal dynasty and the extraordinary deeds of its ancestor Khaye Bumsa of Sikkim may be taken as an illustration. Similarly, the extraordinary theological, tactical and strategic campaigns of Zhabdrung Nawang Namgyal, the founder of the Dukpa theocracy in Bhutan, against his Tibetan adversary may be taken as another example.

Modern Nepal, prior to its consolidation by Prithvi Narayan Shah in the mid-18th century, was divided into dozens of small principalities. Some of them were bunched together for defence or/and marital alliances such as Baisis (a group of 22 principalities) and Chaubisis (another bunch of 22 such units). Many of them had local origins out of Khas, Magar and other dominant communities, but once they established a sizeable domain, most of them claimed Kshatriya origin, invariably from varied Indian princely houses, and tried to sanskritize themselves in the Hindu caste hierarchy. Gorkha emerged from such a situation, and in the course of time she charted a distinct course of her own. And that is how the last ruling dynasty of Nepal, the Shah rulers of the Gorkha kingdom, claimed to have come to Nepal from Chittorgarh in Rajasthan, India, in the 15th century (Hamilton, 1971; Stiller, 1973), whose descendant, Darbya Shah, captured the throne of Gorkha in 1559 and laid the foundation of the Gorkha principality. A descendant of Drabya, Prithvi Narayan (1723–75), moved from Gorkha after vanquishing the little principalities of the Kathmandu Valley in 1769 and laid the foundation of the modern state of Nepal. He was farsighted enough to realize the agricultural and revenue potential of the terai. And with a view to acquiring those territories in the foothills, he mounted armed attacks and even did not hesitate to secure them on rental basis from the British. Once he consolidated himself in the hills, Prithvi Narayan reached in 1769 for the nominal Mogul emperor in Delhi in India and solicited his approval for his rule in the hills. The Mogul emperor obliged and conferred upon him with the title of 'Shah Shasher Bahadur', and thus they came to be known as the Shah rulers of Gorkha, and in course of time to Nepal. His descendants kept on squabbling among themselves and permitted their prime ministers to grow powerful. Moreover, while the royal family was squabbling among themselves over their petty affairs, their social subordinate clan of the courtiers sprang a surprise by causing a massacre of huge proportion in the royal court and usurping the royal authority to rule the land. Thus, Prime Minister Rana Jung Bahadur turned out to be the real centre of power in 1846 and he made his Shah sovereign a helpless captive. Thus, began about a hundred-year rule (1846–1950) of the Ranas, known for its classical exploits, a most suitable example of 'Oriental feudalism'. The Ranacracy was abolished by a joint struggle of the King Tribhuvan Bir Bikram Shah and the political formations such as Nepali Congress in 1951. King Tribhuwan's son, King Mahendra, dismissed the democratic experiment in Nepal and established his personal rule on the name of the party-less Panchayati system, which ran for 30 years. The second Janandolan (democratic movement) brought back a chaotic democracy in 1990, but Shah dynastic rule continued in practice. At last, Prithvi Narayan's 12th descendant, King Gyanendra Bir Bikram Shah, was not only removed as the ruler, but even the Shah dynastic rule was abolished for good by another mass upsurge in 2008.

Similarly, Phuntsog Namgyal (1604–70), a Bhutia migrant patriarch, whose ancestors had migrated from eastern Tibet to Denzong earlier, was crowned as the sacred king by three visiting Tibetan monks in 1642 (Unknown, 1963: 1). It is said that three monks had come to Sikkim from three directions separately looking for new land to establish their theocratic domains. When they could not convince each other of their respective claims, they hit upon the idea of crowning Phuntsog as the Chogyal, the one who would rule as per religion under their patronage. Namgyals ruled over their domain indifferently through the help of the Lepcha and Bhutia Kazis. The little principality was invariably attacked by the Dukpas from the east and Gorkhas from the west, and in the process it lost the bulk of its territories to them. At last, the British colonial rulers came to their rescue after defeating the Gorkhas in 1815 and restoring Sikkimese territories secured as war booty from the Gorkhas. But this reprieve was also short-lived, as the British managed to secure first Darjeeling for establishing a hill sanatorium and its south-western portion, south of river Ramman, in the course of time. By 1888, Sikkim was effectively turned into a British protected princely state under the control of its powerful political officer. Thutub Namgyal, the unfortunate ninth ruler of Sikkim, spent most of his time in captivity along with his Tibetan consort. His son and successor died in mysterious circumstances soon after his assumption of the throne. Tashi Namgyal, the 11th ruler of the dynasty, remained behind the scenes in his first 35 years of rule, leaving the administration in the hands of the British political officers and then to his son, the crown prince, who had dreamt of turning his little kingdom into an independent entity. Palden Thondup Namgyal (1923–82), Phuntsog's 12th descendant, was obsessed with re-establishing the pristine Bhutia rule in multi-ethnic Sikkim in the third quarter of the 20th century. Thus, having failed to resolve the ethnic complexities in his principality, he paved the way for the merger of Sikkim and the Indian Union in 1975.

Zhabdrung Ngawang Namgyal (1594–1651), a Tibetan householding monk from the Brugpa sect of the Lamaism, took shelter in Bhutan in 1616 with a view to avoiding sectarian warfare rising in Tibet and established a theocratic regime in 1641, making himself the head. Before he took to Samadhi (retreat) in 1651, he had made provision for a dyarchical system of authority in the land. That system recognized his incarnations as the sacred rulers of the domain. However, an elected monk for a term of three years would run the secular affairs of the state. This ideal contrivance led to confusion, conflict and civil strife for about 200 years. In such a situation, it was logical that the theocracy was replaced with the Wangchuk monarchy on December 17, 1907, when the first hereditary ruler, Ugyen Wangchuk, was crowned as the king of Bhutan with active support of the British colonial rulers in India. And the fifth descendant of the said Wangchuk was crowned as the fifth Druk rGyalpo, king of Bhutan, in 2008 in a glittering ceremony. He is the only surviving king among the three former Himalayan kingdoms.

First it was the turn of Bhutan to engage in armed conflict with the British, who had taken the cudgel on behalf of their ally, the Koch Behar in 1772–3, leading to George Bogle's mission to Bhutan and Tibet. Within the next four decades, it was the Gorkha Kingdom of Nepal, which clashed with the British over encroachment on the Terai land leading to the Anglo-Nepalese War of 1814–15. This was a decisive engagement by which the state boundaries of Nepal and Sikkim came to be established. The Bhutanese continued to function in oriental perfidy by raiding the Duars, looting the cattle, cash and kind and running away to the interior with captives for enslaving. Then the British retaliated by taking away and confiscating various Duars in reprisal, which did not lead to a satisfactory result for them. In desperation, the British sent an embassy in the form of Ashley Eden to Bhutan for negotiating a satisfactory treaty, but the ambassador was not only insulted but was also made to sign a treaty under duress. Once the embassy returned to its base, the British declared war on Bhutan leading to the Anglo-Bhutan War, 1863–4. The war ended with the signing of the Sinchula Treaty in 1865, by which the Bhutan ceded 18 Duars in the plains and the Kalimpong region in the hills in the west, separating it from Sikkim and denying it a possible link with Nepal through the Morang corridor.

Keeping in mind the possibility of trans-Himalayan trade, the British had decided to take Sikkim under their wings soon after the Anglo-Nepalese War. The Sikkimese territories, surrendered by Nepal in 1815, were in principle restored to it, but in reality, the Morang portion in the plains was simply taken over by the British. Thus the three Himalayan states of Nepal, Sikkim and Bhutan were segregated in the hills and their claims in the plains were simply ignored, as they were supposed to be states in the hills only. Though the hilly tracts on right bank of the river Teesta, Darjeeling Sadar and Kurseong sub-divisions of district of Darjeeling were restored to Sikkim soon after Nepalese surrender. Sikkim lost them to British India by 1861. As per the terms of the Treaty of Tumlong, 1861, Sikkim became a British protectorate and by 1888, they stationed a British administrator, J. Claude White, political officer, in Gangtok, the state capital. All through the 19th century, realizing the fact that Sikkim was located on the shortest possible trade route between Calcutta, the commercial and colonial capital of the British India and Lhasa, the capital and the biggest town in Tibet, the British tried to open a trade route to Tibet and then to China by via Sikkim, with limited success. However, by the end of the 19th century Nepal was autonomous from the British; Bhutan came within the orbit of the British Indian empire, but was not considered as a part of British India and Sikkim turned out to be an Indian princely state.

Slowly and steadily, the British began recruiting the Gurkhas right from 1815 in their armed forces, constabulary, labour corps, tea plantation, forest clearance, watch and ward and for a number of sundry jobs. A number of recruitment depots were established closer to the Nepalese borders in northern India far recruitment of the Gurkha soldiers from Nepal, as Nepal did not formally permit the British to recruit her subjects. Moreover, as soon as Darjeeling was taken up as a hill station in 1835, the Nepalese flocked to it and built it up as a thriving urban, plantation and agrarian habitation. The British encouraged the Sikkimese gentry, who were basically pastoralists with a barter economic base, to invite Nepalese labour to develop agriculture and mining, with the result that within decades the Nepalese overwhelmed the indigenous Sikkimese demographically. The same British advice to Bhutanese court led to Nepalese (Lhotshampas: 'the southerners') settling down on the southern foothills (Duars), turning the jungles into thriving agricultural fields, possibly soon after the Anglo-Bhutan War in 1864.

The eastern Himalayan kingdoms as the buffer states and populist expectations

One needs to read Peter Hopkirk's volumes on espionage moves and counter-moves in the central Asian countries, especially imperial plays, to understand their rivalry to control the trade routes and guard imperial boundaries and spheres of influence across the Himalayas. It goes beyond doubt that the British were paranoid on security of their Indian imperial possession in the 19th century, and for that they evolved an elaborate strategy of "external and internal buffer states" at a considerable cost. Added to it was their obsession with securing trade relations with China across the Himalayas through Tibet. Unlike other Asian states, Tibet was a Lamaist theocracy which had an opaque relation with imperial China, which suited British imperial designs. Thus, they discovered that China was the suzerain power on Tibet. However, they did not hesitate to sign independent treaties with the Tibetan authorities without reference to China. After Francis Younghusband's expedition to Tibet in 1903–4, the British had Afghanistan, Tibet and Thailand as their external buffer states. Similarly, from the Anglo-Nepalese Treaty (1816) to the Anglo-Bhutanese Treaty (1910) they stabilized Kashmir, Nepal, Sikkim and Bhutan as the internal buffer states to their Indian possession. These buffer states were closely guarded so far their external relations were concerned by stationing experienced British officers as the political residents at courts of these states.

But this idealist situation changed drastically between the two world wars. Meanwhile, the struggle for Indian independence was vigorously waged by a variety of freedom fighters. The British had no capacity to hold on their Indian imperial possession after the Second World War. Thus, the British decided to set India free, a situation for which the rulers of Kashmir, Nepal, Sikkim and Bhutan were unprepared. To the contrary, they pleaded for continuation of the same old imperial relations with the British to the only British face known to them, that is, the political officer to continue. However, the Political Officer Basil Gould, in the case of Sikkim and Bhutan, clearly informed them that the continuation of their old relations with Britain was not feasible in the changed circumstances and that they were to negotiate their relations with the successor Indian government. Thus, the two Maharajas were advised to prepare memoranda on issues of their concerns and to meet the Cabinet Mission, sent by the British colonial government, in Delhi. The two principalities sent their respective delegations with their memoranda to wait on the Cabinet Mission in 1946. While Raja Sonam Tobgyel Dorji, the Bhutan agent, led the Bhutanese delegation, Maharaj Kumar Palden Thondup Namgyal led the Sikkimese delegation and arrived in Delhi to meet the Cabinet Mission. However, the Cabinet Mission did not find it convenient to meet the delegates and they were advised to return to their states and wait for the outcome.

The then undersecretary of the Political and Foreign Department of the Government of India, sent a note to the political officer in Gangtok on August 10, 1946, informing him of the government's decision on the memoranda of the two delegations, which was to be intimated to them:

> In practice, it may well prove difficult to secure a tidy solution to the future of Nepal, Sikkim and Bhutan, even to the eastern marches of Kashmir [i.e., Ladakh]. This will largely depend on the future policy and fate of China and hence of Tibet.

> The Government of the [Indian] Union must be prepared for complications on North Eastern Frontiers and evolve a policy to meet them. This may well have to be that of maintaining all the principalities in virtual independence of India, but as buffer, and as far as possible, [as] client states. There may be greater advantages in according Sikkim a more independent status than seeking to absorb Bhutan as well as Sikkim in the Indian Union, adding communal problem of Buddhism . . . The Government will be advised to avoid entering into fresh commitments with any one of these frontier states or seeking to redefine their status. Their importance is strategic in direct relation to Tibet and China, and indirectly to Russia. Such adjustment of relations with the [Indian] Union can fully be affected by those political and strategic considerations . . . account of which, it is hoped, the treaty will take rather than the political niceties, which do not help defence policy.
>
> (quoted in Sinha, 1991: 173–4)

It is apparent that the note reflected the imperial thinking of the British to guard its Indian empire with a chain of internal and external buffer states in the north, which would remain not only in the imperial shadow but would also be maintained as client states. It is also suggestive of the imperial approach to 'the Great Game' in the central Asian region in which the British were significant players. The only thing they overlooked before advising the successor state was that, in the changed circumstances, there were no more imperial interests to guard. Furthermore, although the note appears to be only advisory in nature, it unnecessarily created a stumbling block on fresh deliberations on the issue on the part of the functionaries of the successor government (Sinha, 2013). Perhaps it also assumed that the future Indian successor government would automatically tow the imperial advice thus rendering it in foreclosing its options.

The preceding note contains at least two significant points. One is an advice to the Government of the Indian Union, the successor to the British, for maintaining the status quo in the region. The second is an assurance to the Maharajas of the Himalayan kingdoms against the absorption of their principalities into the Indian Union. It appears that the last British political officer in Sikkim must have adequately assured the two Maharajas of their continuation and simultaneously cautioned the successor Indian Union of the danger in disturbing the British contrived status quo in the region prior to her departure from the scene. Consequently, the Government of India first signed standstill treaties after which, in 1950, the formal treaties were negotiated with the three Himalayan kingdoms based on the same old colonial terms and conditions. We shall see ahead in the next chapters how the common people of India, Nepal, Sikkim and Bhutan would aspire for creating a participative democratic system by waging an anti-feudal struggle against the most repressive regimes in the region and how the newly established Indian Union conveniently followed the British imperial advice leading to reinforcing already decadent feudal states of the eastern Himalayan kingdoms. At this stage, it is imperative to note that the bulk of the commoners of the region did not share the British perception of maintaining the status quo of the autocratic feudal regimes. And in fact, they desired to wage anti-feudal struggles for fashioning a democratic future of their own against their repressive overlords.

Meanwhile, the onrush of the Nepalese settlements to the Himalayan foothills mentioned earlier did not stop with Bhutan; it continued eastwards to Arunachal, Nagaland and Mikir Hills (Karbis) and crossed the Patkoi Hills from Assam to Burma. Furthermore, whenever there was an armed cantonment, the British encouraged demobilized Gurkhas to settle down as a strategic support base. In the course of time, these Nepalese contributed handsomely to the economy, culture, literature and politics of the host societies. However, as long the British were the rulers in India, the issue of Nepalese 'citizenship' was irrelevant, as everybody was a subject of the empire. But as Nepal and Bhutan became sovereign states distinct from India after British withdrawal in 1947, the presence of Nepali speakers turned out to be problematic and controversial. They were charged, and at times not without reasons, with harbouring alien loyalty and even as the precursors of 'Greater Nepal', an alleged sinister design on the part of their mother country. Moreover, it goes without saying that Nepali speakers were the most articulate, organized and politically conscious in 1940s in the eastern Himalayan scene and their stronghold and focal point of their deliberations was that of Darjeeling. However, the eastward move of the Nepali speakers from Nepal begins with Darjeeling, which has been a Nepali-dominated land at least for the last hundred years, willy-nilly it has emerged as the most critical land for the Nepali commonwealth in a variety of ways, which we propose to discuss in the next chapter.

Bibliography

Bose, S. C., 1972, *Geography of Himalayas*, National Book Trust, New Delhi.

Gaige, F. H., 1975, *Regionalism and National Unity in Nepal*, Vikas Publishing House, New Delhi.

Hamilton, F., 1971, *An Account of the Kingdom of Nepal*, Reprint, Vol. 10. Series 1, Bibliotheca Himalayica, New Delhi.

Karan, P. P., 1963, *The Himalayan Kingdoms: Bhutan, Sikkim and Nepal*, Nostrands Torchlight Book, Princeton.

Sinha, A. C., 1987, "Frontier Feudalism and State Formation in Sikkim" in *Tribal Polities and State Systems in Pre-Colonial Eastern and North-Eastern India*, edited by S. C. Sinha, K. P. Bagchi, Calcutta.

Sinha, A. C., 1991, *Bhutan: Ethnic Identity and National Dilemma*, Reliance Publishing House, New Delhi.

Sinha, A. C., 2013, *Social Formation in and Around Sikkim in Middle of 20th Century*, VI Foundation Day Lecture, Sikkim University, Gangtok, July 2, 2013.

Stiller, L. F., 1973, *The Rise of the House of the Gorkhas: A Study in Unification of Nepal: 1768–1816*, Manjushri Publishing House, New Delhi.

Unknown, 1963, *Sikkim: A Concise Chronicle*, Published by the Royal Wedding Committee and Printed by Sikkim Durbar Press, Gangtok.

4

DARJEELING, THE FULCRUM OF THE NEPALESE RENAISSANCE

The archaic, obscurantist and repressive Rana regime of Nepal had stifled the creative spontaneity of the Nepalese at large, as they were afraid of literary innovation from within and outside Nepal. Thus, they neither opened avenues for modern education nor permitted anyone to do so. In such a situation, some of the elite dissenters among them who had moved to Banaras, the ancient holy city of the Hindus on the bank of the river Ganges, were inspired in the second half of the 19th century with the ongoing renaissance in Hindi literature. These initiatives led to the first wave of modern literary trends in Nepali literature. However, literary innovations in Darjeeling, a British hill station with a Christian missionary educational system, the story was different. With spread of Western-inspired education, it soon turned into a centre of Nepali literary creativity, which was initiated by newly emerging white collar and blue coat professionals. Once Nepal opened up, it was the Nepalis from Darjeeling and elsewhere in India who became the vanguard of social transformation in Nepalese society. Within a short span of decades, with support from the state, the Nepalese socio-cultural and literary scene touched new excellence of achievement.

Banaras and initiation in modern Nepali literary form

Right from the time of Prithvi Narayan Shah – and even before – Banaras had been a cultural, religious, commercial and political centre for the expatriate as well as Gorkha literati. We are invariably informed that disinherited/discredited/dissenting Gorkha royalties and difficult/discredited/dismissed functionaries were eased out to Banaras on the plea of earning merit at the holy city of the Hindus. Banaras also happened to be the holy city for elderly, sick and dying Hindus to prefer residence in waiting (Kashi Vas) for their end on or around the banks of the river Ganges. The act of Kashi Vas was considered religiously meritorious and socially honourable even for the most despicable persons among the orthodox Hindus. It is claimed that the sacred water of the Ganges at Banaras cleans all the human sins and failings, once the individual takes shelter in the city of Lord Vishwanath, the guardian deity of the city of Banaras. Thus, the city collects all types of terminally sick, deformed, dejected, deprived and desperate people, who look for relief from their scourge with the blessings of the Lord Vishwanath in residence in Banaras, the master of the universe.

This ancient city is not only known as sacred for Hindus and Buddhists, but the city has also been the abode of the scholars, schools of learning, tradition of classical Sanskrit, Pali and Prakrit languages, its own schools of music and dance and theatres, and centres for learning in the sacred and secular knowledge since time immemorial. There have been scholars in residence at Banaras known for adjudicating on the sacred disputations, Hindu jurisprudence, sectarian debates, music *gharanas* (dynasties of musicians) and such other concerns of the Hindu world. Ever since its evolution, the city is also known as the centre of commerce, handicrafts and fine arts on the one hand; on the other hand, it is also the nerve centre of a variety of literary traditions in a number of languages, whose speakers reside in or visit the city and publish their works. It is famous as centre of dance, theatre, dramas, songs, music and accomplished courtesans. It is as well known for decadence, debauchery and perversity among a section of the gentry. Its impact on the Hindu world has been profound irrespective of the sectarian divisions among them. Naturally, Banaras was the obvious choice for the royalty, courtiers, holy men and men of wealth and influence among the Gorkhas to reside. And when such a bunch of experienced, educated persons with leisure come together, they give expressions of their expertise through their creative writings as well. And that is what happened in case of the Gorkhas of Gorkharajya in Banaras.

When the various linguistic groups were engaged in creative writing and enriching their regional languages in various parts of India, Gorkharajya was groaning under the oppressive Rana totalitarian system. The Ranas were distrustful of art, culture and literature. In the name of literature, what was created locally was an artificial and lifeless adaptation of the classical Sanskrit literature. The Nepalese art of painting and statuary fell in decay, while pieces of the British imitation paintings and sculpture adorned the walls of the Durbar Hall and palaces of the Ranas. The first prime minister, Rana Jung Bahadur (r. 1846–77), discouraged the writing and staging of dramas.

> The educational system in Nepal during the Rana period was in shambles. The aristocratic families engaged European or Bengali teachers, family priests and pundits as tutors to their children. The great bulk of population was poor, ignorant and illiterate. In the year 1894, Prime Minister Rana Bir Shamsher (r.1885–1901) started the Durbar High School at Kathmandu. (Rana) Deva Shamsher inaugurated a number of primary schools, many of which were subsequently closed down. Rana Chandra Shamsher (r.1901–1929) discouraged the spread of liberal education. In 1912 (during the famous Delhi Durbar), he told (the Visiting British ruler) George V during latter's visit to India that one of the consequences of sound educational system in Nepal was that she did not produce revolutionaries like (Bal Gangadhar) Tilak and (Gopal Krishna) Gokhale. The establishment of the Trichandra College (in 1918), Prime Minister Chandra Shamsher (had) cautioned, would dig the grave of the Rana rule.
>
> (Sen, 1992: 75–6)

In such a bleak situation, naturally, it was the holy city of Banaras which provided an intellectual outlet for Gorkha creativity. Bhanubhakta Acharya (1814–69), Raghunath Bhatta (1811–51) and Motiram Bhatta (1866–96), the first crop of pioneering Gorkha literary figures, were nurtured, nourished and associated with local literary upheaval. For illustration, they were closely associated with the pioneering Hindi literary group led by the eminent Hindi poet and dramatist Bharatendu Harishchandra, a Hindi icon from Banaras. Bhanubhakta's *Ramayana*, published from Banaras, became a classic in Nepali literature for all the time to come. Motiram Bhatta has the unique distinction of publishing the first Nepali literary monthly journal, *Gorkha Bharat Jeevan*, in 1886 from his Bharat Jeevan printing press. It is to be noted that Balakanda of Bhanubhakta's *Ramayana* was published in this journal in 1887. Thus, the city gave a fillip to a dozen of up-and-coming Nepali litterateurs, who soon shone on the Nepalese literary horizon. Among them, Lakshmiprasad Devkota (1909–59) was claimed to be something like Sumitranandan Pant, Jaishanker Prasad and Shuryakant Tripathi 'Nirala' (acclaimed Hindi romantic poets of the mid-20th century) rolled into one.

The very name of Banaras enlarged the popular imagination of scholarship and sacredness at the same time. They also had a ready clientele among the teachers and students of the chain of Sanskrit *pathsalas*, where among other things the Sanskrit language and *karmakand* (the procedures of priestly rituals) were taught. The litterateurs trained and published in Banaras got spread far and wide among the Nepali speakers, wherever they were settled. For example, Pandit Padam Prakash Dungana came to Shillong, then the capital of Assam province, and gave a fillip to Nepali literary output through his poetic collections (Rawat, 2003: 271). Similarly, there are instances that modestly educated Brahmins from Banaras turned eastwards to Darjeeling, Sikkim, Bhutan Duars, Assam and even to Burma; they opened modest village schools in the local Hindu temples and began instructing children in not only the Nagri alphabets but also rudiments of the scriptures and elementary education in Nepali. Thus, literati Brahmins kept the hope of classical scholarship, but it could easily be turned secular as and when the impetus was given. In the words of Balkrishna Sama (1902–81), the noted Nepalese literary figure, "in the dark days of Rana rule, architects and lovers of Nepali literature turned to India for enlightenment and inspiration and thus, modern Nepali literature grew on the soil of India".

There is another aspect of the Banaras school of Nepali literary creation: the Nepali literary scene was largely controlled by the high-caste Nepalese, invariably the Brahmins, who had a family tradition of learning classics, the sources of the Hindu epics and mythologies. They produced literature on classical themes, which had a ready-made commercial market. However, in the view of Rhoderick Chalmers,

> despite its manifest commercial success, there remained one over-riding limitation of the Nepali literary scene in Banaras: caste and class domination by the Brahmans who were not reflective of their changing audience. While they managed to cater to popular tastes, there is no evidence of a democratization of the literary world allowing "self-expression of lower (caste and ethnic) groups". Nor was the Banaras Nepali community structured in the same way as the much larger Indian Nepali society of Darjeeling area is. Writing from Banaras engaged with topical issues, in particular Nepal-oriented politics, but was often removed from the pressing issues such as education, employment and administration, which faced the settled Nepali community of Darjeeling.
>
> (Chalmers, 2003: 354–5)

Almost the same expression was voiced by the noted Nepali litterateur of Darjeeling district, Indra Bahadur Rai, who talks about the nature of Nepali literature from Nepal;

> While in Nepal literary writing was begun by elite (Aryan) Brahmans, who wrote in praise of their kings, in India the beginning of Indian Nepali literature was made by common soldiers and labourers, who were mostly from Mongoloid ethnic groups, and who wrote of their actual experiences of battles fought and lives lived in India. Indian Nepali literature can justly be proud of its popular and proletarian beginning.
> (Rai, n.d.: 176)

In a way, the Nepali literary scene in Banaras was inspired by the mediaeval classical tradition, and to a great extent it was addressed to the feudal court culture of Kathmandu. In other words, it was elitist in its approach and geared to the needs of a thin upper crust of the society, in many ways which were decadent and inward-looking.

Darjeeling as the home of the Nepali-speaking communities

Unlike Banaras, a relatively recent urban centre of Darjeeling, as a European favoured hill station, was the nerve centre of the Christian missionary activities in the eastern Himalayan region since its inception, which had a theological mandate to work among Kiratis, Nepalis, Lepchas and Bhotias. And for that purpose, back in 1821, the famous Serampur Missionaries from Calcutta had translated the Old Testament in Nepali. Rev. William Macfarlane and his colleagues such as Archibald Turnbull and Padri Ganga Prasad Pradhan, first among the Nepalis to be converted to Christianity in Darjeeling, were instrumental in publishing Nepali grammar and vocabulary in 1887. Soon the Government of Bengal would decide to merge two government institutions, Government Middle School (established in 1860) and Bhutia Boarding School (established in 1874) located at Darjeeling, and start Darjeeling Government School in 1892. This was the locale where the future Nepali litterateur Dharanidhar Sharma (Koirala) would join and come out with his famous literary collection, *Naivedya*. Darjeeling was inhabited by the migrant Nepalese mainly from eastern Nepal, among whom Newar traders, Rai, Limbu, Tamang and other members of the Kirat commonwealth predominated. Furthermore, it was also the recruitment centre for the Gorkha soldiers to the British Imperial Indian army. Thus, it had a mixed Nepali population who were ranked lower in the Nepalese social hierarchy as per the Nepalese Civil Code, the Maluki Ain. They had Bhutias and Lepchas, the two communities, identified with the land, as the social collaborators of the Nepalis, with whom they jelled well. But it was more egalitarian in the sense that there was no predominance of oppressive feudal court culture and demand from the priestly segment like the Brahmins to confirm to the classical standard by some ancient tradition. The Nepali society in Darjeeling in comparison to Bengalis, Biharis, Punjabis, Tibetans and others was in the process of crafting of an identity of its own. The first problem the community faced was the issue of their language, their lingua franca, and Nepali or Gorkhali came in handy for that. They had to struggle to get it recognized as a medium of instruction at level of the elementary schools to begin with and for that textbooks were to be written.

When Darjeeling was taken over as a barren land in 1835 by the British for turning it into a hill resort, its population was estimated to be about a hundred in all. Surrounding areas were very thinly inhabited by the Lepchas and Bhutia immigrants from Tibet, who were termed genetically less productive for a number of reasons (Risley, 1894). The British needed inexpensive labour to develop the hill resort for a variety of purposes: to lay down tea plantations for commercial production; to cut the cart tracts and roads around for easy communication; and to do the sundry jobs for the residents of the civil station. For that, the Nepalese were ever ready, and thus migration, especially from eastern Nepal, began in a big way. For example, in 1891, out of a total population of 30,458 in the district, there were 15,458 Nepalese plus 3,386 Limbus, who were counted separately at the time. A hundred years later, in 1991, the total population of the district would rise to 405,505, out of which 295,583 were Nepalese. Among other developments, Darjeeling turned out to be the attractive site for the settlement of the Gorkha soldiers after their retirement. These disciplined, hard-working and resolute pensioners began to contribute significantly to the welfare and the future wellbeing of the community. Needless to add that the British had developed a construct of "martial race", in which educated and intelligent Indians were termed "cowards", while unlettered and backward communities such as Gurkhas, Pathans and Sikhs were defined as "martial", ideal to serve the armed forces without asking questions.

There is a long history of the British love affair with the Gurkhas beginning in 1814, when the British colonial regime fought against the expansionist Gorkha kingdom and defeated them. The Anglo-Nepalese War (1813–14) led to the signing of the Treaty of Sugawlee in 1815, which fixed the modern boundary of Nepal in the central Himalayan region. A byproduct of the war was the British discovery of the legendary Gurkha bravery, which suited in their scheme of terming certain communities as the martial race. They got busy immediately in recruiting the Gurkhas in the British colonial Indian army with or without the approval of the Gorkha durbar. To begin with, the Nepalese establishment was reluctant in permitting the British to recruit Nepalese in their armed forces, as they saw them as their adversaries. But once the Rana regime was in place in Kathmandu, a new phase of friendship emerged between the two regimes and the Gorkha kingdom came to the rescue of the British in their hour of needs time and again. They also formally permitted the British to recruit the Gurkhas in their armed forces. And for that, the British opened recruitment depots at Dehradun, Gorkhpur, Laheriasarai, Darjeeling and Shillong, mainly for Gurkha recruitment. Apart from that, a number of Gurkhas were recruited in armed constabulary and police forces in the British Indian provinces of Bengal, Assam and Burma. Having realized the qualities of arduous work of the Nepalese, the British encouraged the non-martial Gurkhas to opt for logging, clearing the forests, tea plantation, grazing on the degraded forests and reclaiming the marginal mountainous and forested lands. Furthermore, the British had a policy to settle the Gurkhas near about the cantonments of the armed forces in the mountainous region for a variety of sundry duties, but in the beginning for their services in their coolie corps. Though India-born Gurkhas, labelled as line boys, were not considered suitable for recruitment to the army, they were encouraged to settle on thinly inhabited strategic locations within the north-eastern part of the empire where they were engaged in a variety of low-paid jobs. Thus, one finds concentration of the Nepali-speaking population right from the Darjeeling hills, Sikkim, the Bhutanese foothills, the foothills in Arunachal Pradesh, the Patkoi Hills and beyond to Upper Burma.

The Nepalese of Darjeeling had petitioned to the authorities for recognition of Nepali as one of the Indian languages for the matriculation examination of Calcutta University, which was accorded in the year 1918. In view of a perceptive scholar, unlike Kathmandu, the Darjeeling social scene had its own challenges:

> Those who constituted Nepali civil society often represented different interest or privilege groups. Non-Nepalis, such as Laden La, Bhutanese royalty, or British administrators, could influence institutions through patronage. Equally, establishment figures from within Nepali community tended to reflect the values of their immediate environment: Banaras-based projects could count on the support of the Pandits, Kathmandu activists might draw in educated Brahmins, members

> of the Rana clans or government officers, and Darjeeling could look to retired army or police officers, contractors and entrepreneurs, and the growing class of those who held formal British educational qualifications and positions in government service.
>
> (Chalmers, 2009: 131)

Parasmani Pradhan began editing the first Nepali literary journal, *Chandrika*, with a view to "*Unnati*" (progress) of the *jati* (community/"nation") in the district of Darjeeling. He left editing the journal in favour of Rashmi Prasad Alley; resigned the job of the manager, Hari Printing Press; and joined as the first teacher of Nepali language at the matriculation level in Kalimpong Scottish Mission School in the year 1920. He joined the government job as the assistant inspector of schools in the district of Darjeeling after two years. Along with another fellow Nepali, Karana Bahadur Gurung, the two would incessantly work on teaching methodology in the Nepali teaching schools in the district. In 1924, Parasmani Pradhan became instrumental in persuading the famous Macmillan Publishing Company to publish Nepali textbooks for the schools, which further added to the standardization of the emerging language.

This one development (the government decision to introduce Nepali as a subject of teaching in the schools in Darjeeling) appeared as a challenge and opportunity to the up-and-coming Nepali intelligentsia in the form of SUDHAPA, a triumvirate of Suryavikram Gwavali, Dharanidhar Sharma Koirala and Parasmani Pradhan. This trio turned out to be the "driving force behind many important developments such as founding of the Nepali Sahitya Sammelan in 1924" at Darjeeling (Chalmers, 2009: 117). Furthermore, they standardized Nepali literary form, edited literary journals like *Chandrika* and *Chandra*, wrote a number of textbooks for the Nepali medium schools, organized publications of the books and journals in Nepali and guided the nascent renaissance among the Nepalis of Darjeeling. They had taken successfully massive responsibilities on their soldiers: they were guiding the ill-educated and economically weak Nepali masses; they were busy in evolving popular literary form for their language; they were laying foundation for various literary, cultural and social fora as support system for the community; and they were soliciting institutional approval from the authorities.

As the saying goes, Darjeeling emerged as the cultural hub for Nepalis. It had many firsts of its own type: first Nepali theatre company, the Gorkha National Theatre Company (1909); first literary and library association, Kurseon (1913); Nepali Sahitya Sammelan, Darjeeling (1924); Nepali Sahitya Sammelan Patrika, (1931); and the first non-governmental organization of its own type, Gorkha Dukha Niwarak Sammelan (1932).

> These developments, and the history of the birth and development of theatre in Darjeeling, have been the subject of detailed analysis of two valuable works: Kumar Pradhan's '*Darjilingka kehi purana natakharu ra Buddha charit natak*' (1982) and Indra Bahadur Rai's '*Darjilingma nepali natak ko ardhasatabdi*' (1984).

The saga of Nepali endeavour for the upliftment of Nepali language passed through three phases: (1) from 1920 to 1952, (2) from 1953 to 1971, and (3) from 1972 onwards which has rightly been termed as the Nepali Bhasa movement (Subba, 1992: 92–8). Though the groundwork for teaching of Nepali was done earlier by Christian missionaries and Nepali pioneering teachers, the first phase of the movement was spent mainly in advocating, petitioning and canvassing for introduction of Nepali as the medium of instruction in the schools in Darjeeling. The Universities of Allahabad (1911) and Calcutta (1918) had already recognized Nepali as one of their native languages to be taught and evaluated. Though the Griffith Committee recommended in 1927 that Nepali be introduced as medium of instruction at the primary level, it was subsequently allowed for higher levels of degrees. In this context, the role played by Nepali Sahitya Sammelan and its pivoting triumvirate of SUDHAPA must be written in golden letters. They not only produced quality literature but also wrote textbooks for the children, an act which is not child's play, and they functioned as standard bearers for the Nepali language.

Darjeeling as an emergent Nepali middle class city

We have noted elsewhere (Sinha, 2013) how Darjeeling emerged as an ideal location of emergent Nepali aspirations. Apart from the literary, cultural and educational contributions, Darjeeling also appeared on the scene where things were happening, such as the location for new types of vocations and professions: teaching, legal practice, the medical profession, trade unions, business and shopkeeping, transport and communication, hospitality management, printing and publications and the like. Some of the Nepali speakers even opted for full-time politics as a vocation. Within no time, a vibrant middle class emerged from among the immigrant underdog Nepalis, who were confident taking all types of challenges. Darjeeling was not only the land of political awakening among the Nepalis, but the dawn of Nepali renaissance also took place in Darjeeling. We shall refer to only a few aspects here which had far-reaching consequences for the region. One, the vibrant Nepali print media gave voice to the common people of the region to express their innermost emotions, dreams of a democratic future, and aspirations of a new India through literature and journalism. By then, Nepali had turned into the lingua franca not only of Darjeeling but also of Sikkim and Bhutan. The other significant development was the vigorous trade union movement around tea gardens, which was also anti-imperial and anti-feudal in its orientation. These two developments brought the intelligentsia as well as the underdogs together on a common platform to organize and fight against perceived injustice, for a better future and even to ridicule the mighty. This was the phase in the regional history to dream wild and die for one's ideals. And it is not for nothing one finds the Banaras-educated, politically hardened and first democratically elected prime minister of Nepal, Bishweshwar Prasad Koirala, travelling to Darjeeling for an apprenticeship to a local legal luminary, Rai Sahib Hari Prasad Pradhan, who became the first chief justice of the Chief Court in 1951. Similarly, Justice Pradhan was appointed the first chief justice of the newly established Supreme Court of Nepal in 1961.

In Darjeeling, the issue of recognition of Nepali language was a rallying point for all the ethnic groups in the hills and this issue strengthened the case for Gorkha identity. In fact, the urge for identity led the Lepchas, Bhutias, Rais, Limbus, Magars and so forth to declare Nepali as their mother tongue in various census operations. Harka Bahadur Gurung pays a handsome tribute to unintended social engineering of the Nepali-speaking Indians, who innovated a somewhat more inclusive social world of their own:

> socio-political processes operating in the two Indian territories (Sikkim and Darjeeling) provide some future indicators (even) for Nepal. In culture, these Nepali speakers, free from the strictures of the Maluki Ain, have created a multi-ethnic society with a modern outlook. In politics, caste elitism has been superseded by a democratic spirit, in which leadership of the state is passed on from a Chhetri to a Limbu and then to a Rai, while the (Darjeeling Gorkha) Hill Council leadership in contested between a Tamang and a Limbu.
>
> (Gurung, 1997: 519)

Nepali identity politics in British India

Since 1907, Darjeeling Gorkhas and their search for an Indian identity had been caught in whirlpool of Indian politics. Their spokesmen, opinion leaders, intelligentsia and literati have been making all types of associations to gain an autonomous status in India. First, they got aligned with the tea planters' lobby, Anglo-Indians, and expatriate Rana aristocrats and demanded for a separate administrative set-up for the district of Darjeeling based on "hill ethnicity" in 1907 (Subba, 1992: 75–101). A decade later, in 1917, they changed it to demand for creation of a separate unit known as the "North Eastern Frontier Province (NEFP)" consisting of Darjeeling, Doors, Assam and present Arunachal Pradesh on the basis of claimed racial, historical, religious and linguistic grounds. Soon after that, the Hillmen's Association led by Laden La of NE+BU+La (the journal *NEBULA*) fame along with the Darjeeling Planners' Association and European Association, sent a memoranda to the then secretary of state for India on October 25, 1930, suggesting that:

> The district of Darjeeling, where the Gorkha population predominate, should be excluded from Bengal and be treated as an independent administrative unit with the Deputy Commissioner as an Administrator vested with much more powers than that of District Magistrate assisted by a small Executive Council, representatives of all interests, in the administration of the area.

Sardar Bahadur Laden La was worried of the worsening intercommunity relations in Darjeeling in 1930s and decided to take initiative in this regard. With a view to removing the internal squabbling among Nepalis, Bhutias and Lepchas, a meeting of about 600 notables from various parts of the district was called at Darjeeling on December 23, 1934. The meeting decided to establish a new forum, Hill People's Social Union (HPSU), with Laden La as president, Rup Narayan Sinha as the secretary and a governing body of 16 notables drawn from the three communities from the region. They decided to publish *NEBULA*, a Nepali monthly journal, with a view to nurturing "the sense of unity and fraternity among the three hill communities". This move was intended to be positive, but the fast-moving events in India did not permit it to last for long.

> Unfortunately, this Union was swept away by the first ever whirlwind of elections that came to Darjeeling. This wind

> began to blow hard in mid-1936, soon after, a seat was offered to Darjeeling for the Provincial Legislative Council and (that) took Laden La's breath before it stopped in 1937.
>
> (Subba, 1992: 83)

Darjeeling: the springboard of political awakening in the region

We have previously mentioned two regional formations with their relevance to the district of Darjeeling and the Nepali-speaking people there: first, activities, programmes and demands of the All India Gorkha League (AIGL); and second, demand for Gorkhasthan on the basis of the right of self-determination of nationalities, proposed by the Communist Party of India (CPI). It is interesting to learn how Darjeeling developed into an important stronghold of the Communist Party of India. A whole-timer of CPI, Sushil Chatterjee, was camping in Darjeeling with a view to opening a district branch of the party in the year 1943. He had heard of a daredevil, fearless, philanthropic and active member of the Gorkha Dukha Niwarak Sammelan (among others, its members used to cremate unclaimed dead bodies), who was universally known as Maila Baje (née Ratanlal Brahmin). Chatterjee managed to meet, argue and eventually convince Ratanlal that what he was doing was the work of the CPI and convinced him that individually Baje was vulnerable. In case he joined the Communist Party, the party would defend him and his actions. Thus, Ratanlal Brahmin, the future trade unionist, legislator and parliamentarian, joined the CPI in 1943 and remained an active ideal member of the Communist Party till his end in January 1989 (Pradhan, 2009). A natural mass leader like Maila Baje was instrumental in the phenomenal spread of the communist movement in North Bengal through its various front organizations: All India Trade Union Congress, Centre of Indian Trade Unions, Cha Bagan Mazdur Sangh, Taxi Drivers Association, Transport Workers Association, Kishan Sabha, Student Federation of India, Teachers Association and so on. Moreover, Darjeeling proved to be something like a springboard to the regional political aspirations – Nepalese, Sikkimese and Bhutanese – which CPI did contribute its own share.

But there was another political party, the Indian National Congress (INC), which was much older, better organized and more effective, and had national leadership and programmes of action. The Congress was founded in 1885 and it was a forum of the educated Indian elite, who used to meet in a big city once in a year, pass some resolutions, give impatient speeches in English, and go back home to meet again in the next year in another city. For the first three decades from its inception, it was more of a debating society among its members than an effective political party worthy of support from the common Indians. And it was Mohandas Karamchand Gandhi (1869–1948), a barrister of law trained in England and with a legal practice in South Africa, who changed the course of action of the Congress Party after his arrival in India in 1914. He took up the popular issues of the peasants' exploitation by the English indigo planters, landlords and money lenders; workers' inhuman conditions in the factories; and iniquitous colonial rules against the Indians at large. He worked out a number of constructive programmes and raised an army of volunteers to work on them. He was against all types of exploitation of man by man and showed ways for economic self-sufficiency through creating a number of self-sustaining institutions. Naturally, he pleaded for the cause of common man to be the objective of the Indian National Congress, and once the masses saw his simple living and high thinking, they joined the Congress Party en masse. Thus, INC turned out not only to be a political party but also a mass mobilized movement throughout the length and breadth of the country inclusive of Darjeeling.

By the year 1933, the Civil Disobedience Movement launched by the Congress against the British colonial rule was over and dejected left-leaning members of the INC formed the Congress Socialist Party (CSP) within the fold of the Indian National Congress. The Communist Party of India (CPI), formed in 1924 in a clandestine way, decided to work within the CSP as a strategy and they continued to do so till 1942's 'quiet India' movement on which they were on the opposite side with the British for their own reasons. Some of the left-leaning Nepalese like Manmohan Adhikari, Tulsilal Amatya and Pushpalal Shrestha used to work with CPI; especially Manmohan Adhikari was a member of the Purnia District Communist Party of India. Ratanlal Brahmin and Ganeshi Lal Subba, two office bearers of the Darjeeling District Committee, were interacting with the striking workers at Biratnagar in eastern Nepal on behalf of the CPI. Similarly, many of the Nepalese members of the Congress Socialist Party like M. P. Koirala and B. P. Koirala used to work as members of the Indian National Congress Party and they even courted arrest for that. And it was these elements, leftist Nepalese like Manmohan Adhikari and Girija Prasad Koirala for example, employed in the jute mills, who took the lead in organizing a workers' strike at Biratnagar Jute Mills on March 4, 1947, in Nepal and which was later taken over by B. P. Koirala and his associates. In this way, Darjeeling emerged as an important centre in the eastern Himalayan region politically, culturally and educationally in general, but it had an aura of Nepali trademark.

But before one turns to political developments in Nepal, the sequence of development requires us to consider new scenario emerging in a different form in Darjeeling.

Gorkhasthan: the first half-hearted effort for Greater Nepal

Dr Kunwar Muhamad Ashraf, a communist member of the All India Congress Committee, condemned as communal the demand for Pakistan raised by the All India Muslim League (AIML), pleaded for "right of self-determination of the nationalities" and also declared Indian Muslims a nationality. The idea was canvassed by the All India Student Federation (AISF), the student wing of the Communist Party of India (CPI) in the 1940s. In May 1941, the CPI took up the cause of Indian federalism on the basis of right of self-determination of nationalities through a letter to the members of the party and suggested that India should be a multinational state in future. The Central Committee of the Communist Party of India moved a resolution in April 1942:

> Every section of the Indian people, which has a contiguous territory as its homeland, common historical tradition, common language, culture, psychological make-up and common economic life would be organized as a distinct nationality with the right to exist as an Autonomous State within the Free Indian Union or Federation, and will have the right to secede from it, if it may so desire.
>
> (Samanta, 2000: 97)

Consequently, the election manifesto of the Communist Party of India demanded in 1946 that as India was a confederation of 17 linguistic states, the British should transfer powers to these 17 sovereign nationalities. Two active and vocal members of the Darjeeling District Committee of the CPI, Ratanlal Brahmin and Ganeshi Lal Subba, with the support of some junior members such as Charu Mazumdar and Sourin Basu (the future founders of the Naxalbari movement) got the resolution passed by the District Committee in 1944. The resolution had proposed regional autonomy for three hill sub-divisions of Darjeeling Sadar, Kurseong and Kalimpong, which was endorsed by the State Committee of the CPI.

> On April 6, 1947, these two leaders (Maila Baje and Ganeshi Lal Subba) submitted on behalf of the Darjeeling District

> Committee of the CPI and with full agreements of their leaders in Calcutta, a memorandum to Jawaharlal Nehru, the then Vice President of the Interim Government and Liaqat Ali Khan, the them Finance Member of the Government and the leader of the Muslim League in the Indian Constituent Assembly. In this memorandum they had made a utopian demand for the Gorkhas, Gorkhasthan, an independent nation comprising of the present day Nepal, Darjeeling district (of Bengal) and Sikkim, excluding its present North District . . . The memorandum noted geographical contiguity, cultural and linguistic similarities within the proposed boundary. It further claims that the "national development of the Gorkha people" can take place only if Gorkhasthan is granted on the basis of (a) plebiscite. Temporarily, or till this was attained, it suggests that there be an "immediate end" of the status of Darjeeling as a "partially excluded area" in Bengal.
>
> (Subba, 1992: 90)

It is interesting to note that at the time of submission of the memorandum to the British Indian Constituent Assembly, Nepal was a "juridically independent State" but de facto subservient to the British, and Sikkim was a separate princely state, considered "independent" like other princely states. But still Sikkim maintained its territorial integrity and independence in respect of internal matters. The point to be kept in mind is that the Constituent Assembly had no power to consider anything pertaining to Nepal and similarly without consent of the ruler of Sikkim, it was simply beyond the scope of the then existing transient authorities to deliberate on the demands of the memorandum seriously. In a vaguely legalistic term, by suggesting lumping Darjeeling together with Nepal and Sikkim, the CPI memorandum had proposed a merger of Darjeeling with Nepali-speaking Nepal on the ground of language and ethnic homogeneity. Was it simply expediency or a well-considered policy of national self-determination on the part of a nationality? Incidentally, nobody asked Ratanlal Brahmin to clarify his stand on the issues all through the long years of his active and legislative politics in the country.

The fast-developing events following the move on the part of the CPI in the aftermath of Indian independence proved the aforementioned suspicions. The CPI led an armed agitation in Telangana; it was subsequently declared an illegal political forum, thus its public activities were banned. The party decided to take part in the electoral process, when the first general elections were announced in 1950–2, and it became the main political party in opposition to the ruling All India National Congress at the centre in parliament, when the ban on its activities was finally lifted. It appears that CPI also forgot its resolution on Gorkhasthan within a few years of its resolve: Maila Baje continued to be an elected member from Darjeeling to the legislative bodies, but he never raised the issue of Gorkhasthan on the legislative fora again.

The All India Gorkha League (AIGL)

It is pertinent to note that Gorkhas, once permitted by the appropriate authorities, travelled overseas in various armed operations, especially during the First and Second World Wars. They did fight for the British empire, but also became aware of the liberation struggles being waged in various parts of the world. They observed that a large number of Indians of different political shades, terrorists, revolutionaries, *satyagrahis* and the like were making extreme sacrifices for the cause of their countries. In their own neighbourhood and working experience, they had seen apart from the Indians, Afghans, Burmese, Malaya, Indonesian, Sri Lankans were struggling against alien exploitation and for the betterment of their lot. Unlettered they were, no doubt, but they were not dumb creatures; many of them realized that the British used them against the Indian dissenters as cannon fodder. This must have rankled the consciousness of at least some of them, who could not keep mum for long. Furthermore, there were descendants of disinherited Ranas settled in India, who were looking for an opportunity to whip up unrest in their home country, and some longed for recognition from among the demobilized soldiers. Very soon they connived with some of the ex-Gurkha soldiers, who took up the cause of organizing the Gorkhas in India.

It is pertinent to note that Chandra Shamsher Rana, the prime minister of Nepal, had asked the British authorities not to promote the Nepali soldiers beyond the rank of non-commissioned officers (NCOs) and insisted on strict observance of Nepali soldiers' rights of ritual purification on their return home. It was not only a humiliating exercise but also a costly and cumbersome practice from which they would like to be free, if possible. One of the results of this insistence on ritual purification was large-scale migration and settlement of the Nepalese in India. Similarly, with a view to stopping politicization of the Nepalese in India, the Nepalese prime minister asked the Government of India not to offer non-military jobs to the Gorkhas so that their alleged fighting quality might be retained intact. In view of Rishikesh Shaha, one of the concrete results of the exposure of the Gorkhas to the outside influences during the First World War was the establishment of the All

India Gorkha League (AIGL) in 1921 at Dehradun (Shaha, 1990: 67). The forum remained apolitical for first few years and tried to foster education and employment among its members before it turned into a political organization. In 1927, Rana Bahadur Shamsher, the son of the former prime minister, Maharaja Dev Shamsher, who was thrown out of Nepal to make way for Chandra Shamsher in 1901 and settled down in Dehradun, was elected the president of AIGL. Thereafter, the League linked itself to the communal political party, All India Hindu Mahasabha. The AIGL offered its services to the Hindu Maharaja of Kashmir in 1927–8 for restoration of peace after a communal strife, allegedly committed by his predominantly Muslim subjects.

The League's sessions were attended by a number of ex-subedars and complimentary messages were received from a number of the princely states. A later president, Thakur Chandan Singh, who had attended the Delhi Session of the All India Hindu Mahasabha, had also taken part in the Non-cooperation Movement launched by the Indian National Congress in 1922, had creditably served in the British Indian Army during the First World War and had acted as the assistant to the His Highness, the Maharaja of Bikaner after the war. Moreover, he was married to one of the daughters of the Maharaja Kharag Shamsher Rana, the former commander in chief of Nepal and an elder brother of the then prime minister, who was dismissed in 1886. Further, he edited a number of Nepali journals to highlight the issues relating to the Gorkhas in British India, such as the *Himalayan Times*, *Tarun Gorkha*, and *Gorkha Sansar*. Later, the AIGL adopted a highly subservient attitude towards the Rana prime minister of Nepal and the British colonial regime in India. It was alleged that Rana Chandra Shamsher had bought them over and thus they not only praised the Rana regime, but also went so far as to condemn the Civil Disobedience Movement launched by the Indian National Congress.

For many years fed up with the partisan attitudes of the leadership, the common Gorkhas forgot about the relevance of the All India Gorkha League. But on May 15, 1943, the Hillmen's Association of Darjeeling revived the old moribund AIGL with new vigour in a formal meeting at Darjeeling and elected Damber Singh Gurung as its president and Ranadhir Subba as its secretary. Through its first constitution, the League pledged to secure the future of the Gorkhas in case India attained freedom and it mentioned Nepal as the "Motherland". However, when the second constitution of the League was adopted in 1948, this stipulation was dropped (Samanta, 2000: 88). It appears that rejuvenated AIGL had decided to take up the cause of all the Gorkhas, wherever they were. For illustration, the following resolutions were passed on May 14, 1944, at the second session of the newly activated AIGL at Darjeeling:

> 2. Gurkhas and Rights: (We demand) to amend the Government of India Act, 1935 so as to enable the Gurkhas to be represented in the Central Legislature and provincial legislatures of Assam, Bengal, Bihar, U. P. and Punjab, where Gurkhas have settled in large number. 6. Gurkha grazers of Darrang and Nowgaon . . . who have settled in Assam for the last 78 years, this session declares it to be an act of the greatest injustice to attempt to oust the Gurkhas from the land . . . by giving settlement of (that) land to the outsiders, mainly the Muslims from Mymensingh (district of Bengal). 7. The Gurkhas in Burma: . . . in any programme of rehabilitation of Burma, the interest of the Gurkhas is of vital importance; hence, this session urges the Government of Burma to take steps to have the Gurkhas represented in the Committee of Rehabilitation.

Over the next five years, D. S. Gurung continued to lead the AIGL as its president and turned it into a vigorous forum of Gorkhalis in India. He kept on filing petitions and memoranda to various authorities and raised the issue of the Gorkha homeland. At that time, AIGL was something like a joint front of Nepali-speaking Indians belonging to various political parties like the Communist Party of India, the Indian National Congress and others. D. S. Gurung entered the West Bengal State Legislative Assembly as a member on the Indian National Congress ticket. However, it is alleged that in 1946 he was requested to pay a visit to his native country, Nepal, and he returned to India as upholder of the Rana regime, causing speculation as to how the change had come to his politics. He breathed his last on April 7, 1948, leaving behind the reign of the AIGL to the third generation of the leadership and to revive its fortunes once more. M. P. Koirala, one of the highly respected leaders and the founder president of the Nepali Congress, who was subjected to public harassment in Darjeeling at the hands of AIGL hoodlums, found them a pro-Rana and pro-British regressive political forum (Koirala, 2008: 97–8).

The link between AIGL and the Bir Gorkha Dal, which changed its nomenclature to Gorkha Parishad in early 1950s, becomes obvious through activities of Ranadhir Subba, its one-time secretary:

> In the small hours on 12 April, 1951 Bharat Shamsher, a grandson of Defence Minister Babar Shamsher, along with

> members of the Gorkha Dal including Ranadhir Subba, an erstwhile leader of the Darjeeling-based All-India Gorkha League, were arrested. But that very day Baharat Shamsher, Ranadhir Subba and a few other Gorkha Dal leaders were brought out of Kathmandu prison by a crowd of supporters and sympathizers who thereafter thought fit to demonstrate in front of the Home Minister (B. P.) Koirala's residence hardly five hundred yards away from the prison. Koirala was reported to have himself shot to death one of the demonstrators, Sukol Dhoj, who was allegedly attacking the Home Minister with a Khukri, but in fact, it was one of his party colleagues who had actually killed the demonstrator.
>
> (Shaha, 1990: 255)

Ranadhir Subba along with members of the Gorkha Parishad was arrested again in 1954, as he was involved in demonstration against the Indian parliamentary mission on May 28 (Shaha, 1990: 308). Moreover, the members of the AIGL were involved in the anti-India activities in 1960s during King Mahendra's efforts in the context of the Federation of the Himalayan Kingdoms.

The AIGL was active in Darjeeling and around in eastern Nepal, Sikkim, Bhutan Duars, Upper Assam, Khasi Hills and even in Burma in 1940s. Trouble in Southern Bhutan started either early in or towards the middle of 1948, when some members of the All India Gorkha League, led by one Sahabir Rai entered Bhutan and started enrolling members for the League collecting money for the party from the Nepali settlers. Raja (Sonam Tobgyel) Dorji, the administrator of southern Bhutan, promptly ejected the League leaders, but Sahabir and his men later managed to get a foothold in Daga Pela and Burgaon in the district of Chirang of south-central Bhutan. They were also working up an anti-government movement among the Nepali community. Raja Dorji sent a body of a hundred Bhutanese militia and had several persons arrested. Most of the leaders of the movement moved to the adjoining tea gardens in northern Assam and West Bengal.

It appears that the representatives of these Bhutanese "refugees" approached the Government of Nepal for help, through Colonel Daman Shamsher, the Nepalese consul-general at Calcutta. Some of them also approached Major General Bijaya Shamser, director general of the Foreign Department, and the Government of Nepal in Kathmandu. Mr D. B. Gurung, the then president of the Bhutan State Congress was one of them. The major general wrote some letters to the political officer in Sikkim (Mr Harishwar Dayal) urging him to look into the grievances of the Gorkha community in Bhutan. Non-committal replies were given to these letters. Some representatives of the community interviewed the political officer of Sikkim and Bhutan at Gangtok with a letter of introduction from Colonel Shamser. The political officer had some informal talks with the Raja Dorji, who assured him that the Nepalese who had left Bhutan in 1948 could return, provided they stood trial in Bhutan.

Kaisher Bahadur KC informs that the prime minister of Nepal, Maharaja Mohun Shamsher, had sent him to Siliguri, Kalimpong, Gangtok and Darjeeling to provide relief to the Gorkhas evicted from Bhutan, apparently the elements associated with the AIGL. In his long-winded and high-sounding hyperbole, he informs the readers how he travelled to the office of political officer in Gangtok and met with Raja S. T. Dorji's wife Rani Chuni in Kalimpong and tried to educate them about the problem of impending Chinese incursion and plight of the Gorkhas in the region. He describes in details how some fake refugees were cheating on Rana prime minister of Nepal as victims of suppression and forceful eviction from Bhutan Duars. And these were the same people referred in the previous paragraph (Kaisher Bahadur, 1976: 8–10). Furthermore, he informs that one R. B. Gurung had received money from Maharaja Mohan Shamsher Rana for rehabilitation of the Bhutanese refugees, who were allegedly evicted by Raja S. T. Dorji. When Kaisher Bahadur asked him to produce receipts from the beneficiaries, he along with one Kaji M. Dhoj produced a huge number of master role and two representatives of the alleged refugees. These two, Mr Dhan Bahadur Tamang and Mr Jagannath Jaishi, "looked much too prosperous and garrulous to be refugees". It was a plot to cheat the Maharaja of the money on the name of refugee relief (Kaisher Bahadur, 1976: 10–11).

The ring leaders with the help of one Lal Bahadur Newar of Matelli Bazar organized the so-called Bhutan State Congress on April 4, 1952, at Patgaon, in the district of Goalpara of Assam, as they were turned out of Bhutan. One Dalmandan Raj Chhetri of Patgaon was elected president and Dhan Bahadur Gurung of Siliguri (related to the Gurung Thikedar family of Samchi and grandson of Garajman Gurung) as the vice president. Its aim was declared to be safe-guarding the interests of the Nepalese in Bhutan and to have a democratic government established in the state. The president of the Dhubri District Congress Committee also spoke at the meeting. The Bhutan Agent Raja Dorji protested against this development (interference in the internal administrative matters of Bhutan against the provisions of the treaty) to the Government of India. The Government of India advised the Dhubri

District Congress leaders to dissociate themselves from the activities of the Bhutan Congress.

Similarly, the obscurantist attitude of some of the AIGL leaders continued unabated in Nepal.

> The leaders of the Bir Gorkha Dal sought to discredit the Nepali Congress and its leaders as creations and puppets of Indian Government, exaggerated reports of Indian interference in the internal affairs of the Government and invoked the spirit of militant nationalism as the basis of their policies.
> (Joshi and Rose, 1966: 128)

This was further corroborated by Bishweshwar Prasad Koirala, who was subjected to the antiques of the Bir Gorkas (Koirala, 2001: 135–40). Leo Rose is of the view that Rana opposition to the Nepali Congress operated in a clandestine manner to begin with. But the Bir Gorkha Dal, especially its later version, the Gorkha Parishad,

> made its appeal to conservative, ultra-nationalists, religiously orthodox opinion, and more particularly the ex-service men, who had served in British Gurkha units or Nepal Army. The Gorkha Dal was able to organize effective opposition to the Congress, especially in some hill districts around Kathmandu Valley, but its emphasis was upon narrow "Gorkha" nationalism deprived it of any significant influence in Kathmandu Valley, Terai, or among the Kirati hill people of eastern Nepal.
> (Rose, 1971: 100–101)

The Gurkha Dal held a conference in the early part of 1952 at Kathmandu and decided to form a new political forum, Gurkha Parishad, as the political party of the alleged Nepali nationalists. Its objective was "to save the country from armed upheavals on the one hand and near dictatorship of the party in power on the other". Though it was loud and clear that this political outfit was controlled by the Ranas' men and materials, at one time it rivalled the Nepali Congress, and within a year of its inception made an exaggerated claim of some 800,000 members. It was intriguing that this arch-conservative Hindu traditionalist forum could import an Indian Christian Gurkha from Darjeeling in Ranadhir Subba to be the founder president of the Parishad. Moreover, the gentleman continued to be the president of the Gurkha Parishad at least up to 1960 and managed to be a cabinet minister from November 15, 1958, to May 26, 1959.

Gorkha National Liberation Front (GNLF) and Gorkha Janamukti Morcha (GJM)

AIGL continued its existence as a political party in Darjeeling and its suburbs and did contest elections at the state and federal levels with limited success. By the 1980s disenchantment came to its support base, and a militant entity in the form of Gorkha National Liberation Front (GNLF) led by an ex-Indian soldier, Subhas Ghisingh, emerged with the same old demand for creation of a separate state of Gorkhaland in Darjeeling. The GNLF aggressive movement and strategy of the security forces led to spate of violence at various levels: frequent inter-political, inter-ethnic calls for *bundhs* (blockage of the road traffic and public life) harassed the public life at large and extensive violence against persons and property. The bundhs created hurdles in the normal flow of human traffic and commercial goods to and from Sikkim and Bhutan. Hundreds of persons lost their lives and infrastructures were burnt, houses of the adversaries were set on fire and democratic functioning of the political parties was stopped through violence and arson (Subba, 1992). At last, a tripartite agreement among GNLF and the Governments of West Bengal and the Indian Union was signed in August 1988. A new body, Darjeeling Hill Gorkha Council (DHDC), was created with 42 members with powers for redressal of local problems. Ghisingh was elected and remained head of the DHDC for next two decades without much development for district. His followers were dejected and deserted him in a large body. At last, one of the main troubleshooters of GNLF, Bimal Gurung, rebelled against his boss, created a new forum, Gorkha Janamukti Morcha (GJM), and literally chased Ghisingh from Darjeeling. GJM too, it appears, is determined to create a separate state of Gorkhaland for the Indian Gorkhas in Darjeeling, which is being opposed by the state government in the same intensity, so much so that the Government of West Bengal seems determined to split various individual ethnic groups such as Tamang, Limbus, Lepchas, Bhutias and so on from the Gorkha commonwealth by providing substantial financial inducement in the name of creating various ethnic cultural bodies. These aggressive strategies do not appear to be working, and only time will tell whether the seeds sown by the AIGL for creation of Gorkhaland will materialize in near future.

It is obvious that the British permitted Gurkha settlements across India without much consideration for future consequences. At most they considered such settlements as transient and anticipated that they might go back to Nepal in future. On the other hand, the Gurkha settlers, who were at one time pampered by the British, began demanding settlers' right in their adopted land. Through the lobbies of Anglo-Indians, Plantation Association, and private British personnel egged on the politically inexperienced Gurkhas, the British establishment ignored their political demands. The Gurkha settlers in India had to make a choice between India and Nepal, once the British had gone back home as colonial masters. For years, there was uncertainty in their minds, but once they made their choice, the Nepalese establishment had no role to play in the affairs of the Indian Nepalis. However, the Indian Nepalis remain suspect in the eyes of Indian political class, as agents of Nepalese expansion, a theme which is bandied about off and on.

Wild popular expectations in the eastern Himalayan kingdoms around 1950

The British recruited more than 200,000 Gorkhas for their armed forces with the ready assistance of the prime minister during the Second World War, and the Gorkhas fought for their masters bravely. The war came to an end in 1945, but so came the end of the British imperial supremacy in India. It so happened that the British Conservative Party under the leadership of Winston Churchill was beaten by its Labour counterpart in the general election held in the United Kingdom. The new Labour government decided to grant independence to India. This move set off alarm among the Indian princely states, which had not prepared themselves for the change and had kept their charge in an outdated mediaeval, feudal and imperial mould. There was panic among them, as their subjects were simply impatient for total transformation of the political representation in the system of governance. Furthermore, the All India National Congress Committee (AICC) had further queered the pitch for them by simply agitating for people's participation in the affairs of the princely states.

Nepal, Sikkim and Bhutan, the three Himalayan kingdoms, were parts of the British contrived "inner buffer states" around the northern borders of the "precious British Indian Empire". The three rulers were guided in their state of affairs by the 'resident' in Kathmandu and 'political officer' in Gangtok, in case of Sikkim and Bhutan. As a policy, the British encouraged the rulers to remain in mediaeval isolation, devoid of transportation and communication to the outside world. The subjects were not only kept deliberately in abject poverty but were also permitted to remain ignorant, illiterate and isolated from the rest of the world. The nervous rulers, having heard the confirmed news of impending British withdrawal, rushed to the political officer for the advice. The political officer in Gangtok advised to the rulers to proceed post-haste to Delhi with their "memoranda" to meet the members of "Cabinet Mission" sent by the British government to prepare ground for their withdrawal from India. Of course, the case of Nepal was at a different level, but Sikkim and Bhutan sent their delegations to Delhi, who cooled their heels there for some days waiting for an appointment with the members of the Cabinet Mission. It is important to note that while the Bhutanese delegation was led by Raja Sonam Tobgyel Dorji, the external face of Bhutan and the future father-in-law the third Druk-rGyalpo, the king of Bhutan, the Sikkimese delegation was led of Raja Dorji's nephew and the crown prince of Sikkim, Palden Thondup Namgyal, who was destined to be the last ruler of the Namgyal dynasty in Sikkim. As the members of the Cabinet Mission were busy meeting the leaders of the political parties and negotiations on future set-up were in an advanced stage, the two delegations were advised to return home and wait for the decision in their respective capitals.

And the decision was communicated to them in the form of a "Note" which stated: "Although Bhutan and Sikkim are not in **pari-materia**, the latter being an Indian State and the former 'in process of becoming one', both are conditioned by their proximity to Tibet and thus to China". Theoretically, Sikkim is expected to bargain itself into a union of India, although as Mr A. J. Hopkinson (then political officer, Gangtok) has observed the recognition of so small a separate unit is problematic and there is no other Indian state, with which it could make a common cause. Theoretically too, it will be for the External Affairs Department of the Union Government to (work out) such relations with Bhutan as would facilitate its admission to the Indian Union (possibly with Sikkim). A Note was prepared by the Deputy Secretary, Political and External, Government of India and sent to them accordingly on August 10, 1946 (see above page 58).

The note reflects the British imperial thinking in strongly recommending to the successor state in maintaining their old structure of buffer states and keeping the frontier states as client states. They appear to overlook the fact that there were no imperial interests to guard across the border in the Himalayas for the new entity. However, the note contains two significant points: one, a recommendation to the successor government, the Indian Union, to maintain status quo in the Himalayas; the other, an assurance to rulers of the Himalayan kingdoms against their absorption in the Indian Union. It is logical to believe that the last British political officer in Gangtok, A. J. Hopkinson, must have adequately briefed the two worried Maharajas and assured them of the continuation of the status quo and cautioned the

Indian Union against disturbing the status quo, which might be detrimental to its interests. Possibly, that is why the Government of India signed standstill treaties first and then negotiated new formal treaties with all three Himalayan kingdoms and signed them in 1950 on almost the same old British terms and conditions. However, unaware of these behind-the-scenes diplomatic negotiations, the common masses in the street were getting restive and were busy organizing anti-imperialist and anti-feudal movements in the second half of the 1940s. And here the people from Sikkim, Nepal, Bhutan and India (especially from Darjeeling, Bengal and Bihar) had taken collective initiatives in all three kingdoms to organize, agitate and take over the administration in their hands so that feudal oppression could come to end. But before that, a little digression on Darjeeling will be relevant.

Today, the political water in Darjeeling has become so muddy that it is difficult to imagine good old days of SU-DHA-PA or *NEBULA*. Writing about two decades back, T. B. Subba lamented:

> the last hundred and fifty years or so of intermixed living (in Darjeeling), the Nepalis had gradually evolved a single society and a single ethnicity. Though they still believed in different faiths and supported different ideologies, they were one and a single community. The divide between the Communists and "nationalists" (GNLF: Gorkha National Liberation Front) was purely ideological. But as the (GNLF) movement broke out, the divide between the two groups grew wider and wider . . . Killing of people and burning houses belonging to one group by another were widespread and the number was staggeringly high. There were also instances of the communist Nepalis fleeing from the GNLF areas and the "nationalists" fleeing from the communist strongholds . . . The mutual distrust and enmity have continued. So much so that now the communists would call themselves anything, but "Nepalis" and the "nationalists" anything, but "Gorkhas".
>
> (Subba, 1992: 201–2)

The issue has gone beyond the preceding description in the second decade of the 21st century with the advent of a new forum, Gorkha Janamukti Morcha (GJM). Subhas Ghisingh, the uncrowned king of Darjeeling for two decades since 1987, proved to be a disastrous leader as far as development of resources of the district was concerned. His creation, Darjeeling Gorkha Hills Council (DGHC), proved to be a fiasco, but he clung to the post of chairman of the DGHC for 20 years without holding election to the body he was heading. There were serious charges of non-performance and defalcation of funds for development. His protégé, Mohan Gurung, rose to challenge the arrogant GNLF boss and literally chased him away from the Darjeeling hills and since then, it is the GJM which is calling the shots in the hills. The Morcha has raised the old demand for creation of a Gorkha homeland, the state of Gorkhaland in Hills and the Duars. They put Jaswant Singh, a leader of the Bharatiya Janata Party (BJP), as their candidate and got him elected for the lone seat for the Lok Sabha from Darjeeling district to the Indian Parliament in 2009 so that they could have an effective spokesman in favour of Gorkhaland. But nothing happened in their favour, as the state government in Calcutta was dead set against the formation of a new state of Gorkhaland. The GJM appears to have not learnt a lesson from their past experience of 2009 and decided once more to support another BJP candidate, S. S. Ahluwalia, for the lone seat from Darjeeling in 2014. The GJM-supported BJP candidate, S. S. Ahluwalia, had been elected to the lone parliamentary seat from Darjeeling. And it will be interesting to watch whether he will be able to deliver on their demand for statehood of Darjeeling.

Bibliography

Chalmers, R., 2003, "The Quest for Ekrupta: Unity, Uniformity and the Delineation of the Nepali Community in Darjeeling" in *Nepalese in Northeast India*, edited by A. C. Sinha and T. B. Subba, Indus, New Delhi.

Chalmers, R., 2009, "Education, Institutions and Elites Building and Bounding Nepali Public Life in Early Twentieth Century India" in *Indian Nepalis: Issues and Perspectives*, edited by T. B. Subba et al., Concept, New Delhi.

Gurung, H., 1997, "State and Society in Nepal" in *Nationalism and Ethnicity in a Hindu Kingdom*, edited by D. N. Gellner et al., Harwood Academic, Amsterdam.

Joshi, B. L., and L. E. Rose, 1966, *Democratic Innovations in Nepal: A Case of Political Acculturation*, University California Press, Berkeley & Los Angles.

Kaisher Bahadur, K. C., 1976: *Nepal After Revolution of 1950*, Sarda Prakashan Griha, Kathmandu.

Koirala, B. P., 2001, *Atmabrittanta: Late Life Recollections*, Jagdamba Prakashan and Himal Books, Kathmandu.

Koirala, M. P., 2008, *M P Koirala: A Role in a Revolution*, Jagdamba Prakashan, Kathmandu.

Pradhan, B., 2009, *Gaphsaphma Ratanlal Branmin* (in Nepali), edited by M. P. Dahal, Pratima Prakashan, Siliguri.

Rai, I. B., undated, "Indian Nepali Nationalism and Nepali Poetry" in *Gorkhas Imagined: Indra Bahadur Rai in Translation*, edited by P. Poddar and A. Prasad, Mukti Prakashan, Kalimpong.
Rawat, G. S., 2003, "Nepali Literature in Meghalaya" in *Nepalese in Northeast India*, edited by A. C. Sinha and T. B. Subba, Indus, New Delhi.
Risley, H. H., 1894, *The Gazetteer of Sikkim*, Bengal Secretariat Press, Calcutta.
Rose, L. E., 1971, *Nepal Strategy for Survival*, University of California Press, Berkeley & Los Angles.
Samanta, A. K., 2000, *Gorkhaland Movement: A Study in Ethnic Separatism*, APL, New Delhi.
Sen, J., 1992, *India and Nepal: Some Aspects of Culture Contact*, Indian Institute of Advanced Study, Shimla.
Shaha, R., 1990, *Modern Nepal: A Political History: 1769–1885*, Manohar, New Delhi.
Sinha, A. C., 1998, *Bhutan: Ethnic Identity and National Dilemma*, Reliance Publishing House, New Delhi, 2nd Edition, Quoted from British India Records and Library: EUR: Secret: 4357: File No. 1: From Political Officer in Sikkim to Foreign Department, New Delhi.
Sinha, A. C., 2013, *Social Formation in and Around Sikkim in the Middle of 20th Century*, VI Foundation Day Lecture, Sikkim University, Gangtok, July 2, 2013.
Subba, T. B., 1992, *Ethnicity, State and Development: A Case Study of the Gorkhaland Movement in Darjeeling*, Har-Anand, New Delhi.
Upadhya, T. N. and R. Adhikari, 2003, "Contribution of the Nepalis of Northeast India to the Development of Nepali Literature" in *Nepalese in Northeast India*, edited by A. C. Sinha and T. B. Subba, Indus, New Delhi.

5

DEMOCRATIC MOVEMENT IN SIKKIM AND SIKKIM STATE CONGRESS

Chronologically, Sikkim was the first among the three principalities where a political party was formed, a popular democratic movement against the feudal dispensation was launched and a popular government was formed. Thus, it is in the fitness of things that we first undertake the analysis of those pioneering endeavours. Sikkim, the smallest and most centrally located among them, was a dynastic theocracy, ruled by the Namgyal family since 1642. It was ideally located on the shortest trade route between Lhasa, the Tibetan capital, and Calcutta, the commercial capital of the British Indian empire. Soon after the Anglo-Nepalese War of 1814–15, the British decided to control the affairs of Sikkim decisively with a view to facilitating the trade across the Himalayan passes, and for that they took a number of steps from 1817 after signing the Treaty of Titalia with Sikkimpati Maharaja. By the end of the 19th century, Sikkim was reduced to a small ordinary princely feudatory strictly under the control of British Political Officer J. C. White, and its ninth Namgyal ruler, Thutub Namgyal, was imprisoned in various locations in Darjeeling. After his demise, his eldest son succeeded him, but he died in mysterious circumstances within a few months. Consequently, his stepbrother, Tashi Namgyal, was crowned as the 11th ruler of the principality, who was destined to rule his kingdom for almost five decades till he died in 1963.

Palden Thondup Namgyal, born on May 4, 1923, and the second son of Sir Tashi Namgyal, was an incarnation of his uncle, Sidkeong Tulku, the Gyeshe Rimpoche (the prince abbot). The prince, popularly known as the Maharaj Kumar, who was supposed to be a Precious Jewel theologically, was held in high esteem. He was schooled for monkhood prior to his brother's death in an air crash and was recognized as the spiritual head of the two important monasteries of Rumtek and Phodang. He was given secular instructions at St Joseph's Convent in Kalimpong, St Joseph's College in Darjeeling and Bishop

Cotton College in Shimla to prepare him as the successor to the Namgyal throne. He was then seconded to the Indian Civil Service (ICS) probationers' course in the Administrative College at Dehradun like princes of similar states (Rustomji, 1987). His friend from Dehradun days, Nari Rustomji, found him to be a complex personality: "a shy, timorous, lonely and lost individual" (Rustomji, 1971: 21). In his considered opinion, Sikkim belonged to the Bhutias – the Kazis were, after all, his courtiers. Lepchas were, in any way, the loyal subjects and the rest (read: ethnic Nepalis) were intruders, and thus the responsibility of the protecting power of Sikkim, that is, the British or Indian government. He was stubbornly opposed to any accommodation of Nepalis in the Sikkimese establishment as he took it as the surrender of his legacy.

The Maharaj Kumar saw himself as a Bhutia ruler of his kingdom, and grudgingly accepted Lepchas as his associate subjects simply because of the fact that if he would not, the mythical legitimacy of his regime would be vulnerable and stand alone among the subjects. Thus, he was determined to make a stand in defence of the Lepcha-Bhutia communities against the democratic aspirations of the Nepalis. He wrote to his friend, Rustomji, on April 12, 1949, when he was only 25 years of age:

> I am all for fulfilling the wishes of our Bhutia and Lepchas, real wishes. But I will be sooner damned than let these mean conspirators and job hunters (read Nepalis) have their way, if I can. We are on the verge of getting our independence of sort like Bhutan and I think we have achieved a miracle in not having to accede [to the Indian Union]. Our greatest drawback is that the P[olitical] O[fficer] and the Government of India seem to favour the other side, and we have to proceed so that we give you people [the Indians] no chance to butt in. The second trouble, which I have a feeling is a common, is the unruly Nepalese element against whom I cannot take action as I would like to have.
>
> (Rustomji, 1987: 27)

So in his scheme of things, Sikkimese Nepalis did not figure in his domain and this stubborn attitude ultimately turned out to be his undoing, as the events of the early 1970s showcased. He saw Sikkim in his own image, and stubbornly believed that others must do the same; this insistent belief eventually resulted in the obliteration of the Namgyal dynastic rule in Sikkim. He appeared to be something like a Shakespearean tragic hero, who lost everything at the end: his wife, the crown prince, the throne, kingdom, patrimony, friends and supporters.

On the other hand, the princely state of Sikkim had an archaic aristocratic system, in which Bhutia-Lepcha Kazis (aristocrats) and Nepali thikadars (contract developers of the allotted land with immigrant Nepalese labour) were not only the landlords but were also permitted to run their own police force, jails, courts and revenue administration. They used to collect land rents from the tenants, and apart from that they used to wantonly administer the forests in their localities. There were four types of unpaid compulsory labour, which every tenant was subjected to and defiance of which led to heavy corporal punishments, confiscation of the property and other forms of indignities. Among them, especially Kalobhari (it was a popular nomenclature among the coolies; the black load, because of the fact that the heavy head load was wrapped in black colour tarpaulin so that it did not get damaged while carrying across the snowbound Himalayan passes) was much abused by the Kazi aristocracy. Normally, most Kazi households used to trade with Tibet and goods were transported by the coolies. The political officer had fixed the rates for hiring the labourers. But the Kazis abused the provision during the period of Second World War, when consumer goods were required to be sent in considerable quantity and within the shortest possible time. Kazis used that provision to transport their commercial goods in considerable quantity with indentured labour free of cost. Naturally, it was resented and when the coolies opposed, they were mercilessly flogged. And any voice raised in opposition to the system resulted in repression and public flogging and no political rights were recognized in the system.

The oppressors had a private police force, jails of their own and the judicial powers to try the alleged criminals. J. S. Lall, the first Dewan of Sikkim, writes in 1949:

> The state police were an ill-trained mob, disunited and openly partisan with one side or the other. As upholders of law and order in the country side they were far less than the local bullies. Many of them freely collected exaction because the people were habituated to submitting to the lessees and their henchmen.

In such a situation, anti-feudal activists such as Tashi Tshering, Sonam Tshering, Kezang Tenzing and others, who had suffered at the hands of Kazis' goons, got together and organized a welfare society, Praja

Sudharak Samaj, at Gangtok in the early 1940s. Kazi Lhendup Dorji, a scion of the Chyakhung Kazi Khangsarpa family, had founded a similar forum known as Sikkim Praja Mandal in 1945. And from south Sikkim, some of the AIGL activists such as Gobardhan Pradhan, Dhan Bahadur Tiwari and others had founded Sikkim Praja Sammelan at Temi Tarku. Though they wished to do some or other social service to keep themselves active, politically these fora were inactive.

Social background of political activists in 1940s

There were three clear trends among the early political activists of the Sikkimese scene. First, it was the elements, which were not only sympathetic to the All India Gorkha League of Darjeeling, but were also active members and functionaries of that body. Among them, the Temi Tarku group of Gobardhan Pradhan and company may be enumerated. The important aspect of this group is that it provided leadership to the Nepali-speaking south district adjoining Darjeeling and the leadership came from leading Newar and literate Brahmin families, who were relatively wealthy and modestly educated, with links outside. One may count Gobardhan and Moti Chand Pradhans, who were past AIGL functionaries and were scions of the earliest land lease holding family of Sikkim, and they were willing to invest in organizing a political forum. Needless to mention that a scion of the extended family, Kashiraj, would emerge as the most formidable leader of the Sikkim State Congress (SSC) in the 1950s and would remain on the Sikkimese political horizon for the next decade, when a type of limited electoral system was introduced in the state. Second, there were persons like Sonam Tshering, Kalzong Bhutia, Namgyal Tshering, and Lhendup Dorji Kazi and others who had personal and collective cause to undertake against the state and the oppressive aristocratic Kazi families. This point will be elaborated later through biographical details of some of main leaders and founding members of the Sikkim State Congress. These people, coming mainly from Bhutia extraction, were good grass-roots organizers, which came handy during street demonstrations in the late 1940s when Tashi Teshring was at the helm of the affairs. Third, there were personal factors such as humiliation, ego clashes, and forceful removal from the post or position, property disputes with the state, ruling family or the aristocratic families. Again among the founding members of the Sikkim State Congress Tashi Tshering, Lhendup Dorji Kazi, Sonam Tshering and others may be enumerated. We shall see that most of these leaders were self-serving demagogues who were organizationally weak and failed to establish effective political contacts with sister organizations outside Sikkim, a weakness which cost them dearly in early 1950s.

Before we take the analysis of the events leading to the founding of the Sikkim State Congress, it will be imperative to inform the background of some of the key functionaries of the SSC, as many of them would lead other political parties in Sikkim in the course of time.

Tashi Tshering, the founding president of the Sikkim State Congress (SSC), was born sometimes in 1889 in a Sherpa family in the district of Darjeeling, but claimed to be a Bhutia. He started his career as a supporting staff of the political officer, Gangtok, in the early years of the 20th century and rose to be the head clerk. At the age of 40 years, "he was Casanova enough to seduce the wife of Kazi Raibahadur Norbu of the Residency", and for that offence he was forced to leave the service. In 1929 he set up a curio shop in Gangtok bazaar and for that he had sold his first wife's ornaments. He was known for skills in draftsmanship and turned out to be advisor and teacher to the Maharaja Tashi Namgyal for some time.

> The Ex-pupil went to the extent of sending files to the bazaar for his former teacher's notes, which were then copied into the files by the Maharaja. Tashi Babu, as he was universally known, ensured that the arrangement was profitable to him and for some years, [he] led an apparently contended and an affluent life.
>
> (Prasad, 1954)

It was mainly due to Raibahadur T. D. Densapa, the then private secretary to the His Highness, that the above arrangement came to an end. Naturally, Tashi Babu never forgave the Raibahadur for that. Forced to live by his wits again, he launched into politics and made the Raibahadur Densapa as one of the main targets of his political outfit, the Sikkim State Congress. When the Sikkim State Congress was formed on December 7, 1947, Tashi Babu became the unquestioned leader of it, in which he was stoutly supported by Sonam Tshering, a former rifleman of the Indian army. He had cultivated bazaar shopkeepers and second grade state officials, with whom he would drink and gossip. He slanged easily in English, Nepali and Tibetan with his hate and untamed ego. When the Maharaja appointed three secretaries from among the public men to assist him in administration in 1948, Tashi Babu decided to remain a dictator to them from the outside. When the party under Tashi Babu instructed them to resign, some of his protégés such as Sonam Tshering refused to resign, as they had tasted the benefits of the office. The Sikkim State Congress launched public demonstrations in February 1949 with limited success. Another prolonged and concerted demonstration that May catapulted him to the chair of the chief minister. Obviously this was an experiment without precedent, powers and privileges of the cabinet and any formal rule of its functioning, but the office of the ministry made the inexperienced ministers giddy with unknown powers. Orders were issued without authority causing chaos and disorder in the administration. The Maharaja, prompted by the crown prince, appealed for the help from the political officer, who dismissed the ministry on the name of the Government of India and took over the administration in his hands.

Tashi Babu launched agitation against the move, but the Government of India was well prepared this time and they sent an experienced officer, J. S. Lall, as the Diwan to administer the state. The Maharaja was advised to negotiate with the political formations for establishment of some sort of popular administration. Meanwhile, Crown Prince Palden Thondup managed to lure Sonam Tshering, Tashi Babu's former ally and now adversary, to his political adversary, Sikkim National Party (SNP). At last, an agreement was negotiated among the political parties, the Durbar and the political officer on January 11, 1952, for equal representation of the Nepalese and the Lepcha-Bhutia combine in the State Council, which came to be known as the 'parity system'. Tashi Babu vehemently opposed the agreement and threatened to repudiate it. His stand very nearly put him and the bulk of the Nepali community in the opposition camp to the formation of the State Council. However, elections were held for the State Council in 1953 and without preparing for the ground, active Lepcha-Bhutia leaders of the Sikkim State Congress such as Tashi Babu, Dimik Singh Lepcha, and Lhendup Dorji Kazi stood as the candidates from the predominantly tribal areas of North and East Sikkim against the Sikkim National Party candidates, who were put up by the crown prince. The result was on the expected lines as per the designs of the Durbar and the Sikkim State Congress candidates were defeated by the lesser known candidates of the opposition.

Tashi Babu lost the election against the sinister campaigns of his former protégé, Sonam Tshering, by then the president of SNP and the crown prince of the state, who saw in him a great threat to his designs. The Durbar managed to win over the suave Kashiraj Pradhan of the Sikkim State Congress in its favour and that faction managed to elect Kazi Lhendup Dorji as its president leading to side-lining of the founder president of the party for good. Once the State Council and the Executive Council began functioning, Tashi Babu's opposition to them were not taken seriously. Tashi Babu refused to draw any lesson from his lapses and his own creation, Sikkim State Congress was hijacked by others in spite of all his efforts. His failures were double-fold. Neither did he go to the Sikkimese masses to educate them politically, nor did he reach the leaders of All India Congress Committee from the neighbouring states in India for their support. He led a delegation to New Delhi around 1950 to convince Prime Minister Jawaharlal Nehru on the demands of his party. C. D. Rai, another delegate, reminisced that Pandit Nehru was talking to them on their demands in a very cordial, relaxed and animated way in Hindustani, a language Tashi Babu was not possibly well conversant with. He asked the prime minister to speak in English, which he did in a formal way, with disastrous results for the visitors. Thus, Tashi Babu's ego was his biggest enemy and he died a sad man in 1956. And within a decade of his meteoric rise, this colourful politician of Sikkim was forgotten for all practical purposes.

Sonam Tshering

Sonam Tshering was believed to be a Lepcha, but claimed to be a Bhutia and also represented the Bhutias, and was born in the last decade of the 19th century. He had joined the British Indian Army as a rifleman and had seen the action during the First World War. He joined Sikkim state service after his retirement from the Army rising to be the head clerk of his department. He had landed property at Tathangchen village near Gangtok. He had some disputes with the local lessee, the Gangtok Kazi, in which he was made to suffer a lot financially and corporally, turning him into a staunch anti-Kazi for good. And for that purpose, he was one of the key organizers of Praja Sudharak Samaj at Gangtok. He enthusiastically joined the Sikkim State Congress and was one of the three joint secretaries appointed by the Durbar after the expressed public demand to begin with, but soon disenchantment emerged to Sonam Tshering because of the demand of majority rule in Sikkim on the part of SSC. The crown prince was looking for such an opportunity and he enticed Sonam to his side for launching a political front under his control as an antidote to SSC. Sonam began as the vice president of Sikkim National Party when it was established in 1948, and he soon became the president of the party by ousting the nominal founder president, Gyaltsen Tshering, in 1951.

He outsmarted his onetime mentor Tashi Babu's nominees in negotiating favourably for the Lepcha-Bhutia combine with SSC negotiators such as Kashiraj and Dimik Singh Lepcha for sharing seats in the State Council. Furthermore, while the SSC leaders boasted of popular support without working on ground, he showed shrewd tactics and organizational skill during the State Council elections in 1953, causing defeat to the SSC stalwarts. He formed the Executive Council along with Kashiraj Pradhan and both of them worked as a team alongside the crown prince in belittling the fortunes of SSC. His self-service soon earned him the wrath of the crown prince and both executive councillors were charged with corruption by end of the term of the Council. He contested and won the second State Council elections in 1958, but an Election Tribunal found him and his brother executive councillor, Kashiraj, guilty of electoral malpractices and corruption and both of them were debarred from holding the similar office. He would leave SNP soon to join L. D. Kazi, first to form Sikkim Swatantra Party and then Sikkim National Congress (SNC) in 1960. He would leave SNC in the early 1970s and support the ruler along with most of the Bhutia notables. Finally, he was the ceremonial speaker of the second State Legislative Assembly, 1979 to 1984, during the chief ministership of Nor Bahadur Bhandari of Sikkim Sangram Parishad (SSP), prior to his demise.

Dimik Singh Lepcha

Dimik Singh Lepcha was born in the last decade of the 19th century, joined the British Indian Army, rose to retire as an honorary captain and became secretary to the Sikkim Soldiers Board (SSB).When the SSC was founded in 1947 he was the natural choice as the Lepcha face of the party to be appointed as its vice president. He resigned as the secretary of the SSB in 1948 to work full time for the party and joined the administration as one of the three secretaries. He, along with Sonam Tshering and Rughubar, joined the administration as the secretaries to the government, which accomplished nothing tangible leading to popular agitation for its dissolution. He was known as unavoidable crowd puller with his roaring slogans and booming voice. He was also famous for being a competent and popular football referee during tournaments. He remained loyal to both Tashi Babu and Kashibabu till his last. Like other Lepcha-Bhutia leaders of SSC, he was allotted the North Central Lepcha-Bhutia Constituency for the State Council elections in 1953 by the party, which he lost. At last, he met with his end in an automobile accident near Namchi in Sikkim South in early 1950s and died in hospital at Kalimpong.

Kashiraj Pradhan

Kashiraj Pradhan was born on December 11, 1905, in one of the branches of the famous Newar families, who came to Sikkim in 1867 after securing land lease to develop it with imported Nepalese labour.

Kashiraj was the second graduate in the state of Sikkim. He was one of the four brothers who had divided their landed properties: Kush Naraian got Duga estate in Sikkim, Gobardhan to Timi holdings, Kashiraj got his shares at Biratnagar in eastern Nepal and the fourth brother received what they had at Kurseong. Educated at Darjeeling, Banaras and Calcutta he served as a teacher and then as the headmaster at Tashi Namgyal High School, Gangtok. He wore many hats: teacher, journalist, litterateur, small-time entrepreneur and politician. As the most educated, articulate and polished politician of the SSC, he rose to several positions of power and honour: vice president of SSC (1949–56), president of SSC (1957–67) and state councillor and executive councillor (1953–9). When the Maharaja of Sikkim capitulated in May 1949 after prolonged agitation of the SSC, he arrived from Biratnagar post-haste in response to Tashi Babu's call, only to find that the 'Ministry' for which he had intended had already been given to another Nepali member of the SSC, Chandra Das Rai. Not to be outdone, a post of secretary to the chief minister was created for his benefit for a 29-day-long ministry.

Once the negotiation for ethnic representation in the proposed State Council was on, D. S. Lepcha and Kashi Babu were representatives on behalf of the Sikkim State Congress. It is alleged that two SSC representatives were cajoled by the crown prince and the political officer to accept the parity between the Nepalis (with two-thirds of population in the state) and the Lepcha-Bhutia (with about one-third of population of the state) combined against the express mandate of the party. When the president of the SSC threatened to repudiate the agreement, the Durbar changed its tack and announced that in fact the two SSC representatives had signed the agreement not as the representatives of their political party, but as the representatives of their respective communities. While bravado, loud talk and demagoguery were left to the lot of the Tashi Babu, Kashiraj coolly established his full control on the party apparatus. He became its "undoubted brain and presented a perfect example of how one man can have two dozen faces". In such a situation, it was easy for him to manage to field four members of his family and relatives as the candidates for six seats meant for the Nepalis in the State Council election in 1953 and convince his apparently ambitious Lepcha-Bhutia party competitors to fight from such constituencies, which were strongholds of the opposition. The result was foregone conclusion: while Tashi Tshering, D. S. Lepcha, L. D. Kazi and others lost in their contests, Kashiraj's candidates were victorious. He along with Sonam Tshering was elevated to position of the executive councillor, a position which ensured him monetary return and proximity to the power to be.

In such a situation, the sincere Lepcha, Bhutia and other members of other communities left SSC and Kashiraj was instrumental in proving the crown prince's charge of the Sikkim State Congress to be the political outfit of the Nepalis. Suffocated of partisan antics of Kashiraj's clique, L. D. Kazi, the respected aristocratic Lepcha face of the party, as well decided to leave SSC and float his own political forum, the Sikkim Swatantra Party in 1958. Worst was yet to come to Kashiraj's door. He stood as a candidate for contesting State Council bye-election in 1959, with holding posts of executive councillor and president of the SSC in the past against the secretary of his political party, SSC, C. D. Rai. His humiliation was all the more pronounced when the results were announced; he was not only defeated in the election by his younger colleague but he also lost his security deposit. By then, the SSC was no more even a Nepali party, but had earned the nickname of the Newar Party under his stewardship. However, he was busy building up his nephew, Nahkul Pradhan, as his successor, who eased him out as the president of the party in 1967. In spite of all that, he continued to keep his ears attuned to the soundings from the Darbar. The Namgyal establishment acknowledged his services by awarding him with the second civilian award, Pema Dorji, in 1971. Even after that, he was one of the most sought after personalities of Sikkim. This one of the most versatile minds of Sikkim breathed his last at the age of 85 in 1990.

Lhendup Dorji Kazi

Lhendup Dorji Kazi, born in 1904, may be remembered as the most colourful and innovative leader of 20th-century Sikkim. He was a scion of the famous Khangsarpa Kazi household of Chyakhung, which had worked in opposition to the Sikkim rulers in the 19th century. As a price for that, he was defrocked as the head lama of Rumtek monastery allegedly on trumped-up charges. Quite early in life, he along with his elder brother, Kazi Phag Tshering, had founded the Young Men Buddhist Association (YMBA) at Darjeeling. Two brothers started a number of elementary Nepali medium schools in western Sikkim and introduced some social reforms. They undertook to business and commercial activities and very soon Lhendup became the managing director of Western Sikkim Transport Company, which was later "taken over by the Durbar" to form a part of the Sikkim Nationalized Transport (SNT). He founded the Sikkim Praja Mandal (SPM) in 1945 with a view to organizing social reforms among the villagers and he was one of the founders of the Sikkim State Congress in 1947 by merging his voluntary forum.

It appears that he chose more polished and sophisticated style in politics by allying with Kashiraj Pradhan to boisterous histrionics of Tashi Tshering. But soon he learnt that for Kashiraj's politics was a means for personal convenience and not as a vehicle of public service. Kicking off the presidency of SSC, he opened a new front against his old associates of the Sikkim State Congress as well as the Durbar pet political front, the SNP, by founding a political party, the Sikkim Swatantra Party in 1958. Soon a number of fellow travellers and old warhorses joined him after deserting their political formations: Sonam Tshering, C. D. Rai and B. B. Gurung, to name a few. Thoughtful churning among them led to founding of a new political forum in 1960, the Sikkim National Congress (SNC). The new party had a clear manifesto, party structure, register of ordinary members, its own occasional publication on political resolutions and a head office at a central place. At the top of it, it had a very experienced, articulate, enthusiastic, theatrical and capable media manager in Kazini Eliza Maria Dorji, the indomitable Belgian better half of the Kazi.

Meanwhile events began to change fast in placid Sikkim. The Crown Prince Palden Thondup Namgyal decided to marry for the second time after demise of his Tibetan wife. He chose to marry Hope Cooke, a young American girl in March 1963 against the long-standing Sikkimese convention. This nuptial ceremony went ahead in spite of the opposition from the monk body and the Kazi aristocracy against the convention to marrying a foreigner. The prince was 40 by then and his lady love was half of his age; it was a scandalous wedding to say the least. By the end of the year, Sir Tashi Namgyal, the ruler of Sikkim, breathed his last in December 1963. The crown prince along with his American queen got busy in making hectic preparation for their much published and waited formal crowning, which was accomplished in May 1965 with all international glare and attention of some international guests. The couple immediately espoused the cause of the international personality of Sikkim with an eye on recognition of little Sikkim from the United Nations Organization (UNO) against the wishes the protecting power, the Indian Union. However, his biggest bugbear was Lhendup Dorji Kazi and his consort, Eliza Maria Dorji, who went on mocking at the hollow moves and counter-moves of the Namgyal couple in this regard. By then the democratic display of State Council elections and procedure for choosing executive councillors were taken to the limits of absurdity. The last election for the State Council was held in January 1973, which was challenged on the ground of malpractices in voting and counting procedures, which were brushed aside by the powers that be. On the contrary, the ruler went ahead with the arrangements of celebration of his 50th birthday, ignoring the public protests.

Naturally, the Sikkimese masses lost all their patience, took to the streets and attacked the law enforcing apparatus, leading to collapse of the administration in the better part of the state. Within 25 years, it was the second time when the ruler was constrained to request the Government of India to take over the administration and establish rule of law. By then there were drastic differences in the opposition to the feudal dispensation. In place of idealistic Jawaharlal Nehru, it was his more pragmatic daughter, Indira Gandhi, as the prime minister of India and in place of tall-talking Tashi Babu of SSC it was organizationally shrewd L. D. Kazi at the forefront of agitation. It was the famous Lhendup Dorji Kazi who was leading the anti-establishment movement on behalf of his newly created Sikkim Congress after merging the SSC, SNC and Sikkim United Front. The next two years were marked with moves and counter-moves by the ruler to fight for retention of the autonomous status of Sikkim and his opponents to sabotage his moves. What ultimately resulted in was the merger/annexation of Sikkim to India and Lhendup Dorji Kazi taking over the chair of the chief minister of the little state as a part of the Indian Union. At the end, it was sweet revenge for L. D. Kazi against the former crown prince turned the last Chogyal of Sikkim for getting the Kazi defrocked and removing him from the august office of the head lama of the significant monastery decades back.

However, Kazi's tenure as the chief minister was shrouded in controversy from the beginning. Inefficiency, corruption, factionalism and dissention in the party, interference by the bureaucrats on deputation, arrogance and interference of the MLAs in the administration were some of contributory factors to his downfall. Above all, Kazi's frequent change in political affiliation to the tune of the fast changing national political alignment in New Delhi in the second part of 1970s caused havoc to the expectation of the Sikkimese. He failed to control the young brigade of three members of the Legislative Assembly from running amuck: Nar Bahadur Khatiwara, Ramchandra Podyal and Krishan Chandra Pradhan. The vested interests in the form of feudal elements and the former ruler were waiting for the opportunity to strike at the weakest moment. An inapt and irresponsible statement of the then Prime Minister Morarji Desai on the merger of Sikkim to India further emboldened the sagging morale and wild expectations in Sikkim. They identified Nar Bahadur Bhandari, a former schoolteacher, who had opposed the merger of Sikkim with India and for that he had to suffer as the tool in their hands. It was the same Bhandari who had coined the catchy slogan: "Batiso Chor and Des Bechwa"

(32 members of the legislature, who had stolen the country and those who sold the country).

The result of the second election to the Sikkim Legislative Assembly held in 1979 was a foregone conclusion. One but all 32 candidates including the Kazi lost the contest badly and Nar Bahadur Bhandari formed the government as the chief minister. The rest is not a long story. Though the Kazi continued to call himself a Congress man till the last, the Indian National Congress never took him seriously for an effective role in state politics thereafter. He remained in the news at times by giving statements on political developments and did attract a number of visitors looking for nuggets of old world political snippets. He survived about another three decades prior to breathing his last on the last day of July 2007 at the age of 103. The grateful Indian Union had recognized his services to the cause of Indian nation by conferring on him "Padam Vibhushan", the second highest civil award to distinguished civilians.

Birth of the political parties

The preceding brief biographies of some of the significant actors of the first flush of democratic upsurge in Sikkim, who championed the cause of the people at large against the ruler and his courtiers, are suggestive of the contours of the Sikkimese politics, which would take in the second half of the 20th century. The British political officer and the Namgyal courtiers had created such a reign of terror that nobody could openly dare to assemble for any public cause. Thus, inspired by the movement for independence in Indian plains, some educated and enlightened Sikkimese such as Tashi Tshering, Kezang Tenzing and Sonam Tshering met to discuss state of affairs in Sikkim on the pretext of a picnic party at Bhotia School, Gangtok in 1947 and they decided to form a reformist forum, Praja Sudharak Samaj. Earlier they had petitioned to the authorities against forced labour and oppression of the landlords. And they pleaded for paying land rent directly to the state bankers instead of the lessees, as was the practice till the 1940s. Their petitions were not only ignored, but they were also charged with spreading Nepalese communalism. In course of time, the Samaj leaders such as Sonam Tshering were physically assaulted by the Kazis' goons for openly raising the cause of the forced labour. Similarly, two Nepali thikadars, Gobardhan Pradhan and Dhan Bahadur Tiwari of Temi Tarku in south district, who were exposed to populist movements in Darjeeling, stealthily met at Thakurbari at Rangpo on plea of worship and picnic. However, the police inspector smelt a rat, paid a surprise visit to the picnickers and went back to report that there was nothing objectionable being done. On that day, August 14, 1946, they established another such forum, Sikkim Praja Sammelan, for redressal of the plight of the commoners (Subba, 2012: 63–4).

A descendant of illustrious Cheebu Lama, the Lepcha Kazi of Chyakhung, Lhendup Dorji Khangsarpa (or L. D. Kazi) and an ascetic turned politician, Krishna Das Ray Chaudhury, established a third organization called Sikkim Praja Mandal in western Sikkim in 1945.

> The Praja Sudharak Samaj of Gangtok had the benefit of the seasoned counsel of Tashi Tshering, an English educated former employee of the Political Office, who alone of all the champions of change, had understood politics and administration, and had the gift of articulating his views. The Gangtok party (Sikkim Praja Sudharak Samaj) decided to hold a public meeting at Gangtok football ground – then known as Polo ground – on the 7th December 1947. The two parties from Temi Tarku and Chyakhung were invited to participate. Tashi Tshering (had) composed his pamphlet, '*A Few Facts about Sikkim*', which was translated into Nepali by Chandra Das Rai, who also took upon himself to cyclo-style enough copies for distribution among the masses.
>
> (Basnet, 1974: 76)

Among the other speakers, there were Tashi Tshering, Kezang Dorji Tezang, K. D. Ray Chaudhury, Helen Lepcha, née Sabitri Devi, and Captain D. S. Lepcha.

That was an unprecedented political meeting at which the Sikkimese heard their first political speeches. Again, Basnet informs us what happened in the meeting:

> Appearing with the stalwarts was a young man, Chandra Das Rai, 24, from Namchi. He was asked to read the Nepali version of the paper, '*A Few Facts about Sikkim*', which he did with gusto, lacing his reading with witty remarks. The crescendo of applause that followed his speech marked him as a budding hero in the inchoate politics of Sikkim. All the speeches were in Nepali language, the language of an overwhelming majority of the population and the *lingua franca* of Sikkim. Later that evening, the three associations formally merged together and formed a new party called the Sikkim State Congress (SSC). Tashi Tshering was elected President of the party, Dimik Singh Lepchpa as the Vice-President and

> Kashiraj Pradhan as the General Secretary, consciously disabusing the charge of possible Nepali Party by the Durbar. It was decided that a five-member delegation should call on the Maharaja and present the "three-fold" demand of the Sikkim State Congress. The three-fold demands were: (a) abolition of landlordism; (b) formation of an interim government as a precursor of a democratic and responsible government; and (c) accession of Sikkim to the Indian Union.
>
> (Basnet, 1974: 77)

It appears that the Sikkim State Congress was organized as the Sikkimese counterpart of the Indian National Congress (INC) and affiliation to the parent body was sought. (Tshering, 1960) The party petitioned to the ruler for a drastic change in the political structure (Memorandum, 1960: 7) with their three-point demands. Apart from formulating and presenting political issues of radical significance, the Sikkim State Congress started to impart political education to the masses through campaigns and movements. In no time, it became the party of masses, reflecting their aspirations. Though its popularity was more among the Nepalese, the State Congress took special care to appear as the forum of consensus and avoided any overt identification with a particular community. This was the political forum, which was careful to represent all the important ethnic groups and region of the state. They launched agitation in favour of their demands.

Columnist Sunanda K. Datta-Ray, Palden Thondup Namgyal's self-proclaimed durbar chronicler, refurbishes his image as a great visionary, who could envision a "federation of the Buddhist units such as Sikkim, Bhutan and Tibet" in 1947 (Datta-Ray, 2013: 64–6). And with a view to counteracting Namgyal's alleged strategy to galvanize Lamaist conclave against India, a nervous political officer, Harishwar Dayal, drafted Tashi Tshering out of a mob to organize Sikkim State Congress. The author had heard this formulation once before from a scion of the Libing Kazi, Tashi Tobden, in 2008, a few months prior to his unfortunate fatal road crash. Mr Datta-Ray would have profitably read the solicited advice of Tobetologist Sir Basil Gould, Hopkinson's predecessor, on the steps to be taken in the uncertain situation after the Second World War and impending British withdrawal from India. It was Gould's idea to think of a Buddhist Federation of Tibet, Bhutan and Sikkim and send a representation to the Cabinet Mission in Delhi, which Sikkim and Bhutan did. This was the argument with a view to justifying the crown prince's known role to get Sikkim National Party organized to counteract the efforts of the Sikkim State Congress.

After a lot of prevarication, the ruler appointed three secretaries from among the State Congress activists: Sonam Tshering, D. S. Lepcha and Raghuberdas, apparently with a view to representing the Bhutias, Lepchas and Nepalese subjects. Neither of the three appointees nor the administration cared to work out the rules and functions of their respective office. In the process, it was a frustrating experience for them as well as the party they represented. Naturally, there was clamour for their recall and the party president asked them to resign and come back to the party fold. Out of ill-experience or pleasure of the office, they were reluctant to resign and that was the opportune moment for the crown prince to entice Sonam Tshering from SSC to his fold by highlighting the alleged risk of the 'one man: one Vote' demand of the SSC. And since then to his end, Sonam Babu had a distinction of being a significant functionary of all the political formations in Sikkim one time or another.

Durbar reacts by organizing, Sikkim National Party

Andrew Duff, an author, sympathetic to the cause of the Durbar, writes that the aforementioned demands of the SSC "posed irritating challenge [to the Crown Prince, Thondup]". He could accept the first demand: "he knew that the land laws needed to change, but he also knew that the problem was deeply ingrained and could not be addressed overnight. As for the second, he was willing to consider change, but he also had grave concerns. For decades the ethnic make-up of Sikkim had been altered with the wide-scale immigration from Nepal. Any move towards more representative government would give Nepalis more power. Thondup was deeply concerned by the obvious implication – that the Buddhist community might lose its strong connection with the land in the face of the growing Nepali population . . . It was the third demand, however – that Sikkim should join India – that Thondup found most frustrating. He was certain that such a move was incompatible with Sikkim maintaining its identity separate from India" (Duff, 2015: 34–5). And thus, alarmed at the impressive popular response and organizational success of the State Congress, the impulsive 24-year-old Maharaja Kumar got the Sikkim National Party (SNP) organized in April 1948.

This party had few clear political objectives. It was an organization of the aristocrats and the neo-rich Bhutia courtiers and sought to safeguard Lepcha-Bhutia interests against the alleged Nepali-dominated Sikkim State Congress. The Sikkim National Party stood for an independent Sikkim with special treaty with India. This party could not assume the character of a mass party, did not spell out any ideological commitment, and was mainly a defender of the status quo in Sikkim. It was a political forum floated by the crown prince against the expressed advice of the political officer. It was not only funded by the Durbar, but even the paperwork such as the resolutions and so forth were also drafted by the crown prince; not those half-wit functionaries such as Gyaltsen or Sonam Tshering, who had never accomplished such exercise in their lives. However, the brain behind the facade of the political forum, worked out the following resolutions on April 30, 1948:

1 Resolved that with regards to the question of abolition of landlordism in Sikkim, the party would approach His Highness the Maharaja for an early consideration . . . a time-honoured institution, like the one in question, cannot be suddenly wiped out of existence root and branch, without giving rise to graver consequences, such as, administrative difficulties and disruption.
2 Resolved that the proposal of introducing a responsible government in Sikkim, at the present juncture, is not administratively possible. For under the existing state of circumstances, a responsible government would be quite impracticable.
3 Resolved that Sikkim shall not under any circumstances accede to the Dominion of India.

(Documents, 1960)

From its very inception, it remained a party under the leadership of the affluent Bhutias with the backing of the lamas from various monasteries. The National Party leadership was convinced that the State Congress was committed to wresting power from the ruler and establishing the "tyranny of the majority". Indomitable Tashi Tshering rightly termed it as the "anti-thesis of the State Congress".

As an answer to the mechanization of the crown prince, the Sikkim State Congress organized its next session at Namchi on October 22, 1948, and reiterated its three-fold demand and decided to agitate for that. And for that, the SSC decided to open its branches in every village, canvassed in favour of three demands against abolition of Kazis and Zamindars, establishment of people's government and joining India as a democratic move. They pleaded with the people that they were not against the king, but they were certainly against the oppressive administration run on the name of the king. The Durbar ignored their plea and went ahead with sabotaging SSC by placating the Sikkim National Party. Out of desperation, the SSC sent its president, Tashi Tshering, and one of the general secretaries, Chandra Das Rai, to Delhi in December 1948 to impress upon Pandit Jawaharlal Nehru to act in their favour of their demands. Nehru gave a patient hearing to his visitors and explained the intricacies of their demands and advised them to go back and strengthen their movement among all sections of the Sikkimese.

The State Congress organized a series of no-tax campaigns, non-cooperation movement and non-violent agitation against the autocratic administration. Its leaders courted arrest in favour of their three-point demands. They also lobbied to convince New Delhi of the urgency of drastic political change in Sikkim. To some extent they were able to impress upon New Delhi about the partisan attitude of the ruler towards the Sikkim National Party. Armed with organizational experience and fraternal assurances from the politicians in New Delhi, the State Congress embarked on the second Satyagraha movement in May 1949. The demonstrators barricaded the royal palace and the ruler ran away to take shelter in political office. The hyperactive crown prince tried to drive from the palace to the political office for confabulation, but the agitating volunteers of the SSC blocked his way by lying in front of his vehicle. Indomitable Namgyal Tshering, the vice president and C. D. Rai, the general secretary of SSC mounted on the hood of the jeep being driven by the prince and managed to secure the keys of the vehicle, forcing the beleaguered prince to stage a retreat to the palace.

Figure 5.1 About 3,000 Congress demonstrators, led by Vice President Namgyal and Gen. Sec. C. D. Rai, demanding formation of Interim Govt. with the intervention by Indian Political Officer, Mr. Hareswar Dayal. The Chogyal accepted the formation of Interim Government.

Source: Courtesy of Mr C. D. Rai.

As the popular agitation continued unabated, the Maharaja was forced to hand over the administration to the political officer, who advised him and the SSC to negotiate among themselves to break the stalemate. After prolonged negotiation, the Maharaja agreed to instal a five-member interim government inclusive of two of his nominees. In this way, the first popular government of Sikkim was installed on May 9, 1949, under the leadership of the president of the Sikkim State Congress, Tashi Tshering, and it included Dimik Singh Lepcha and C. D. Rai of State Congress; Dorji Dadul and Reshmi Prasad Alley were the two nominees of the Durbar. This ministry was installed without defining the scope of its power and functions. On most important issues, the Durbar and its nominees disagreed with the chief minister. Moreover, Durbar's nominees proved to be unenthusiastic about the popular government, which was also not in a position to liberate the masses from the feudal autocracy. The ruler refused to introduce agrarian and administrative reforms insisted by the chief minister. Out of desperation, the State Congress leadership embarked on questionable political gimmicks with vulgarity. Meanwhile the Maharaja Kumar had been trying to convince New Delhi that popular government in Sikkim meant anarchy and political instability. This led the Government of India to act "in the interest of law and order". All of a sudden the political officer sent for all the five ministers on June 6, 1949, and curtly announced the summary dismissal of the ministry in the name

Figure 5.2 Interim Government was formed on 9th may, 1949.
Left to right: R. P. Alley, C. D. Rai, Tashi Tshering, Capt. Dimik Singh Lepcha & Dorjee Dadul.

Source: Courtesy of Mr C. D. Rai.

of the Government of India. This action on the part of the Government of India came as a boost to the Durbar and a rude shock to the democratic forces, which had not traded for such a strong reaction from the New Delhi (Sinha, 2008).

The Indian government explained that the "threat of disorder might not have come from the State Congress, but it might have come from the Maharaja's side". Thus, the government had little choice but to act in any case. However, the executive power of the State was proposed to be transferred from the erstwhile ministry to a Dewan (quasi-chief minister), selected from among the Indian administrative cadre "for the good of Sikkim, but that his (the Dewan's) administration would be for the briefest possible period" (Patterson, 1963: 233). Consequently, an Indian administrator, J. S. Lall, was appointed Dewan of Sikkim on August 11, 1949. The Dewan undertook to apply remedial measures to alleviate the hardship of the agrarian people immediately. The lessee system along with the privileges of the leaseholders was abolished. The peasants were protected against frequent eviction from their patrimonial holdings. Effective steps were taken to recast the judicial, legal and revenue administration. These steps eased to some extent the tension between the Durbar and the masses.

As regards the status of Sikkim vis-à-vis India, Sikkim was bound by the declaration made by the Viceroy Lord Wavell in anticipation of a transfer of power in the subcontinent, which envisaged new political arrangements between the princely states and the successor governments. Sikkim attempted to negotiate on her future status along with other members of the Indian Chamber of Princes. The Constituent Assembly of India adopted a resolution on January 22, 1947, to the effect that a committee should deal with the special problems of Sikkim and Bhutan, negotiate with the Chamber of Princes and duly report to the Assembly. Later, a standstill agreement between the Sikkim Durbar and the Government of India was signed on February 27, 1948, by which "all agreements, relations and administrative arrangements as to the matter of common concern existing between the Crown and the Sikkim State on August 14, 1947" were deemed to continue till a new treaty was negotiated.

The Ministry of External Affairs, Government of India, issued a statement on March 20, 1950, on the principles on which the new treaty was to be signed. Both the parties agreed that Sikkim would continue to be an Indian protectorate in respect of external relations, defence and communication. Though Sikkim would have her internal autonomy, maintenance of good administration and law and order would be the ultimate responsibility of the Government of India. Both the parties also decided to follow a policy of "progressive association of the people of the state with her government" and institute a system of village council. The Indo-Sikkimese Treaty enshrining the above principles was signed at Gangtok on December 5, 1950, by the Maharaja Tashi Namgyal and Harishwar Dayal, the political officer in Sikkim (Coelho, 1971: 25–6). The popular political leaders were sceptical towards the treaty. In fact, it was such an odd mixture that all political activists could find some aspects of the treaty to be in their favour. The Sikkim State Congress held that the autonomous status of Sikkim was identical with that of the Indian state of Jammu and Kashmir with the exception that the latter had joined the Indian Union formally, while the former did not.

Sorry state of affairs of the Sikkim State Congress

On the populist front of Sikkim, there was utter confusion in the Sikkim State Congress, the oldest among the political parties of the three kingdoms. It was apparently a multi-ethnic forum to begin with but the leaders of the party were politically illiterate, novice and innocent of the power constellations in the state administration. They had neither the idea of power politics nor did they try to identify and work out a strategy to overcome their handicaps. Moreover, they took it for granted that the Indian national leaders, who belonged to the All India National Congress and to which they presumed to belong to, would instantly support their cause. It did not appear that they ever seriously tried to reach out to the regionally significant Congress leaders in their neighbourhood, who really mattered and had linkages to the prime minister. There is no evidence to show that the SSC ever tried to reach Gopi Nath Bardoloi of Assam, B. C. Ray of West Bengal, or S. K. Sinha of Bihar, the significant INC leaders in their neighbourhood. Neither did they have any contact with national leaders of the new regime in New Delhi. Incidentally, unlike other princely states in India, which were handled by Sardar Vallabhbhai Patel, the home minister, Sikkim and Bhutan were being looked after by the Ministry of External Affairs, that is, the prime minister cum foreign minister, Jawaharlal Nehru, who was a terribly busy person.

On the other hand, the Maharaj Kumar of Sikkim, a shrewd and scheming man, soon got his courtiers around on a stark communal platform, enticing the anti-Kazi populist Bhutia face from among the SSC, Sonam Tshering, assistant general secretary. He offered him from his pocket product, the position of president of the new party, Sikkim National Party, with a view to guarding his fief. In spite of the contrary advice given to by the power to be, he did not hide that it was he who was the SNP and that the rest were his factotums. He did not sit idle after creating the SNP and busied himself into buying amenable elements from among the SSC. Soft-spoken and second graduate of the state, and a scion of the Pradhan clan, Kashi Raj Pradhan was his first target. Whenever he realized that things were getting hot for him in New Delhi, he would dispatch one of his sisters to cultivate the file-pushing bureaucrats, who mattered in hours of crisis. On the other hand, leaders of SSC helped him immensely through their omissions and commissions. Impetuous Tashi Tshering, loudmouth Dimik Singh Lepcha, and the overall unruly SSC members strolling around the streets of Gangtok bazaar in euphoria of great expectation, did not endear themselves both to the commoners and the political guardian deity in Sikkim, the political officer. It appears that the Government of India appeared to be concerned with ongoing development in Sikkim. They apprehended that the affairs of the state might be slipping into chaos through the so-called popular agitations launched by the SSC and they stopped taking much interest in its 'popular' programmes. Thus, the goal of the democratic struggle, which appeared within grasp in the beginning, kept on shifting further and farther, testing the patience of the commoners, who had invested their immense optimism in the anti-feudal struggle in Sikkim.

Two Indian ICS officers, Harishwar Dayal and J. S. Lall, posted in Sikkim to represent the democratic Indian Union, behaved exactly as they used to do during the colonial period. They kept filing regular reports lashed with colonial biases: Tashi Tshering was termed as a Casanova, drunkard and gambler, running a bric-a-brac shop in Gangtok, as a cashiered head clerk of the Residency, and an arrogant and ambitious braggart. Dimik S. Lepcha was similarly labelled as an army ranker, who prided in his loud voice, empty mind and extravagance. Kashi Raj Pradhan was described as a soft-spoken, amenable and slippery personality with a dozen hidden faces. His overriding concern was to export rice to Tibet through Sikkim, illegally imported from Nepal. Gobardhan Pradhan, who had merged his Praja Sammelan with the SSC and an ardent follower of the AIGL, continued to attend AIGL sessions. The Maharaj Kumar was found openly talking about his Tibetan option on the ground that there was no difference between 'Sikkimese' (Bhutias) and 'Tibetans', claiming that Rongs (Lepchas) and Tsongs (Limbus) were in his pocket, as they were Buddhists (Lall, October 1953). In his estimate, Nepalis were the responsibility of the Government of India, who should or should not think about them. He believed that except some Limbus from the west district, all Nepalis in Sikkim, including the Pradhans, were immigrants and they had no place in his 'Sikkimise' kingdom, which meant a Bhutia kingdom, forgetting conveniently that even the term 'Sikkim' was taken from the Limbu language.

When the newly appointed Dewan arrived in the state capital, he found to his utter surprise that the state treasury was empty, as taxes had not been collected for about two years. He instantly cancelled the leaves of school teachers and put them on the duty of tax collection. He came to know that the most significant move on behalf of the SSC was that of 'No Rent' campaign, launched most effectively in southern Sikkim under the leadership of Chandra Das Rai. Thus, no such collection could be made in the southern part of the state. He decided to visit the most deviant defaulters in the densely settled southern district of Namchi, but there was no road leading to it. So he travelled in circuitous way by jeep through the district of Darjeeling. He found the way blocked by the SSC agitators on a strategically located water stream (*jhora*) on the way just before Namchi bazaar. The agitators were shouting slogans in the name of Mahatma Gandhi, demanding the abolition of house tax, forced unpaid labour, land rent, and the introduction of the rationing of food as well as other issues that affected the life of the commoners. On reaching the spot, the Dewan tried to understand the immediate cause of the agitation from the leaders of the movement. When he talked to their leader on the spot, he was requested to address the agitators. The Dewan not only did so, but he promised to order the abolition of house tax, the compulsory unpaid labour, and promised to order the collection of land rent through the state bankers of Sikkim immediately. The agitators also demanded the rationing of food, supply of kerosene and actions against the hoarders and black-marketeers in essential commodities. The Dewan's orders had a solitary effect on the agitators. He also ordered the creation of administrative block at Namchi and ordered Dorji Dahdul, the first graduate of the state, to be posted as the Tahsildar of the block. Attending to these popular demands went in a big way to assuage the ruffled feelings of the commoners and the Dewan, who was seen as a strange intruder to begin with, began to be seen as the effective tool for the welfare of the people against the backdrop of the Kazi and lessees' autocracy and ruler's inaction. However, such moves blunted the aggressive agitation of the Sikkim State Congress and efficacy of the ruler's authority.

Dewan J. S. Lall was an experienced administrator, who knew how to deal with the chaotic situation. He took immediate steps to tone up the administration. Police force was trained and organized on a priority and a central control was put in operation. Administration was established by dividing the principality into two districts, Sikkim Eastern and Sikkim Western and qualified sub-divisional officers (Tahsildars) were appointed. Administrative roles of the lessees were taken away; unpaid labour was abolished forthwith; house tax was removed; forests were taken over from the charge of the lessees and separate forest department as a government branch was organized for the first time. At last, the lessee system itself was given a go-bye and villagers for the first time had a sense of being administered for their welfare by the state. Ration shops were opened for various essential provisions such as cereal, cloth, kerosene, salt and so forth during the post-war critical days of scarcity. Strict orders against the black marketing were issued to the shop keepers and the administration saw to it that they obey the orders. Once the administration started functioning in normal ways, a large many complaints of the commoners were taken care of. And that too created numerous problems, which made many quarters uneasy.

For the first time the SSC leadership was confronted with the real challenge with reasoned administrator and diplomat like J. S. Lall and Harishwar Dayal, who worked on the scene in the full knowledge of the Government of India. On the other hand, the scheming Palden Thondup had a political party at his beck and call to counter the Sikkim State Congress populist moves. Out of inexperience and lack of handling the populist cause, the SSC began to display factionalism within its rank, which was further fanned by its opponents. At the top of it, the Government of India was suspicious of the link between the Nepalese leadership within the SSC and the mechanization of the Gorkha League under the influence of the Ranas of Nepal. While the crown prince kept on harping on the imagined internal autonomy of Sikkim, the Government of India itself was suspicious of the activities of some leaders and their links between the SSC and Gorkha League. In the circumstances an ethnic compromise was in the offing, which was neither effective, nor democratic, nor was even it permitted to work under the presidency of the Diwan. Consequently, the scheme of ethnic parity fall prey to the manipulation of the crown prince.

Democratic fraud of the parity system

On the other hand, there was hardly a known public move on the part of any political party in India to understand what was going on in Sikkim, with the exception of some stray efforts by the Congress Socialist Party of India (CSP). But these efforts were sporadic and, in fact, it indirectly created problems for the already belaboured Sikkim

State Congress. The maverick socialist Ram Manohar Lohia regularly visited Darjeeling to organize the Congress Socialist Party. His style of speech was popular in the hills, but his association with the Marwari businessmen did not present him with a positive image. This was because of the fact that his political hosts perceived the Marwaris as hoarders and black-marketeers and of being in league with the rich anti-people zamindars of the region. In their bravado, the Indian Socialist Party began to believe that they were an alternative political force to the Indian National Congress, the ruling party in India, which rightly claimed to be the inheritors of the freedom struggle in the country. This led to the creation of bad blood between the two, and in the process it was the SSC which was made to suffer for the strenuous links with the Indian socialists, who were not only internally divided but were also badly beaten in the first general election held in 1952. Similarly, attendance of SSC sessions by B. P. Koirala in December 1949 at Rangpo and his brother, G. P. Koirala at Malli, strengthened the imaginary link of the SSC with that of Nepal and made it easier for its detractors to label it not only as a Nepali party, but also to claim that the SSC was sponsored from Nepal. There were many individuals such as Dil

Figure 5.3 At the invitation of Sikkim Congress, the Prime Minister of Nepal B. P. Koirala, attended the Annual Session Sikkim State Congress at Rangpo. On the right side Kalimpong Gandhi Jungbir Sapkota, Kashiraj Pradhan, Nakul Pradhan and Adhiklal Pradhan. From Calcutta the socialist leader Shivnath Banerji attended the Session. On the left side standing are Gen. Sec. C. D. Rai, Parsai and Capt. Dimik Singh Lepcha, Sitting on the front, Vice President Namgyal Tshering and Lai Bahadur Thegim (23rd December, 1949).

Source: Courtesy of Mr C. D. Rai.

Bahadur Gurung, D. B. Tiwari, Gobardhan Pradhan and others who were actively associated with the AIGL and who also took part in SSC activities. Thus, as far as the Government of India was concerned, they took a formal stand, apparently in line with the advice left behind by the British colonial functionaries, to wait for developments across the border in Tibet or China, mentioned previously.

The AIGL did not honestly try to reach out to Sikkim in a big way for two reasons. First, knowing full well the feelings in the Durbar, the British political officer in Sikkim would have refused permission to the Nepalis to engage in political activity in Sikkim. This would not have been easy to defy with impunity as there was no appreciable number of ex-Gorkha soldiers, the potential support base of AIGL, in demographically small state of Sikkim. On the other hand, the Sikkimese Kazis and lessees were ruthless in their suppression and treatment of the tenants, another potential support base of the AIGL. As soon as it became clear that the days of the British rule were numbered, various social fora formed an apparently multi-ethnic political party, the Sikkim State Congress, and positioning itself in opposition to it would have been counter-productive for the AIGL. It appears that the above quoted prescription by the Government of British India was known and understood by the rulers of the kingdoms and the functionaries of the Indian Union in Sikkim, but the political leaders were not aware of it. Moreover, communication apparently came handy to the new rulers in Delhi to fashion their approach to the Himalayan kingdoms and also emboldened the Bhutan agents, father and son: Dorjis and the Maharaj Kumar of Sikkim to actively oppose the democratic aspirations of their people in the late 1940s and early 1950s.

At times, the Maharaj Kumar of Sikkim appeared defiant and he took a huge risk by openly organizing the Sikkim National Party. In fact, he was determined to get independence for his little fief without thinking of international complications and its financial viability. It appears that the Government of India could not actively oppose the move because they were not sure of the democratic credentials of the Sikkim State Congress. In the process, the Government of India permitted the Maharaj Kumar to blackmail her simply because of the treaty that was signed, and by which India was not to interfere in the internal administration of the state. On the teeth of the uncompromising anti-Nepali stand of the Maharaj Kumar, the Government of India had to willy-nilly agree to a compromise. Hence the late lamented ethnic parity between the two socio-cultural blocks of Nepalis and Bhutia-Lepcha, the parity system, was contrived with which no body was fully satisfied. With the exception of Tashi Tshering, there was no voice from among the Lepchas or Bhutias in opposition to the parity system in the state as a whole. Unfortunately for Sikkim, Tashi Tshering, by then, was completely discredited as a foul-mouthed agitator by the vested interests and even his ethnic identity, Bhutia, began to be questioned. The last nail, so to say, in his coffin was his contesting the elections for the State Council and losing it miserably in 1953. The problem was further compounded for the Government of India because of the fact that the Sikkim State Congress did not have a creditable Bhutia leader to stand against the antiques of the Maharaj Kumar.

A Nepali scholar described the process through which the "parity system" was contrived:

> In May 1951, the matter of communal representation was discussed by the representatives of three parties: Maharajkumar Palden Thondup Namgyal represented the Maharaja; Sonam Tshering represented the Bhotia-Lepcha interests as projected by Sikkim National Party; the State Congress was represented by Dimik Singh Lepcha and Kashiraj Pradhan. The Congress representatives had been deputed by Tashi Tshering with clear instruction that they were to discuss things . . . and were not to take any decision, which was left to the Party High Command. The representatives sat whole night through, drinking expensive liquor from the Maharaja's cellar. And the next day the "Parity Formula" was signed by the four whereby the elected seats in the future State Council were to be divided equally among the Bhutiya-Lepcha and the Nepalese communities, and the Maharaja was to appoint five nominees. Tashi Tshering refused to ratify the agreement signed by the two Congress representatives. The Sikkim Durbar, however, gave out that Dimik Singh Lepcha had signed as the representative of the Lepchas, while Kashi Raj Pradhan had signed as the representative of the Nepalese. All Tashi Tshering's protests were of no avail.
>
> (Basnet, 1974: 99)

The founding assistant general secretary of the SSC, Sonam Tshering, had already deserted the party and D. S. Lepcha was silenced, as his support base was shifting. The polished and less communicative Kashibabu was won over, while the tenacious Tashi Tshering was totally ignored and allowed to cool his temper with strong liquor. It was a credit to the hard bargaining done behind the scene by the "power to be" that some electoral device was introduced in favour of the Nepali speaking Sikkimese and an acknowledgment was secured that they too were legally Sikkimise subjects. There is no doubt that the provisions of the State Council, the Executive Council, Electoral College, voting system and counting procedures, and role of the Dewan were far from democratic, but those were not mean achievements in the given situation of the transitional phase of the regional politics, which had not known a democratic tradition of its own.

The above folklore mentioned by Basnet on the back-door bargaining on the part of the Durbar with the SSC leadership speaks volumes on the quality of the men and the means purportedly offered to them. It appears that there was a tacit understanding with the Government of India on this vital issue. We should like to remind our readers that the colonial prescription of maintaining status quo in the Himalayan region, which was reduced to absurdity soon after "liberation of Tibet" by People's Republic of China. In fact, in the changed scenario, all the areas on the southern slope of the Himalayas mentioned in the above advice were being claimed by China as five fingers of its Tibetan palm of the extended Chinese hand. But New Delhi was still pursuing the dead horse of Himalayan buffer states by boosting dwindling edifice of the dynastic rulers at the cost of the democratic political formations. Consequently, Sikkim State Congress was left in the lurch and New Delhi mandarins permitted the crown prince to bolster his factotum, the Sikkim National Party, at the cost of its opponents. Thus, a contrived electoral process was evolved in which about one-fourth electorate could dictate its partisan verdict on three-fourths of the voters. While the SNP leadership under cunning Sonam Tshering worked out electoral strategy on the ground by organizing the electorate in its favour, front leaders of the SSC such as Tashi Tshering, D. S. Lepcha, L. D. Kazi and others believed in bravado and tall talk. Furthermore, its secretary of the Sikkim Congress, Kashi Raj Pradhan, managed to get four tickets to himself and his three kinsmen from the Nepali-dominated constituencies in the south and west of Sikkim. What resulted in the victory of candidates of SNP on the Lepcha-Bhotia seats and similar victory of all six Nepali candidates put forth by the SSC in the Nepali-dominated constituencies, thus, validating the Maharaj Kumar's charge that the Sikkim State Congress was essentially a Nepali party.

No one was surprised when Sonam Tshering and Kashi Raj Pradhan were sworn in as the two executive councillors. They realized soon that they had very little to do and both of them got together with their patron, the crown prince, to find ways and means to do away with office of the Dewan, whose handling of the state of affairs left little scope for three political actors to be politically visible. There were charges of corruption, but they continued in their office for full term of five year. After the second general election to the State Council in 1958, there were serious charges against both the executive councillors, which were proved valid after investigation of an election tribunal, rendering both of them to be disqualified from contesting elections for six years. However, the Maharaja was good enough to condone Kashi Raj's disqualification to only six months, making him eligible to contest the bye-election caused by his disqualification. But public disgust to his dealings was so pronounced that the secretary of the Sikkim State Congress, C. D. Rai, was made to contest as an independent candidate against the SSC president Kashiraj Pradhan. The honourable President Pradhan of the SSC not only lost the bye-election to his own one-time secretary, but lost his security deposit also (by 3,013 to 634 votes). The SSC was by then divided into two factions: C. D. Rai with four councillors and the official faction of Nahkul K. Pradhan with two. By then, in the popular perception, the SSC had been further reduced from the alleged charge of being a Nepali party to label as the "Newar party". Within a decade of its inception, this most promising multi-ethnic democratic party of the Himalayan region was turned into a pale reminder of its previous self. In such a situation, a number of disgruntled active members of the SSC left it to join the newly floated political forum in 1960, the Sikkim National Congress. In total, the Sikkim State Congress had a life of about 25 years from December 1947 prior to its merger into the Sikkim Congress in early 1970s, but its ethos was dead and its thunder was stolen by 1958. For the next 15 years it continued to linger and was useful to some vested interests to let it survive, but it was barely the skeleton of the mass-based public spirited political party of the late 1940s.

Limits of the multi-ethnic politics in a small feudal state

What assessment does one have of the leadership of the Sikkim State Congress from among the Nepalis? Unfortunately, those who were in the helms of affairs were known as the weathercocks, behaving as per convenience and wishes of the power to be. I have records from 1948 to 1956 showing that the Sikkim State Congress kept on passing resolutions and sending delegations to Delhi for merger of its outfit with the Indian National Congress, which were ignored. Finally, Kashi Raj Pradhan, apparently a fraternal delegate to the Durgapur session of the Indian National Congress, was advised by the president of the INC and Prime Minister of India Jawaharlal Nehru not to attend the

Congress sessions in future, as it created problems for them with the Durbar. The message was loud and clear: the Sikkim State Congress had lost its relevance in the eyes of New Delhi. All these years in early 1950s, the crown prince had been objecting the alleged links of the SSC with India and Indian political parties as interference in the internal administrative matters of the Sikkim against the spirit of the treaty. In these politically muddy waters, two individuals stood consistently and unwaveringly for their chosen politics till the end without changing sides: Netuk Tshering and Lhendup Dorji Kazi. Netuk Lama (Tshering), was a common muleteer, who had joined Sikkim National Party in 1948 and remained a royalist all through his life. Lhendup Dorji began his career on the side of democracy and had various political incarnations and he died as a democrat after a cheered political career in Sikkim.

It is interesting to note that most of the first generation leaders of political fora in Sikkim had military background: Tashi Tshering, Sonam Tshering, D. S. Lepcha, Nahkul Pradhan and much later, Lal Bahadur Basnet. Some others came from feudal background such as L. D. Kazi, Kashi Raj Pradhan and Gobardhan Pradhan. Such leaders had no time or experience of mixing with the commoners as one among them. These were the people who were used to issuing orders to others to be obeyed; they could collect the crowd but did not know to address commoners for popular cause. They could not organize a mass movement against the feudal oppression and sustain it for a period. They could arouse the emotions and sentiment for or against some issue or individual, but could not work out an agenda for a sustained mass movement with a cause for the benefit of the commoners. The result was that the crown prince could always beat them in their game of politics with his better resources and still superior skill. Without sounding the Indian National Congress, they appeared to have believed that the leadership of the Indian National Congress would be willing to endorse their movement and extend their instant affiliation, which did not come on their way, as there was possibly a change in the priority of the Government of India in the region.

It appears that the credentials of the Sikkim State Congress were suspect in the eyes of the Indian national leadership. An interesting episode of the Sikkim State Congress movement was its charter of demands, multi-ethnic leadership and mass movement against feudal anachronism, patterned on the footings of the Indian National Congress to begin with. However, it is intriguing that even after four decades of Sikkim's merger with the Indian Union, no serious efforts have been made to write democratic history of Sikkim and integrate it with that of the national democratic history and similar movements in other princely states in the country. Furthermore, we have noted above, the presence of the Koirala brothers on the occasion of the annual conferences of Sikkim State Congress prior to 1950 as an article of fraternal support, but such public support had not been visible once the Nepali Congress leadership launched armed revolution in southern Nepal and subsequently joined the government under the Rana prime minister. It appears that the Nepali Congress leadership either got caught in the power politics of their country, or there was a change in their policy and priority. Thus, the phase of politics in the first two decades of Sikkim State Congress with its participation in the State Council degenerated to a stinking cesspool of non-performance and that its dysfunction itself created contradiction leading to its end and its creator, the principality of Sikkim.

Bibliography

Basnet, L. B., 1974, *Sikkim: A Political History*, S. Chand, New Delhi.

Coelho, V. H., 1971, *Sikkim and Bhutan*, Vikas Publishing House, New Delhi.

Datta-Ray, S. K., 1984, *Smash and Grab: Annexation of Sikkim*, Vikas Publishing House, New Delhi.

Dutta Ray, S. K., 2013, *Smash & Grab: Annexation of Sikkim*, Tanquebar, New Delhi.

Documents, 1960, "Inside Sikkim", *Mankind*, February, New Delhi.

Duff, A., 2015, *Sikkim: Requiem for a Himalayan Kingdom*, Random House India, Gurgaon.

Lall, J. S., 1953, *Fortnightly Report, Private Papers of Baleshwar Prasad*, Nehru Memorial Museum and Library, Teen Murti House, New Delhi, Sub File No. 18.

Memorandum of the Sikkim National Congress, submitted to Shri Jawahar Lal Nehru, Prime Minister of India, submitted at New Delhi on August 23, 1960.

Patterson, G. N., 1963, *Peking Versus Delhi*, Faber & Faber, London.

Prasad, B., 1954, *Private Papers, Nehru Memorial Museum and Library*, Nehru Memorial Museum and Library, Teen Murti House, New Delhi, Sub File No. 18.

Rustomji, N. K., 1971, *Enchanted Frontiers: Sikkim, Bhutan and Northeast Frontier of India*, Oxford University Press, Bombay.

Rustomji, N. K., 1987, *Sikkim: A Himalayan Tragedy*, Allied, Bombay.

Sinha, A. C., 2008, *Sikkim: Feudal and Democratic*, Indus, New Delhi.

Subba, P., 2012, *Sikkimma Dosro Kranti 1973* (in Nepali: The Second Revolution in Sikkim, 1973), privately published by the author, DPH Road, Gangtok.

Tshering, T., 1960, "A Few Facts About Sikkim", *Mankind*, February, 1960.

6

NEPALI CONGRESS, MUKTI-BAHINI AND DEMOCRATIC EXPERIMENT IN NEPAL

> There had been no agricultural revolution in Nepal. The restoration of monarchy (in 1950) was neither a result nor the cause of such a revolution. So, there was no large scale capitalist farming, no prosperous peasantry, no landless labour and certainly no proletariat or working class. There was not even a floating population of unemployed in the towns or countryside as all "vagabonds" and deserter "villains" trekking to India to become sentries in Indian business houses or soldiers in the army. There had been no industrial or even a mercantile revolution in the country. We know that in the absence of waterways, roads, rails, or communications, overland routes are hazardous, freights high and risks of trade numerous. Consequently, internal markets are small and primitive and foreign trade restricted to luxury goods. There are few statistics of any kind available in Nepal till today. So an appraisal of her economy or class structure cannot be made with scientific accuracy, but only rich class in Nepal with some accumulated wealth has been the feudal nobility, which invested its capital in cash and stocks mainly in adjoining India. This section of nobility in course of time grew strong enough to demand some elbow room to become more respectable and grow richer. It resented the curbs imposed by arbitrary Ranas and monopolies exercised by the ruling clique and its courtiers . . . In addition, there was no civil service and no national consciousness as distinct from tribal loyalties. Whatever national cohesiveness the country possessed was symbolized in the person of the King.
>
> (Goel, 1966: 48–9)

This was the most appropriate overall picture of the Nepalese landscape in 1950.

The Nepalese administration or the Rana regime was so repressive that even mild reformist moves and welfare-oriented programmes could invite harsh punishment. And thus many a disgruntled individuals, even from the aristocratic background, who wanted to do anything a new, were forced to live a life of exile in India. Some of the students, who came to study in India in the 1920s and 1930s, did get attracted to ongoing anti-imperialist struggle in India and they found it thrilling to join that. Similarly, many of the ex-Gurkha soldiers, who had seen combat in different parts of the world during the two world wars, were just not happy with their pension and at times many of them desired to join their Indian brethren in their struggle against the colonial oppression, so that they could get away with anachronistic treatment at the hands of the regime, once they could get back home after their retirement.

The story of the Rana repressive machine has a long history. After demise of Prithvi Narayan Shah in 1775, his squabbling successors squandered the opportunity to establish a stable regime within next seven decades. There was so much bloodshed, factional fighting and intrigue within the royal household that one of the lesser known but dangerously ambitious characters, Rana Jung Bahadur, seized upon the opportunity in 1846 to take over the regime.

> He was responsible for the infamous Kat (kot) massacre in which 500 of the nobles were murdered at the queen's instigation. He was the son of Kaji (zi: a courtier), a Nepalese official, and, entering the military service while still young, he rose rapidly to the rank of Colonel, when, as personal attendant for the young prince, he became queen's lover. The (British) Resident at that time, Major (later Sir Henry) Lawrence, mentions him as an intelligent young man, particularly expert in all military matters but, though young in years, profoundly versed in intrigues. Following on the Kat massacre Jung Bahadur emerged as the most powerful man in Nepal, with the support of the army and his six brothers. The Rani, who had hoped to use Jung Bahadur for her own purposes, had to flee to Benares. The king tried to regain power and even led an attack against Jung Bahadur in 1847, but none of the plots against Jung Bahadur were successful, the agents were put to death and the king declared unfit to rule, and on 12th May, 1847, he was deposed and the heir-apparent put on the throne. Jung Bahadur had got rid of every opponent, had married members of his family into every influential

> family in the kingdom. In 1849 he had offered six regiments of Nepalese troops to the British for service against the Sikhs, and while this offer had been refused, it had brought Nepal into a more favourable light with the British authorities. He even sent one of his grandsons to Darjeeling to be educated by an Englishman, (former the British Resident in Kathmandu) Brian Hodgson.
>
> (Patterson, 1963: 133)

Ranacracy or Ranarchy: the traditional political system of Nepal

Rana Jung Bahadur had risen to prominence from very modest background. He and his family later created for themselves a new class, which was completely cut off and isolated from the Nepalese society at large. Like the founder of the modern Nepal, Prithvi Narayan Shah, who prided himself to be the king of the Magar (Magar Ko Raja Mai Hu) and his land was pure land of the Hindus (*yo asil Hindustan ho*), Jung Bahadur paid homage at the Hindu shrines in India on way to Europe. This was further advanced by his descendant like Chandra Shamsher who accepted Saka and Vikram samvat, borrowed from ancient India, as the official calendar in 1911 (Gurung, 1997). To begin with, Jung Bahadur introduced the first civil code (Maluki Ain) in 1854 based on classical Hindu Dharamshastrik law, which provided rationale for one of the most repressive and retrograde regimes in the world. Another innovation of his was introduction of the law, making his office of the prime minister hereditary in the family without abolishing the institution of monarchy. It was so designed that the eldest of the surviving brother would succeed to the office of the prime minister with a view to ensure that no minor would ever come to the office of the prime minister. Furthermore, he got the kings married to the daughters in his family, an act by which he ensured that the kings would remain within the full control of the prime minister. The system of Rana administration was primarily oligarchy that circumvolved within family.

> In one century that Ranacracy that existed in Nepal, the history has been of plots, assassinations and fights for power within the family. Probably to appease his brothers with whose help he had assumed power or to share the spoils, Jung Bahadur laid down a system of succession peculiar to the land . . . Instead of the system of primogeniture "the role" would go from the elder brother to the younger one. When one generation terminated,

> the eldest of the succeeding generation would assume the title of His Highness the Maharaja, the Prime Minister, the Supreme Commander-in-Chief or Marshall.
>
> (Koirala, 2008: 19)

Moreover, the Ranas would not marry into a commoner's family. Their mode of behaviour, language and overall style of conduct bore audacious insolence. They would always speak in the royal plural, which they knew that they were not entitled to. They married their daughters to the royal princes or else to the scions of the princely states in India and their sons to the daughters of the royal household. Thus, they were completely cut off from the common Nepalese and had in fact alienated themselves from the Nepalese commoners. They took most care that there should be no spread of education. They believed that education not only leads to spread of new ideas and novel visions but also creates a middle class of new occupations such as doctors, engineers, professors and teachers and the like who could challenge their obscurantism. The prime ministers looted the wealth of the country shamelessly in every form, may it be land or jewels or cash. The first commoner prime minister, M. P. Koirala, informs that Prime Minister Padma Shamsher, who had abdicated after a short rule of 18 months, had confided in him that he had taken to India over Rs. 6 million in cash alone when he remitted the office (Koirala, 2008: 21).

However, all the precautions could not ensure Jung Bahadur that his own descendants would necessarily become prime ministers after him. Jang Bahadur's sons were earlier involved in conspiracy against their uncles for the purpose of bringing prime ministership in the family and consequently, their names were struck off from the successors' list for ever. One of the junior brothers of Rana Jung Bahadur, Dheer Shamsher, held military posts after Jung Bahadur's demise in 1877, while the eldest surviving brother, the issueless Ranodip, was the prime minister. It is claimed that Dheer was ambitious, scheming and had a brood of 17 sons to back him up. He could not acquire power of prime minister during his lifetime, but wished to his sons that the desire he could not accomplish in his life should be completed by them. The power must come to his family. And for that his sons enacted another Kot massacre on the night of November 22, 1885, by killing ruling prime minister, (uncle) Ranodip and their cousins, who were in the capital. Henceforth the Ranas were divided into two classes: outer, 7 brothers' families and 17 brothers' inner families, who availed all the powers of the state. There was a third occasion in 1934 soon after the devastating earthquake when nearly another Kot massacre was enacted. Rana

Rudra Shamsher had risen to the post of commander in chief and was naturally in line for the prime ministership. After him were his brothers and General Hiranya Shamsher, the son of Prime Minister Bhim Shamsher. Thus, the turns of the sons of Chandra and Juddha appeared much lower in the 'roll' list of incumbencies. They were getting old and were less likely to succeed to the highest post. This led to a conspiracy among the sons of Chandra and Juddha, as it was question of now or never. The earthquake provided a god-sent opportunity to them: on the pretext of inspecting the devastation thus caused, most of the important generals were dispatched to distant destinations and rest were intimidated at the point of bayonets and desired succession was secured. And thus from 1846 to 1951, there were 10 Rana prime ministers who ruled over Nepal in three generations with their terms ranging from four months to 31 years; an average rule of the Rana prime minister was 10 years and about four months.

Jung Bahadur's agnates had disqualified and disinherited his descendants from the high office, as promiscuity practised by the leading families in Nepal, and proliferation of children inside and outside wedlock, necessitated a modification of the agnate system introduced by Jung Bahadur. It was Prime Minister Chandra Shamsher Rana who came out with innovative idea to disinherit many of the alleged undesirable Ranas from the list of significance, which ultimately led to demise of the system in 1951, in the following:

> Those born in wedlock were known as Class A Ranas, and only they alone were entitled to succeed to the highest offices; children born of mothers whose marriage with Rana husbands were legitimatized after birth were known as Class B Ranas; those born out of wedlock were known as Class C Ranas, and were not entitled to succeed to the highest offices. Naturally the Class C Ranas became very numerous, and as they were usually wealthy, too, because of their anomalous circumstances, they were usually in a position to do a great damage by supporting intrigues. In addition, the Class A Ranas were divided into several factions, and these sought the support of Class B and Class C Ranas to whatever their ambitions might be.
>
> (Patterson, 1963: 135–6)

It is needless to add that the Class C Ranas such as General Hiranya Shamsher and his sons, General Subarna Shamsher and General Mahabir Shamsher, played a pivotal role in the anti-Rana struggle led by the Nepali Congress in 1950.

In the words of a British journalist, George Patterson, Nepal in 1950 was a protuberant rather than a compact form, had no geographical individuality, comprising 56,000 square miles, was about 520 miles long and 90–100 miles broad, with a diverse population of 8,473,478.

> It was primarily a country of small villages with a total of 28,780 cities, towns and villages scattered throughout the country. Of these 85 percent had fewer than 500 inhabitants and only ten cities had 5,000 or more residents within their municipal limit. Of these ten cities, five were located in the Kathmandu Valley; four were in the eastern Terai and one in far western Terai.
>
> (Patterson, 1963: 139)

Traditional law of the land

At the top of it, with a view to give law to lawless Nepal, Rana Jung Bahadur called a meeting of the Council of the knowledgeable persons of the Gorkharajya to frame the laws based on the *Dharamshatra* (the Hindu scriptures) and *lokdharma* ('customary laws' of the land) for the state. It came to be known as the Maluki Ain (literally, "law of the land" civil code of the country), which was signed by 219 "notables" of land belonging to the Court Council (*bharadari kausal*) 31, Thakuris 4, Brahmins 31, Chhetris 100, Newars 8, Gurungs 3, Magars 4, and 4–5 other ethnic groups. It was promulgated on January 5, 1854, and since then it had laid elaborate hierarchical social structure for the country, which was to be governed as per the provisions of the Ain (Hofer, 2004). With little modification, it continued to be in practice for the next 110 years, when it was replaced by new Maluki Ain by King Mahendra in 1963; since then Ain has been drastically changed first in 1990 and then in 2015. However, it is instructive to understand the basic social provisions of the original Ain, which was created with a view to providing the exploitative nature of the civil code.

All the social units in the high hills, midlands and the foothills, and the traditional indigenous communities and migrants were placed in the following hierarchical order of five-fold division, in which caste/ethnic groups were ranked as per *Dharamshastrik* provision of purity and pollution: (1) *tagadhari* (wearers of the holy cord); (2) *namasinya matwali* (caste groups of the 'Non-enslavable Alcohol-Drinkers'); (3) *masinya matwali* (caste groups of 'Enslavable Alcohol-Drinkers'); (4). *pani chalanya choi chito halnunapranya* (impure but 'touchable' castes); and (5) *pani nacalnya choi chito halnuparnya* (untouchable castes: Hofer, 2004: 9). The Rajguru, the royal preceptor, was ranked above the Maharaja Dhiraj, the king, and the Maharaja the prime minister; rest of the Brahmins, Chhetris (Kshatriya), Vaishyas and other castes and ethnic groups were placed in a ritually ranked order. Though Maharajadhiraj ranked the highest in principle, his royal red seal (*Lal mohar*) with authority to use on the royal behalf was usurped by the Jung Bahadur and since then it remained in the hands of the subsequent prime ministers till 1951. Similarly, on the charge of the heinous crimes, even the Brahmins, who were not to be hanged, might be awarded capital punishment with the royal seal of the Maharaja. Rest of the castes and communities were slave for the Ranas and there was rampant slavery and serfdom in the country. Rana infants were born "generals" and they used to get promoted with age, not with any type of professional training and corporal exercises. Similarly, chunks of territories in the kingdom were appropriated as the private property by the Rana prime ministers and commanders in chief during their rules. It was not only a poor country, but it was also an illiterate country, as any type of educational instruction was not encouraged and those who tried to defy the edict, were harshly punished, so much so that one Kishan Lal had written a book on maize cultivation, in which he had pleaded for indigenous seeds instead of imported one, as it was common modest maize on which ordinary people lived on. And for that, he was imprisoned. His relatives pleaded to the Rana prime minister to release him on the ground of sickness, prompt came, the response from the latter: "I did not send Kishan Lal to prison in order to survive".

Early socio-political stirrings

The privileged Brahmins were permitted to travel to Hindu shrines in India, especially Banaras, for acquiring scriptural learning and instructions from the traditional orthodox (*Sanatani*) establishments. By the second half of the 19th century two developments were taking place simultaneously. First, the Rana establishment was slowly getting closer to the British colonial rulers. And second, a group of literate Brahmins were busy developing and enriching Nepali vernacular language and they started composing texts in Nepali language. In this way, apart from the classical Sanskrit scriptures, the sacred and mythological writings in vernacular Nepali began to be recited on ritual and festive occasions. For illustration, Bhanu Bhakta's Nepali Ramayan, published for the first time in Banaras in 1880s, became a household sacred scripture for most of the literate Hindu households within no time. Though the Ranas kept a strict watch on such developments, the urge to write on the sacred and classical themes soon turned towards composing secular literature, especially in close by Darjeeling district in Bengal, in adjoining British India. Within no time, essays and poems on social, cultural and political aspects began to be produced. Incidentally, it was a development, different from Brahaminical endeavours of Banaras in the sense that the lead in the production of the secular literature in Darjeeling was invariably taken by the communities known as the Kirat.

In such an atmosphere, Nepal could not remain untouched from the above scenario. It is a fact that the Ranas in their own ways tried their best to insulate the royal family from all types of social, economic and political interests of the country. However, in spite of their virtual captivity, Shah Sovereigns kept on trying to reach to the elements hostile to the Ranas to reclaim their patrimony from the usurpers. In February 1882, an anti-Rana conspiracy was discovered and as much as 31 higher caste individuals were severely punished for that and their families lost their properties and they were ex-communicated from the caste fraternity. Though the Rana commander in chief, Dheer Shamsher, dared not physically harm the Prince Narendra Bikram Shah, he got him imprisoned by their British benefactors for the life in Chunar Fort in India. That was also the time India was under the spell of an Indian social reformer, Swami Dayanand Saraswati, who had pioneered a socio-religious movement known as Arya Samaj, which had been challenging the orthodox style of religiosity among the Hindus. Pandit Madhavrao Joshi got inspired by the Arya Samaj movement and began preaching social reforms in Kathmandu Valley in the first decade of 20th century. The preacher and his associates were awarded with imprisonment for long years and when they were released, they were banished from the country for good.

Another element comes in the picture in the form of the disinherited Ranas living a life of exile in India during 1920s, when Mahatma Gandhi's Swadeshi movement was on. Thakur Chandan Singh, a relative of an exiled Rana from Dehradun and an ex-Gurkha soldier of the British Indian army, was instrumental in organizing the All India Gorkha League as a forum mainly for the ex-soldiers, but other Nepalese working in British India also flocked to it. Ranas were happy for that, as the Gorkha League invariably worked in concert with the Anglo-Indians, British industrialists such as the tea planters and the British administration. The forum raised demands for better living conditions for the Nepalese living in India and demanded creation of a Gorkha homeland in Darjeeling district for the Gorkhas in India. Ranas would use the forum for their purpose in the 1940s and King Mahendra did the same by recruiting some of its active members in the

1960s in his administrative structure. In this context, it is instructive to note that drawing inspiration from the similar experiences in India, Umesh Bikram Shah, Khadagman Singh Basnet, Captain Khandman Singh, Maina Bahadur, Rangnath Sharma and others organized Prachand Gorkha, a clandestine armed revolutionary forum in 1930. The objective of the forum was an armed revolt by dynamiting the Ranas and seizing the power from them. Once the secret was leaked out, the involved individuals were ruthlessly punished and then expelled from Nepal for life. This was also the time, when a number of Nepalese were in contact with the Indian political leaders such as Rafi Ahmed Kidwai, Mahatma Gandhi, Jaiprakash Narayan, Shibanlal Saxesena, Madan Mohan Malvia and Jawaharlal Nehru; many of these individuals would play active roles in waging anti-Rana agitation in 1950.

There were some conscious persons like Krishna Prasad (Upadhyay) Koirala even in the first quarter of the 20th century, who was forced to leave his home and hearth in Nepal and live in extreme poverty for cause of the wellbeing of his Nepalese brethren (Koirala, 2001, 2008). He was born at the village Dumja in Singhuli district and had managed to learn Sanskrit, Persian and English on his own. He was running business in the Terai; established the town of Biratnagar and ran customs posts on contract from the Rana regime. In the words of his eldest son:

> His was a flourishing business extending from the eastern hill border of Nepal to the western most point of Nepal Tarai. Besides, he owned properties and land extending in several districts of the eastern hills and Tarai . . . My father was the sole distributor of all brands of imported cigarettes in the whole of Nepal before it was taken away from our family . . . We had several horses and ponies in our stables and hundreds of cattle in our cowsheds and our early yield of grains from our land would run to several thousands of mounds. For his beliefs and convictions, he had staked these all.
>
> (Koirala, 2008: 4–5)

How did he lose everything he had? His only crime was his audacity to having arranged to send a parcel of torn and tattered dress of the common Nepali women and men, to the spouse of the Rana Premier Chandra Shamsher in 1919 on the auspicious day of Dasai as conventional salutation. This was the way he thought he would draw attention of the most powerful person in the land towards appalling poverty rampant in the country. And for that his entire property was confiscated and he was forced to live a life of extreme poverty in India for the next 10 years. Moreover, he had two wives, five sons, a number of daughters and many dependents to support. For the next decade this man was buffeted from one place to another and lived a life of utter want and poverty. His status was partly restored by Chandra's successor in 1929, but this proud philanthropist preferred to die in Rana jails than making any compromise on his principles. His stand was vindicated by the events in Nepal, when three of his sons would be elected to the post of prime minister in days to come. Political exiles such as Krihna Prasad Koirala were invariably supported by the Indian and Nepali benefactors, who were themselves not necessarily affluent. These politically conscious persons had formed various small political parties in the Indian cities and used to work against the Rana regime in a clandestine manner as much as their resources could permit.

When Krishna Prasad Koirala was being temporarily rehabilitated, Prachand Gorkha movement was active and Ranas were busy in ruthlessly suppressing the suspects. Reasons were very simple: its impact, whatever it was, was limited to the Kathmandu Valley, which could be easily controlled. However, some of these elements got inspired to organize a more sophisticated forum in the form of the Nepal Praja Parishad in 1936 with clandestine support from the then almost captive King Tribhuwan Bir Bikram Shah. The activists of the Parishad used to draft anti-Rana leaflets and stealthily reach them at the doors of Ranas in the night. They took help of Pandits Shukhrarj Shashtri and Murlidhar, who were adept in mass recitation of sacred texts with motives to rise against tyranny. Such well-versed theological exponents were marshalled in spreading the message of waging war against the treacherous Rana regime. Pandit Sukhraj Shastri and his associates had met Mahatma Gandhi in India and sought his support against the Rana regime. Gandhi inspired his visitors to wage non-violent agitation in Nepal. However, the moment Shastri and company returned to Kathmandu Valley, they were imprisoned.

Arrest of the respected Shastri led to huge resentment among the tradition-bound Nepalese, which further made the Ranas worried. At last, the regime announced heavy prize of Rs. 5,000 to anybody providing information against the alleged conspirators, who had formed the Parishad. And it worked; it was Shastri's younger brother, Ramji Joshi, who provided list of the members of the Parishad to the administration out of greed of the prize money. That led to imprisonment of around 500 suspects in 1940 and many of them were awarded with capital punishment, which was carried out with extreme ruthlessness to create maximum terror among the commoners. Among the associates of the Shastri who suffered most were Dhasrath Chandra, Dharambhakta and Gangalal. But the members of the Parishad did not lose heart and chose captive Tanka Prasad Acharya as the president in absentia. The Ranas tried to implicate the king in conspiracy against them, as he had advised the government to hold the trial in public instead of spontaneous trial of the suspects. Ranas were so taken aback by the king's advice that they decided to implicate him in the alleged plot against them. However, it caused so much resentment among the people that they had to devise another scheme to remove him from their way. The scheme was to replace the king with that of the Crown Prince Mahendra and banish the king along with rest of the family to their ancestral place, Gorkha, in custody. But even this plan could not materialize for fear of popular resentment. That event among others made the king determined to find ways to end of the Rana regime for good.

Public moves to organize political parties

By and large, Nepal, with its width of more than 500 miles, has been a south-oriented country. Its former functionaries, the nobility and commoners all alike, found it convenient to settle down in the Indian cities close to its borders such as Dehradun, Lucknow, Banaras, Patna, Ranchi, Calcutta and Darjeeling, from where they could remain in touch with their country as and when required. Moreover, the border between the two was open to the subjects of the both the countries to travel freely for pilgrimage, trade and social intercourse such as marital alliance. We have already mentioned Rana prompted All India Gorkha League of Thakur Chandan Singh above. Formerly disinherited Class C Ranas, who were invariably posted on the district administrative headquarters in the southern Terai locations, did not have much love to the then ruling closed club of the Ranas. For example, one of the great grandsons of Rana Jung Bahadur, Rana Shiv Jung Bahadur, was with the Nepali Congress revolutionaries in the anti-Rana movement in 1950 (Koirala, 2008: 86, 159). Many of them were educated in India and they had close friends among the Indians and, in fact, most of them were closely watching ongoing Indian freedom struggle against the all-powerful British colonial power. In fact, some of them did not hesitate to make a common cause with their Indian brethren by taking part in the agitations, getting lathi charged, courting arrest, and going to jails for the cause of Indian independence.

Broadly speaking, there were two strands of Nepalese political activists in 1940s working with the Indian National Congress:

the Patna-Banaras-based Koirala brothers and their associates and Lucknow-Calcutta based group of Rana Mahabir and Subarna Shamshers and their associates. There were individuals in both the groups who had courted arrest during the 1942 'Quit India' movement of the Indian National Congress. Likewise they also had very close friends among the Indian freedom fighters, who came to positions of power in the late 1940s. There was a third strand represented by Biratnagar based Manamohan Adhikari and his friends, which was oriented towards Darjeeling and Calcutta based Communist Party of India (CPI), but because of its collaboration with the British during the Second World War, it was suspect in the eyes of the ex-Gurkhas at large, who were involved with the anti-Rana movement. There were discordant elements such as Tanka Prasad Acharya, Dili Raman Regmi, Kedarman Vyathit and Prem Bahadur Kanskar, who had limited social base, but acted as if the entire edifice of the anti-Rana movement would collapse in their absence. Thus, they invariably bargained on all occasions for something or other without getting involved in struggles with the masses. They were careerists to the core and many of them came close to King Mahendra's extra-democratic Panchayati Raj move.

A large number of politically conscious Nepalese got naturally involved in the activities of the Indian National Congress. For illustration, Bishweshwar Prasad Koirala, Dilli Raman Regmi, Udayraj Lal, Hari Prasad Pradhan, Kashi Prasad Shrivastava, Surya Prasad Upadhyaya and many others were arrested at Patna, Banaras, Darjeeling and Calcutta. Prior to that, Bishweshwar Prasad Koirala was one of the founder members of the Indian Socialist Party in 1934. Moreover, he was in the Hazaibaug Central Jail along with other prominent Indian Congress leaders like Dr Rajendra Prasad, Dr S. K. Sinha, Anugraha Narayan Sinha, Jagjivan Ram, Jaiprakash Narayan, Rambriksha Benipuri and others. Moreover, his elder brother, Matrika Prasad Koirala, was the secretary of the Bihar Provincial Congress Committee (BPCC) in the 1940s. Surya Prasad Upadhyaya, Kashi Prasad Shrivastava, D. R. Regmi, Dr K. I. Singh, Mahendra Birbikram Shah and General Subarna Shamsher were closer to the Lucknow-based Indian National Congress, especially Rafi Ahmed Kidwai. Some politically conscious persons organized in a clandestine way Nepal Praja Panchayat in Kathmandu in 1947. Prior to that, D. R. Regmi and B. P. Koirala changed old Nepali Sangh into Nepali National Congress, got it inaugurated on January 25, 1946, in Calcutta (Shrivastava, 1955: 133) and as a token to honour to captive Tanka Prasad Acharya, languishing in Kathmandu jail, elected him president of the Congress in absentia, while B. P. remained the working president. Congratulatory messages were received from the Congress president, Acharya J. B. Kirpalani, and others on the occasion. Within a few months, the labourers in a jute mills (Biratnagar) went on strike on March 4, 1947, for which B. P., Tarini and Girija Koirala, and Manmohan Adhikari were arrested and taken to Kathmandu. Soon after that, the non-cooperation movement spread in Kathmandu, Illam, Dhankuta, Lumbini, Parasi, Jaynagar and other locations. Simultaneously, Dr K. I. Singh, Krishnadas Bhakta, Udayraj Lal, Dasrath Prasad, Koulpati Devi, Ram Baran Verma and other organized bands of agitators at Parasi, Butwal, Bhagwanpur, Jhandenagar and other places in the western Terai.

B. P. Koirala was kept in jail in a miserable condition without basic facilities, which led to deterioration in his health. His two younger brothers, Tarini and Girija, were kept in jails separate from him. Having learnt miserable conditions of her son, B. P.'s mother arrived in Kathmandu to attend on him, which was refused. He was released after resorting to long hunger strike, when the Indian prime minister intervened with the Nepalese authorities on humanitarian ground. He went to Bombay for treatment of throat cancer, an ailment, from which he suffered till last. By the time he came back to Banaras from Bombay, he learnt that the Nepali National Congress was inactive. Ganeshman Singh, Krishna Prasad Bhattarai and Gopal Prasad Bhattarai egged up B. P. to take up the leadership of the party from inactive president. On the other hand, Kathmandu Group, with P. B. Kanskar, Pushpalal Amatya, S. P. Upadhyaya, K. P. Shrivastava was resolute in favour of D. R. Regmi. Regmi refused to see that he was holding on the post of president in absence of its working president, B. P. Koirala, who was available at the moment. Finding the judicial side in B. P.'s favour and in consideration that Mr Regmi was more an academic than a man of action, M. P. Koirala joined B. P.'s group. And this was the background in which Jaynagar Working Committee of the NNC was held. However, what resulted in after that was:

> This split in the (Nepali) National Congress later gave birth to a new party. This new party was named Nepali Democratic Congress (NDC). Mr Regmi's erstwhile ardent followers such as Prem Bahadur Kanskar deserted him to join the new party and Pushpa Lal and few others chose to join the Communist Party (of Nepal). With its headquarters in Calcutta and later in Patna, the Nepali Democratic Congress came into existence in the middle of July 1948 (with Mahendra Birbikram Shah as the president and Surya Prasad Upadhyaya as the General Secretary).
>
> (Koirala, 2008: 99)

They appealed to D. R. Regmi and B. P. Koirala to co-operate with them. And the NDC resolved to follow Gandhian non-violent ways with a view to bringing democracy in Nepal. They had goodwill of the Indian national leaders and possibly they were able to establish a channel of communication with that of the Maharajadhiraj Tribhuwan in Kathmandu for a future potential anti-Rana move.

Birth of the Nepali Congress

Two parties (NNC and NDC) had unique problems. While Nepali Democratic Congress (NDC) had no dearth of money, as the party was backed by two resourceful Rana brothers, Mahabir Shamshere and Subarna Shamshere, but it lacked field operators and it was suspect in the eyes of the commoners as Ranas' outfit. On the other hand, devoid of sizeable financial support, the Nepali National Congress (NNC) had more field workers and network of party cadres in various locations. In such a situation it was logical for both to join hands for the larger cause of democracy. The president of the NDC, Mahendra Bikram Shah met the president of the NNC, M. P. Koirala, at Jogbani in Bihar and they discussed possibilities of getting together. Conveniently, the office of the NNC was located at Banaras, but B. P. Koirala had his residence at Patna. In this way, it was convenient for S. P. Upadhyaya, the general secretary of NDC to take up the issue with B. P. Koirala at Patna. When behind the scene negotiations culminated in a broad agreement, it was decided to give a formal shape to the confabulations between the two political bodies.

It was decided to include as many political elements as possible in the new formation and an appeal was made with that effect inviting all political fora to a conference to be held in Calcutta. Only response from inside Nepal came from Gopal Prasad Rimal, Chairman, and Action Committee of Praja Panchayat, who decided to dissolve his forum and merge it with forthcoming organization. One may have a glance at B. P. Koirala's version of the merger proposal:

> Then Surya Prasad Upadhyaya came to me on behalf of Subarna Shamshere, proposing that we merge our parties. We called ourselves the Nepali National Congress at that time, and they were Nepali Democratic Congress. They wanted to join forces . . . Our work at that time was concentration on distributing pamphlets inside Nepal, developing contacts, and establishing local committees wherever possible. Dr. K. I. Singh joined us from his base in Nautanwa in United Provinces,

> where he had homeopathic medical practice. Slowly our party character began to reflect more and more of Nepal, whereas earlier we had a stronger base in Darjeeling and Calcutta. With arrival of the *Jayatu Sanskritan* (Victory to Sanskrit) activists such as Kashinath Gautam, Sribhadra, Rajeshwar Devkota and others, we finally began to make inroad into Nepal. In the Tarai, we had people like Rameshwar Prasad Singh, Pathak, and others. Kashi Prasad Shrivastava was also with us. Then the matter of merger came up, and I said it was a good idea, but it would have to be discussed with Matrika Babu, our president. Surya Babu asked me to come along, so he and I went to Jogbani. There we decided that two working committees would meet separately and come up with a plan for assimilation. Three main points to be decided were: What would be the flag? Who would be the president? And finally, what would we name the amalgamated party? My own concerns were centred on who would appoint the officers within the party, such as the Secretary.
>
> (Koirala, 2001: 96–7)

The leaders of the National Congress and the Democratic Congress assembled in Patna and negotiations for the merger of the two parties, name of new forum, the flag, location of the office, the mouthpiece newspaper, and most importantly, the office bearers, especially the post of president were taken in earnest. The main hurdle among the delegates was the post of the president of new party. While B. P.'s camp with spokesmen like Ganesh Man Singh, Rudra Giri and Bhattarai brothers advocated his candidature, NDC president, Mahendra Bikram Shah, and general secretary, Surya Prasad Upadhyaya kept on arguing against that. Finally, the D C group mounted an open threat to M. P. Koirala: "If you do not accept the job (of the president), the negotiations would be broken down; the unity between the two parties would not be possible" (Koirala, 2008: 107–8). Thus, even B. P. Koirala came round to accept the fact that M. P. Koirala would be the most acceptable candidate for the president of the new party. M. P. Koirala goes on further to inform us:

> Finally, it was decided that I should be the president of the newly merged parties, while the flag *of the NDC* would be adopted for the new emerging party. Also the mouthpiece paper, *Nepal Pukar*, would remain the same as it had with NDC. The Executive would be so nominated that it would

> give adequate representation to both the wings. The main points of negotiations having been agreed to, it was decided to give everything a final and formal shape. The Working Committees of (both) the parties ratified the proposal and a joint statement of appeal by the presidents of the two parties was issued. The two parties announced a date to meet in a national convention in Calcutta.
>
> (Koirala, 2008: 108)

Realizing the compulsion of the situation, the delegates of the Nepali National Congress and the Nepal Democratic Congress met at Tiger Cinema in Calcutta on April 8, 1950, and debated on the terms for the unison of the two political parties. At last, it was agreed that new party would be known as the Nepali Congress with Matrika Prasad Koirala as the president. It was also decided to adopt the flag and mouthpiece, *Nepal Pukar*, of the Nepal Democratic Congress for the new party and its headquarters would be located at Banaras. Dr K. I. Singh was opposed to the merger of the two parties and some of the active members were so much distrustful of the Ranas that even association of the two Rana brothers was resented. Among all the NNC, Balchand Sharma was upset, as he could not be accommodated among the office-bearers of the Nepali Congress. The NC decided to explore the possibilities of even armed insurrection and exploring the possibilities of securing arms for the purpose.

Mukti Vahini (guerrilla fighters) in operation

Keeping that in mind, a Conference of Nepali Congress was held on September 26, 1950 at Bairgania in Bihar adjoining the border with Nepal. After a long discussion, certain very vital decisions were taken. A Mukti Vahini was to be raised to liberate Nepal from the Ranas and for that, a Supreme Command Council with M. P. Koirala as its Supreme Commander and two regional Commanders, B. P. Koirala and General Subarna Shamshere, for Eastern and Western Fronts respectively were designated. Some arms from Shaikh Muhammad Abdulla of Kashmir and anti-Nizam activists in Hyderabad were collected. But they were not found adequate to wage a war with the well-armed Rana forces. It was decided to procure arms from Burma, which was under the control of a friendly Socialist Party. The Burmese leadership agreed to provide the requisite arms, but the issues emerged who would be qualified enough to choose them and how would they be transported to the party headquarters before they would be dispatched to the field of action. General Subarna Shamshere's nephew, Thilbam Malla, who was trained in Indian Military College, Dehradun and Bhola Chatterjee, a socialist academic from Calcutta with knowledge of the arms, travelled clandestinely to Rangoon for the purpose. The arms were shipped by the Himalayan Airways aircraft of General Mahabir Shamsher to Bihata airfield near Patna. And they were collected by B. P. Koirala, transported secretly across North Bihar and distributed to the fronts where guerrillas were in action. On the human front, common farmers, ex-Gurkhas soldiers and ex-Indian National Army (INA) of Subhash Chandra Bose such as Puran Singh and G. B. Subba or Yakthumba, made a common cause with the Mukti Vahini. Nepali Congress leadership air dropped leaflets containing its publicity materials appealing to the Nepalese to rise in revolt against the Rana autocracy and made appeal to them to join the Mukti Vahini against the Rana's exploitation. They also improvised a clandestine radio station to broadcast news relating to their actions from the battle front under the charge of Phanishwar Nath Renu, a volunteer from adjoining Purnia district in Bihar, who would be a famous Hindi literature in days to come.

Earlier it was decided that armed revolt against the Ranas would be launched in November 1950, but the intelligence trickled down that the Maharajadhiraj was getting restive to come out in open against the Ranas. With a view not to be seen as a reactive force to that eventuality, the Nepali Congress decided to advance their armed revolt to October by taking over treasury, arms store and jail and mounting an attack on the governor's residence at Biratnagar, Morang in the eastern Terai. However, the Governor Rana Uttam Bikram had fortified his residence and kept on firing relentlessly on the rebels. The guerrillas retreated thereafter, regrouped as a strategy to assess their gains and improvised an unused tractor into a battle tank with a view to breaking open the walls of the governor's residence. Meanwhile the guerrillas had mounted surveillance on the advancing Rana forces sent from Kathmandu to relieve the pressure on the Morang governor and attacked them so ferociously at the most unexpected location that they ran away after throwing away their armaments. Thus, Biratnagar was captured and the governor was made a captive by the Mukti Vahini; similarly Jhapa, Rengeli, Dharan, Illam, Dhankuta, Saptari, Mahottari and Rajviraj from eastern Nepal were captured by the Mukti Vahini. In a recent study, Binayak K. Thapa has shown how two ex-soldiers, Naradmuni Thulung and Ram Prasad Rai of Bhojpur, organized Mukti Vahini at their own and after capturing Bhojpur proceed to east and west from there unopposed (Thapa, 2017: 40).

Within no time, "Nepali Congress voluntary forces struck at nine different fronts. Parasi, Kanchanpur, Bhairahwa in the west and Udaypur, Pashupatinagar, Mahottari and Jhapa in the east were places where mukti vahini volunteers had struck before the end of November 1950" (Koirala, 2008: 147). M. P. Koirala informs the his readers the invaluable encouragement, sympathy and tacit support he got from the chief ministers of Bihar, West Bengal and Uttar Pradesh in their anti-Rana liberation struggle.

Earlier in November Thirbam Malla led the Mukti Vahini at Birgunj and captured the town and the fort along with arms and treasury with cash amounting to Rs. 5 million and some jewellery. The victorious forces proceeded to Amlekhgunj, the rail terminus in north on way to Kathmandu, but met with stiff resistance. However, Thirbam Malla, the hero of the victory operation, was martyred in Duncan Hospital at Raxaull. Two commanders, B. P. and Subarna, took the treasury in their control, brought it to their headquarters at Patna and carried it to Delhi for handing over to the king. There was a rumour that it was done at the behest of the Indian ambassador, Sir C.P.N. Sinha. Handling of the cash captured from treasury at Birgunj would lead to a number of unpleasant controversies among the activists and even with the Government of India (Shrivastava, 1955; Koirala, 2001: 113–14, 2008: 140–3). Meanwhile, Mahendra Bikram Shah mounted an attack on Nepalgunj in the western sector and Dr K. I. Singh had taken over Bhairwa in spite of his limited arms. In this way, the Mukti Vahini was surging ahead on various locations capturing various landmarks in a furious way.

It may be remembered that the Nepali Congress had decided in its Calcutta session to launch the armed revolution with a view to overthrowing the Rana regime and introducing a democratic dispensation. And for that, the Nepali Congress had decided to seek support of the Indian Socialist Party and, in fact, the veteran socialist leader, Jaiprakash Narayan was something like the patron of the party and whenever, they ran in problems, they would turn to seek his counsel. Required arms were secured through the good office of the Indian socialist leaders from Kashmir and Burma. The call for an armed revolution was given first in the south-eastern part of the country at Biratnagar as a strategy, which had already seen industrial workers' strike at the local jute mills in the past. Soon the revolution spread in the middle of the Terai to Birgunj, then to the west to Nepalgunj. Many of the leaders of the Nepali Congress like Matrika Prasad Koirala, Bishweshwar Prasad Koirala, S. P. Upadhyaya, Kashi Prasad Shrivastava and others happened to be the members of the Indian National

Congress at one time and had taken parts in its non-cooperation movement against the British. When the armed revolution was launched in Nepal, large many Indian political activists took part in it and some of them such as Tarapada Babu, Kuldeep Jha, Balbhadhra and others met with their end in the action in Nepal (Renu, 1977).

On the other hand, the leadership of the Nepali Congress was not cohesive enough for launching a revolutionary struggle. There were factions: B. P. and M. P. groups; socialist armed revolutionaries and Gandhian pacifists; there were feudal elements like Mahabir and Subarna and diehard anarchists like Dr K. I. Singh; there were idealists armchair dreamers like D. R. Regmi and difficult egocentrics like Tanka Prasad Acharya. Even eastern and western Terai divisions were at times created problems. Two factions from NDC and NNC were still not well integrated into a cohesive political organization. Even the Koirala brothers were faction ridden: while M. P. was self-conscious, pompous and scheming, B. P. was apparently arrogant, cliquish and impulsive in his behaviour and this apparent personality clash led to continuous bickering between the two affecting the party. For illustration, M. P. had no hesitation to be the commander in chief of the armed guerrillas, but would not like to store arms and ammunitions at his residence as he was non-violent Gandhian. On the other hand, B. P. sought Gandhi's blessings for their anti-Rana struggle a few days before Gandhi's death, but he informs his readers collecting half a dozen explosive bombs from Ram Manahar Lohia in Calcutta at the neck of the time, when poor Gandhi was shot dead by his assailant in Delhi. Both the brothers had ambivalent attitude to each other. M. P. had cultivated an image of being a moderate in politics and invariably instigated others against "impetuous and hot tempered" B. P. Koirala. M. P. gave the impression that as the party president and elder statesman, it was he who should be the prime minister. The moment opportunity emerged; he rushed to be the first commoner to be the prime minister of Nepal without even sounding the mood in the party.

The Nepali Congress realized that they were fighting a popular war against the Ranas in favour of the Maharajadhiraj with a view to establish a democratic order, but they had no access to the king. And for that purpose, they dispatch a small group of leaders led by Ganesh Man Singh to Kathmandu, who was intercepted and put behind the bars. The Nepali Congress leadership was desperate to establish contacts with His Majesty and to know his mind and acquaint him of their moves for cause of the country. And then, they learnt on November 7 that the king had sought a political asylum in the Indian embassy in Kathmandu, which had been promptly granted. This development created a great diversion for the armed revolutionaries fighting in the field in very adverse circumstances with extremely limited resources. Since then, the attention of the world had shifted from the progress of the armed guerrilla operations to an absurd drama unfolding in Kathmandu in which, the usurper Ranas would depose the rightful ruler from his inheritance and enthrone his infant grandson as the king.

The king makes a historic restorative move

Meanwhile something significant was happening in Kathmandu in the royal palace. Having realized the gravity of the situation, the king decided to play a gamble. The king had somehow maintained a liaison between the Indian embassy and himself. The contacts were doctors Devendra Dasgupta and Hazra, and B. L. Sharma, a confectioner who would supply sweets to the Royal House. They would transmit messages, as the occasion demanded. It was through these agencies that the king had got assurance from the Indian side that he could take political asylum in the Indian embassy, in case an emergency demanded it. When the situation became hot enough, the king decided to make a final bid for freedom and as previously arranged the king, in ruse of hunting expedition, gave a slip to Ranacracy and took the shelter in the Indian embassy on November 7, 1950.

> A string of cars streamed out of the Royal Palace towards north, carrying three generations of the royal family. The four year old second son of the Crown Prince, Prince Gyanendra, was the only member of the family who was not included in the entourage . . . With the entry of the King and his family into the Indian Embassy and his reception by the Ambassador, history was corrected. One hundred and four years and fifty-two days earlier, when the Kot massacre was being perpetrated by Jung Bahadur, King Rajendra in that night of terror, had sought asylum in the British Residency; but the doors were not opened and a century of Rana thraldom on the people as well as the King was imposed. This time, the opening of the gate of Indian Embassy, opened the floodgates of democratic upsurge and consequent freedom to the people as well as of the King, which for the past century was denied to them.
>
> (Koirala, 2008: 127–8)

The Ranas were taken aback; the prime minister hurriedly called a Durbar for confabulation. They sent General Vijaya Shamsher, the youngest son of the prime minister, to request the king to return, who was refused an audience to the king. Then they sent General Arjun Shamsher, the king's nephew (sister's son), who went to meet and request his uncle, the king to return to the Royal Palace armed with a revolver. Again the audience was refused and messenger returned empty handed. The desperate prime minister met the British chargé d'affaires and expressed his intention to mount an armed attack on the Indian embassy with a view to releasing the king. He was advised otherwise and it transpired that inadvertently left behind, the king's infant grandson, Gyanendra, would be crowned as the king after duly deposing King Tribhuwan. Prime Minister Mohan Shamsher called an informal meet of army officers, civilians and civilian officers and declared his intention to instal the baby king and sought their opinion. Gaya Prasad Shah was the only solitary person, who had courage, in spite of the show of the armed strength, to give his honest opinion. He asked why there should be such a hurry to instal the 'baby prince'. A delegation consisting of different persons from different walks of life should wait on the king and should seek his intentions and request him to return. When he uttered these words, a Thapa, a senior colonel in army and very close to the prime minister, chided him with these words, "You Madheshia, you do not know the ways of Nepalis. The throne cannot be kept vacant". After that there was nothing to discuss and assembled crowd had purported to have passed a resolution with the following:

> Having been asked our opinion by His Highness (the Prime Minister) on the present situation, we represent that according to our law and tradition, even the dead king's funeral pyre cannot move unless his successor has ascended the throne and since the present King has vacated the throne and taken asylum in a foreign embassy and thus (not only) the throne has fallen vacant, such action of His Majesty the King has caused insult to the nation. His Royal Highness the Crown Prince in normal course should have succeeded him and should have been enthroned but he also has left together. Efforts should be made to bring back the eldest son of the Crown Prince, who is a minor and in case he is not given back for the purpose, the youngest prince (Gyanendra), who has been left behind in the palace, should be brought and placed on the throne because the throne should not remain vacant according to our tradition.
>
> (Koirala, 2008: 130–1)

The above document was signed by 258 individuals. Among them, 193 were military officers, 56 civil officers, and nine were non-serving personnel, possibly the alleged members of the legislature. On the same day (November 8, 1950), at 2:45 p.m., Prince Gyanendra was enthroned the king of Nepal at the Durbar Palace, Hanuman Dhoka, where traditional throne is placed. This was heralded by a 31-gun salute reverberating through the city. That very day a large procession came out in Kathmandu, decrying the Rana's action and shouting pro-king slogans. The procession was, of course, dispersed by club wielding armed police force. This farce of crowing a new king was ignored by the entire world, but for the British. When they expressed their readiness to recognize the baby king at the insistence of the Rana prime minister, the Indian Union threatened to leave the Commonwealth of Nations in that eventuality and that was end of the farce. In this context, the statement given by the minister of home affairs, Sardar Vallabhbhai Patel, Government of India, clarified the position amply:

> The Government of India recognizes Maharajadhiraj Tribhuwan Birbikram Shah as the rightful King of Nepal. Only a mentally unsound person will recognize Mohan Shamsher's proclaimed baby king. And an aircraft of the Indian Air Force is being sent to bring the Maharajadhiraj (from Kathmandu) to India undisturbed. Any interruption in this exercise will not be tolerated.
>
> (Renu, 1977: 30)

King Tribhuwan along with his family was airlifted to New Delhi on November 11, 1950, and India accorded him an honoured political asylum. Prime Minister Jawaharlal Nehru impressed on Prime Minister Mohan Shamsher that he should open negotiations with the king and settle the matter amicably. The Rana prime minister sent his representatives to meet the king and in this way an intricate process of negotiation started. Possibly on the advice of Jawaharlal Nehru, King Tribhuwan made an appeal to the Nepali Congress to ceasefire on the battlefront and the Rana group to come together to find a way out of the predicament peacefully. It appears that the king was under control of India and it looks India had decided to help restore the king to his rightful throne after removing the usurpers. The Nepali Congress was an unknown and untested political commodity to the king, who was unaware of the extent of the ongoing political turmoil in the country. On the other, the Ranas felt it was below their sense of propriety to talk to the commoners such as Ganesh Man Singh, Koirala brothers and Class C Ranas like Mahabir and Subarna. It appears that the king had developed trust in Jawaharlal Nehru and would listen to his advice attentively. However, India had enough bad publicity because of the Western press, especially the British, which reported Nepali Congress advances as Indian efforts addressed to merger of Nepal into Indian Union. What the Nepali Congress was doing in the field without taking New Delhi in confidence was willy-nilly had to be defended by Government of India to the world. In such a desperate situation, leadership of the Nepali Congress tried to reach the king in Delhi. However, they could meet only the royal princes and the private secretary to the king, but they failed to meet the His Majesty. Perhaps New Delhi did not want to create undue public controversy on the Nepalese quagmire and they wished to resolve it by the earliest at the best possible satisfaction to everybody.

It was at this stage that the Indian ambassador to Nepal, Sir C.P.N. Sinha, requested the Nepali Congress leadership to come to Delhi for a tripartite meeting. But the said meeting was never held in a manner in which three parties sat together to thrash out the issues because of possibly the above factors. Probably, it also suited New Delhi to have its way as all three parties were suspicious of one another. This is what B. P. Koirala had written about the Delhi Agreement:

> When they talk about the Delhi Agreement, this is all there was. We never had a discussion with Mohan Shamsher's delegation about the procedures leading up to the agreement. All the talk was done via the medium of Jawaharlalji, and Jawaharlalji himself did not make any concrete interventions. The King took no part at all, although if he had talked to others, I do not know of it. What is presented as the "Delhi Agreement" is something imaginary. But constantly, whenever I raise a point, the Indian side would say, "This is according to the Delhi Agreement".
>
> (Koirala, 2001: 129)

Same was the assessment of the president of the Nepali Congress, M. P. Koirala:

> In Delhi we never sat across the table to iron out our differences and so-called tripartite conference as such never took place. The representatives of the Government of India would convey to us the views of the Ranas and of course the King was out of picture till the finalisation of the parley.
>
> (Koirala, 2008: 176)

M. P. Koirala confronted General Vijaya Shamsher, son of the Prime Minister Mohan Shamsher and emissary to the 'negotiation' in Delhi, and asked him why the two sides could not sit together in Kathmandu to iron out their differences. And he got the response: "(Look), it was a job for me to make my old ones agree even to negotiate in to Delhi, let alone directly with you people, whom they think much below their status and dignity".

The supreme commander of the Mukti Vahini, M. P. Koirala, declared ceasefire on January 17, 1951, without consulting anybody (Shrivastava, 1955: 162), which was resented by at least some members of the western front. This news created confusion on the various fronts, where volunteers were advancing ahead in most difficult circumstances. Even on the eastern front, the home base of the Koirala brothers, there was opposition to ceasefire. Out of desperation, a Rana activist of the revolution, Shivo Jung, a scion of Rana Jung Bahadur, took to the arms, overpowered some of his colleagues, captured some ammunition and refused to surrender before the insistent senior colleagues. The commander on the spot, Yakthumba, was forced to calm him by physically overpowering him. Similarly, Dr K. I. Singh refused to lay arms in the western front in spite of the appeal made by the leadership. There was utter confusion in the minds of the common volunteers, who had staked everything for the cause of the revolution. They felt at a loss as their mission was incomplete and the same leadership, which demanded them to make all possible sacrifices, was asking them to stop it in between. There was desperation and demoralization among the cadre of the Congress. Simple revolutionary failed to understand that if there had to be negotiations with the Ranas, what was the purpose of intense and violent conflict leading to loss of life. For the fighting forces very mention of words 'negotiation' and 'compromise' smacked of contempt. Moreover, they were unable to comprehend the reasons for such a compromise with people's enemies after sacrificing hundreds of young men and capturing about one-third of the Nepalese territory (Renu, 1977: 87).

Because of some misinformation, the Nepali Congress leadership reached Delhi only on January 14, 1951. The Rana Prime Minister Mohan Shamsher had agreed on January 8 to accept the King Tribhuwan as the sovereign ruler of the kingdom and the Ranas and the Nepali Congress to be a part of the democratic dispensation. After that, everything was settled quickly: the king would return as the sovereign head of the state to Kathmandu; there would be a cabinet of 10 ministers headed by the then Prime Minister Mohan Shamsher with five members each from the Ranas and the Nepali Congress; B. P. would be the leader of the NC component in the cabinet and the home minister with second rank. And if any of the two components dissociated from the cabinet, the cabinet would get dissolved. Finally, "after secret negotiations in Nepal and India between the King, the Ranas and the Nepali Congress, they signed an agreement on 12th February, 1951, to form a coalition Government". These details trickled to Kathmandu; political fortune seekers and office hunters like Dilli Raman Regmi, Tanka Presad Acharya, Khagda Man Singh and the like descended to Delhi and went round sounding for possibility of their inclusion in the cabinet. Though everything was settled after a lot of negotiation and bargaining, but these elements felt themselves important enough to insist their inclusion in the cabinet. On the other hand, Ganesh Man Singh had made it a point that he would not join a cabinet under a Rana prime minister. And for that, name of Tripurwar Singh Pradhan was settled with a view to giving representation to the Kathmandu Valley. On February 8, 1951, the president of India gave a party at Rashtrapati Bhawan, New Delhi, to the leaders of the insurrection as well the Ranas and their representatives. By this time, everything was already agreed upon from both sides.

The king returns to Kathmandu and appoints the cabinet of ministers

The king, along with his family and the leaders of the Nepali Congress, came back to Kathmandu on February 15, 1951, to a tumultuous welcome, and after two days a coalition government was sworn in. Though Ranas were coerced to agree to the settlement, they were still unwilling to share power with anyone, including the king. On the other hand, working arrangements among the constituent units and various ministries were unknown. Neither the king nor the ministers had any idea how to function as colleagues in the cabinet system. While the Rana ministers behaved as they used to do in the past, most of the NC ministers tended to act out of inexperience like the Ranas in their administrative works. There was no trained bureaucracy at any level to assist the ministers in their duties by providing appropriate papers. It was possibly the Indian strategy to stabilize Nepalese system on some formal administrative structure in place of the Ranas' autocratic informality. Prior to that there was no institution of administration with an office, no administrative cadre with secured service and perks, and Nepal had blissfully no administrative rules as such. Neither did they have any system of keeping administrative records or filing procedure. Most of the functionaries, when appointed to some or other offices, functioned from their residence.

Populist regional print media began labelling the king as the great democrat and his efforts of seeking shelter in Indian embassy as revolutionary one. But in reality,

> for what had taken place in Nepal was not really a revolution but a restoration (to the King of his dynastic privileges). The King's was the struggle against the Ranas, and the rebels had also fought on his name. The Government of India had supported the King. The Nepali Congress were thus viewed as auxiliaries of the King, and the Ranas suspected shrewdly, and not without considerable justification, as later events to show that as soon as the King had access to the traditional instruments of power, the army, the police and administrative machinery, he would be in a position to get rid of the organization and its leaders.
>
> (Patterson, 1963: 140)

B. P. Koirala recounts how the 'democrat King Tribhuwan' got an upper hand on the populist lump of leadership and showed his true colour when the first opportunity occurred:

> We told (Kiran Shamsher, the Deputy Commander-in-Chief of the elite armed force), "Go to Singha Durbar and move the troops out of there (to Narayanhiti Durbar)". Other than Singha Durbar, only Narayanhiti Durbar, the Royal Palace, had the kind of barracks that could hold them (the Bijuli Garat: or the crack force of the armed forces), and these were presently empty . . . . The next morning, without my (the Minister of Home) knowledge and informing no one else, the King took the salute of those troops. It was as if the king were telling them; henceforth show me loyalty you have shown Mohan Shamsher. Looking out of my window, I saw the King receiving the salute. I was there as a guest (of the King), and at very least should have been informed, but he did not see it fit to do that . . . From that day onwards, the King had an upper hand, and democracy lost a notch. We would have retained room for manoeuvre if the force had stayed back at Singha Durbar. From the moment that the battalion came into his hands, the King's attitude changed. From that day the King became powerful.
>
> (Koirala, 2001: 142–3)

The Rana ministers would act in the same old pompous style and demand privileges for their seniority against the agreed understanding, but confronted of their own agreement in private, they would break in tears and plead for patience on the name of honouring the old ones. The king, the crown prince and the princes were part of the same Rana feudal system of upbringing, court culture, clique, conspiracy, false sense of prestige and belief in a mystique divine right over the subjects. The King Tribhuwan was an extrovert, he would like dancing and having fun against introvert Crown Prince Mahendra. They had no social life of their own. B. P. Koirala records in his posthumous biography in King Mahendra's words: "You know, my life has been spent very much alone. My childhood was rather lonely. I had no friends and I developed intimacy with no one. I grew up among servants, and it was my ***bubu*** nurse who brought me up. Singers and performers used to come to the palace, and from them I tried to learn to sing". Further, the king confided in B. P.: "You have been my first personal guest". Continues B. P.: "This was what his father had said as well, when I had stayed as his guest at the Narayanhiti Royal Palace". Here was King Mahendra, repeating the same thing. "You have been my only personal guest. All others have been official guests" (Koirala, 2001: 201–2).

Naturally, the Ranas were not reconciled to the loss of the power, prestige and arrogance so soon. It is learnt that Hari Shamsher, King Mahendra's father-in-law, and the royal brother-in-law, Rana Kaisher Bahadur K. C., organized Gorkha Dal and popped up 'Robin Hood' Dr K. I. Singh from the prison to create problems for the otherwise chaotic government. In any way, the coalition government was not working to anybody's satisfaction. Some type of crisis would crop up almost every day. The Government of India would intervene through its ambassador, who had poor image among the concerned intelligentsia and political class in Nepal. Ambassador Sir C.P.N. Sinha would tilt invariably towards the feudal pack familiar to him and invariably demand accommodation from the representatives of the Nepali Congress. This went on for some time, but tempers were rising high and his acts were seen as Indian intervention in the routine internal affairs of Nepal. On the other hand, the impetuous B. P. Koirala failed to see that it was a provisional and transitional government, which deserved patient handling from an experienced politician and a politically educated person like him for any success. Unlike others, unfortunately he had a higher stake in the success of that experiment, which he failed to appreciate. Undoubtedly he was politically and physically attacked to provoke him frequently. There were cliques among the Ranas, a bunch of discredited politicians and there were individuals even in his own party waiting in the wings for him to falter. And he did falter, when he announced his resignation from the cabinet publicly before submitting it to His Majesty the king. And at that moment, he lost King Tribhuwan's trust and favour for all the time to come as an unreliable character. B. P. Koirala resigned as the home minister on the 'revolution day', November 11, 1951, the day King Tribhuwan had left Kathmandu for India, after working as the first home minister of Nepal for eight months and 22 days leading to dissolution of the coalition cabinet.

Democratic experiments leading to Panchayati Raj

Apparently, the moderate face and president of the Nepali Congress, M. P. Koirala, was invited by the king to form the government. It is alleged that even Jawaharlal Nehru had written to the king in favour of M. P. Koirala as the prime minister, but he was asked by his party to choose one of the two options he had: president ship of the Nepali Congress or the prime ministership of Nepal. But it appears that the Nepali Congress president was reluctant to forgo the either of the two. The issue was discussed at length in the party forum formally; it was put to vote and M. P. lost badly. He had to resign from the prime minister's post in the absence of support from the Nepali Congress. Within a week, he formed his own political forum, Rashtriya Praja Party and within no time, he was sworn in as the prime minister and he could collect politically light weight individuals as the ministers. However, the Nepali Congress went on asking for holding the promised election to the Constituent Assembly. He could continue in office as long as King Tribhuwan was alive, but the moment Crown Prince Mahendra succeeded his father as the king, his days were numbered. B. P. had suggested to him to do something dramatic in favour of the common people prior to his departure from the office so that people would remember him for the good cause (B. P. would himself commit the same mistake before he was removed from the post of prime minister by King Mahendra in 1960). But M. P. would not believe that he would be removed so soon. Have a look at what actually happened:

> A few days later, even as the cabinet was meeting, news came from the Royal Palace that Thuldaju (the eldest brother in Nepali, an address of endearment) had been removed from the office. An envelope arrived from the Singha Durbar, which he opens, with Mahabir Shamsher and all the other persons present. He reads the letter and then announces, "I am no longer prime minister. You are no longer ministers. This cabinet is no more". Thuldaju immediately left for home, asking the flag on the car to be sheathed. At his residence, the military guard was

> already packing up and would not give him the salute. His phone line had been cut and the electricity disconnected; this is how he was disgraced. He spent the night in darkness and without a phone. As Thuldaju used to say later, "I just don't understand the Royal Palace".
>
> (Koirala, 2001: 173–4)

King Tribhuwan died in Europe on March 13, 1955, and Mahendra had taken over as the sovereign of the country. It was commonly known that the relation between the father and son was barely civil. Whatever the late king stood for, Mahendra detested: the king appreciated the role of the Indian establishment in restoration of royal status in the kingdom, which Mahendra saw as interference; the king appreciated democracy and would have preferred the Nepali Congress among the faction-ridden variety of political groupings in the kingdom. Mahendra was out and out a monarchist, who saw democracy and political parties as the nuisance on way to his ambition. Both had minds of their own, but the king was accommodative to the opposite, while Mahendra, once he would make up his mind, no possibility of accommodation would be left out. B. P. Koirala records a clash between father and son over the latter's choice of a life partner. B. P. pleaded Mahendra's case with the king, who could agree perhaps unwillingly, but cautioned all concerned, "This is what B. P. said, but mark my words this crown prince will make you all sob; he will make you weep. I know him, and he will make you weep" (Koirala, 2001: 239).

Unlike his father, King Mahendra had his own ideas about role of the king, nature of governance and people's participation in the affairs of the state. He believed that the ruler was the source of authority, and there cannot be another such entity in the state and thus, he wanted to reign and rule himself. After he assumed power, he raised a debate regarding democracy: "They say democracy is here but is still in infancy. But how is it then that an infant is so crafty, greedy. There is no innocence of a child in this democracy". However, he went on show of forming and removing cabinets by egocentric persons with limited support of the people possibly to expose their incompetence. After dismissing M. P. Koirala, he announced a five man Council of Advisors with all members drawn from the Rana extraction, an unusual step in the given situation. Then on January 27, 1956, Tanka Prasad Acharya, who was not even president of his rump political forum, was invited to form the government. Within six months Acharya resigned as the prime minister on July 13, 1956. The king took about a year to find another worthy for the post of prime ministership. And thus, Dr K. I.

Singh was appointed as the prime minister on July 26, 1957, and after rousing enough heat and dust, he too resigned on October 6, 1957, within three months.

At last, General Subarna Shamshere was asked to form the government and initiate steps for writing the constitution for Nepal. And for that, Sir Ivor Jennings, who had drafted the constitution of Ceylon, was commissioned. He worked on his drafts and his two drafts were rejected on the ground that he had given too much power to the legislature. An exasperated Jennings submitted a third draft and made it clear that he had enough of it: "I will not submit another draft. I am leaving". It was a peculiar document, which had protected the king's power, at the same time, maintained the legislature's authority. That is how that document reached for a balance. Truly, a constitutional monarchy rests less on what is written and more on how much responsibility is exhibited by the king and the prime minister. The draft document by Sir Ivor Jennings was approved and elections were held on that basis in the summer of 1959.

And for that,

> on 12th February, 1959 the King announced the first Constitution for Nepal. It provided for the establishment of two Houses of Parliament. The lower House was to consist of 109 members elected from single member territorial constituencies and the Upper House, or the Senate, of thirty-six members, of whom eighteen would be elected by the Lower House and eighteen nominated by the King. The Cabinet was to consist of the Prime Minister and not more than fourteen Ministers, a Supreme Court and fundamental rights to ensure personal liberty, equality before the law, and religious freedom.
>
> (Patterson, 1963: 147)

Moreover, the king would retain discretionary power in respect of the selection of a prime minister, appointment of the members of the State Council, dismissal of the prime minister and temporary suspension of the cabinet in special circumstances.

Triumphs and tragedy of the Nepali Congress

The Nepali Congress was the only organization in the country, which had presence in almost every part of the country. It had cared to prepare an election manifesto with a 13-point programme of agrarian reforms. It had promised to start heavy industries in the state sector and cottage industries through the co-operative societies of the members. In its foreign policy it pleaded for establishing friendly relations between Nepal and other countries on terms of equality and mutual respect. The Nepali Congress had fielded its candidates in almost every nook and corner and the leadership had undertaken extensive tours to the countryside in favour of its candidates. The canvassing for electioneering was intense and electorate was promised a stable government, if elected to power. The result of the election was a foregone conclusion: the Nepali Congress came victorious winning 74 out of 109 seats for the Lower House, the Pratinidhi Sabha. But even after a month and half, the Congress leadership was not invited to form the government. It appears that the king had not expected the Nepali Congress would get majority in the parliament after the elections. However, on the basis of popular support, B. P. assured the king that he would get a senior leader like Subarna Shamsher to be elected as the leader of the legislature or anybody else if he would like. The king's response was clear:

> I have worked with Subarna Shamshere for more than a year. He is a bit sluggish. I am a dynamic person, and you are also dynamic, so I am keen to work with you. For that reason, you are acceptable to me. I have already tried out Subarna Shamshere. The rumours (distrust between the two) in the alleys are false. I would like to see you as prime minister; it will have to be decision of your party. That was the king's reply, and later he called on me to form the government. "I had already contacted Jawaharlalji".
>
> (Koirala, 2001: 190)

He was elected leader of the legislative wing of the party and he was invited to form the government. B. P.'s democratic routes may easily be traced to Indian freedom movement, in which cause, he was imprisoned by the British along with a galaxy of Indian leaders, and some of them became president, chief ministers and cabinet ministers in the states and the federal ministers later in life. His political apprenticeship, chiselling of the leadership qualities and an abiding faith in the masses may be traced to his growing up as an Indian Congress volunteer during his formative period. It appears that unconsciously he adopted Jawaharlal Nehru as his model for the prime ministership. He tried to chart an independent foreign policy: reaching to China diplomatically to reduce Nepal's over-dependence on India; joining Socialist International as a political support system; establishing diplomatic ties with Israel on socialist ideological ground and doing the same with Pakistan to display national autonomy. But he forgot the fact that Nehru had an old political party with experienced leadership to back and a vibrant Parliament to review and even cross-examine him on his actions. And the head of state, the president, a really ceremonial head, was another very senior Congress man. On the other hand, Koirala had to humour an egoist, a despot and an opinionated king who was suspicious of his prime minister's accomplishments. Moreover, he had nothing much to show on the agrarian front, his major constituency, during his prime term of slightly better than a year and half. The king was watching from the wings rather impatiently that his prime minister was stealing the show right under his nose and most of the focus was shifted to his prime minister. King Mahendra had never bargained for anything like that and he got active to undo which was unpalatable to him. There was no dearth of intrigue loving courtiers, as political culture of the country continued to be feudal. But the king was constantly in touch with the loose balls from B. P.'s camp such as Surya Prasad Uppadhyaya, Bishwabandhu Thapa, Tulki Giri, Bhadrakali Mishra, Rishikesh Shaha and even dear 'Thuldaju', who could reach the king's ear invariably with 'invented' or distorted information, which latter would prefer to listen as sinister designs.

There were rumours in the air in Kathmandu that something was afoot. Rishikesh Shaha had warned B. P. about it and so had done Surya Prasad in his own ways. Before taking leave for visiting Calcutta from his prime minister, Subarna Shamshere had warned him that something was afoot, but that might not be immediately. But the most puzzling was the information, which Bharat Shamshere, the leader of the Opposition in the House (Pratinidhi Sabha), communicated to B. P. in a dramatic way. He had rushed to B. P.'s bedroom, when he was not even dressed properly; occupied the couch in front and blurted out:

> "Something very strange happened today".
>
> Bharat Shamshere did not tell B P what signal he had had, all he had said was: "Something very strange (had) happened. For so many days I had been asking for an audience with the king, saying that he should also give some time to the leader of opposition and he had not obliged. Suddenly, I got a call last night asking that I present myself before His Majesty in the palace at 3 pm today. I have to leave for Calcutta for a programme today at 11 am and I have already bought the ticket".
>
> "So you can go to Calcutta tomorrow".

> "The king will ask questions. He is, to my mind, a critic of the government".
>
> "You, too, can criticise the government, say what you think is appropriate. But if he seeks your advice, you must tell him that this democratic institution we have, the parliamentary system, this should not be strangled. That after all, it is also in your interest".
>
> "That, of course, I will put before him. I just wanted to know if there is anything else to say". Bharat Shamshere then left B P's house, but not before asking: "So then, shall I stay?"
>
> B P replied that he should. And that dialogue between the two had occurred on December 15, 1960 at 10 in the morning.
>
> (Koirala, 2001: 251)

Prime Minister Koirala was attending a delegates' convention of the Tarun Dal (youth wing of his party) attended by a good number of delegates on the same evening, possibly affiliated to his Party. And that was the opportune moment chosen by the power to be. Surendra Bahadur Shah, the chief of the general staff, with a band of 300 jawans surrounded the venue and came to Koirala and said, "The King has given instructions, we had better (to) go" (Koirala, 2001: 252–3). What actually happened on that day:

> On 15th December 1960, the King Mahendra announced that he had taken over direct rule and had put the Prime Minister and other political leaders in jail, giving as his reason the corruption in the Congress Party and the deterioration of the government administration . . . In taking the action the king actually went beyond powers granted to him in the Constitution, for not only he dismissed the Cabinet, but also ordered arrest of all members of the council of ministers. He also imprisoned the Speaker and the Leader of the Opposition, and arrested every person who could be regarded as political.
>
> (Patterson, 1963: 150–1)

Soon the political parties, rather everything political, were banned; armed forces were posted at all the critical positions; and Singha Durbar turned into the royal secretariat in letter and spirit. The courtiers, sycophants and hangers-on flocked to the king within no time. Deprived Ranas, who had been desperately waiting in the wings, jumped on the opportunity and they provided much needed expertise of a certain type to run the administrative machinery. Externally, democratic world showed disappointment with the development. Perhaps the king had taken New Delhi in confidence to the extent that the prime minister would be replaced. But India was for a shock when she learnt that the parliament was dissolved; parliamentarians were jailed and political parties were banned. It was the king's personal rule, though there was no doubt that he was the sovereign ruler of the kingdom. Active politicians were rather puzzled as they had not anticipated such a drastic turn of the events and they turned inactive or over-reacted by wild condemnation of the act. Even the royalists could not gauge properly as to how much they would go with the king and how long would the new situation continue.

After the initial shock, whatever was left of the Nepali Congress outside Nepal regrouped in exile; they condemned the king's act and promised to go to the people and organize resistance. B. P.'s associates, the Indian Socialists, over-reacted and tried to help the rump NC in whatever the ways they could. In fact, there was a talk of armed resistance and some feeble efforts were made in that direction. Subarna Shamshere was the first senior politician of Nepal, who condemned the takeover and denounced the royal efforts as the suppression of democracy. He recounted how King Mahendra's father had helped to establish democratic traditions in feudal Nepal and wondered when efforts were being made to strengthen democracy by an elected parliament, why the king was to take such a retrograde step. However, bulk of the leaders of most of the political parties continued to be in jail in inhuman conditions for many years. Though the king gave the impression that he could not care for any criticism, but the international pressure began to work on him and slowly the captives began to be released. However, B. P. remained in captivity for about a decade before he was let out in precarious health.

After attending to the problems of poor health, B. P. assessed the prevalent political situation inside and outside Nepal and called for arms resistance to the king's autocracy garbed as the Panchayati Raj. He noted two weak points in Subarna Shamshere's taking up of arms against the king. First, he was himself located outside Nepal and was dependent on assistance of the others such as India, which limited his autonomy and the Nepalese struggle became part of India's strategy vis-à-vis Nepal. Second, he found that the Nepalese people wanted change, but they were scared of the uncertainty and were not convinced that a determined revolutionary group would be able to assume leadership. He did try to reach the Socialist International for support.

In this context, he mentions his meeting with two members of the Socialist International: Hans Janitschek from a Scandinavian country and Berect from Israel. Both of them responded to his request for the arms in the cause of restoring democracy: "We cannot help you without India's consent, and if India is in such a frame of mind, you do not need our help at all". "However, we will give you all diplomatic support you require" (Koirala, 2001: 295).

After that very little was left unclear and B. P. reached the prime minister of India, Indira Gandhi, straight and made the request to her, "I need a crore (of) rupees and some weapons. I see a mature situation for revolution in Nepal". In response, she said, "That is not a problem. You build your organization; I will make arrangements for what you ask" (Koirala, 2001: 294). And after that there is no evidence that B. P. ever reached the Indian prime minister or for that matter her successors. And that takes us to the condition mentioned by Indira Gandhi. What type of party the Nepali Congress had turned out after the king's crackdown in December 1960 on politicians and political parties? We do know that a group of young men had mounted armed insurrection in the bordering southern locations, exposing them as the foreign agents or the bandits. There was even a dramatic hijacking of a small aircraft, but the Nepali Congress as a party was dysfunctional. While old revolutionaries of 1950 vantage were already a tired lot and part of them had already been co-opted to the king's court, and the younger recruits to the fold lacked the fire of B. P. Koirana, Yakthumba, Thirbam Malla, Dr K. I. Singh and the like. It appears the Congress committed two cardinal mistakes. First, it never seriously challenged the well-entrenched feudal social order inclusive of the royalty and concentrated on building an independent national image, which collided with the king's ambitious project. Second, an avowedly socialist Nepali Congress had nothing to show on the agrarian front, and like other hill-based entities, Nepali Congress too ignored totally the Terai and the Madhesis, from where he had learnt a primer of politics. In spite of the avowed socialist NC ruling under B. P., there was no evidence of agrarian reforms in spite of the promised electoral manifesto. In fact, his supporter had nothing tangible to show to the commoners what relief B. P.'s government had brought from them at the grassroots level.

What could be more demoralizing than B. P.'s Thuldaju, Matrika Prasad Koirala and the founding president of Nepali Congress, informing him in captivity that he was going to the United Nations Organization (UNO) and the United States as the royal ambassador, who would be defending the royal takeover and sing the "song of

Panchayati Raj". What a tragedy it was? While the entire popular face of Nepali Congress was in prison, its founder president and the commander in chief of the guerrilla forces was singing the song of the royal takeover in the UNO. Even Matrikababu's better half saw the apparent embarrassment of the situation and asked B. P. to request his elder brother to refuse the officer. The Nepali Congress over-lived B. P. in a clandestine way for some time and resurrected itself publicly after the second democratic upsurge in 1990. Not only that: its nominees became prime ministers thereafter many a time. But this was not the Nepali Congress of its glorious past spirit. It persists even today and possibly it is still in a better shape among the political parties in the country and is still basking in the past glories of the revolution. B. P.'s youngest brother and five-time prime minister, Girija Prasad Koirala, who prided himself to have taken part in civil disobedience movement launched in 1950s, burnt his fingers in quagmire of the anti-feudal Lhotshampas' agitation in Bhutan in 1990s, an affair to which we turn in the next chapter.

Bibliography

Goel, N., 1966, *Political History of the Himalayan States*, Cambridge Book and Stationery Stores, New Delhi, 2nd Edition.

Gurung, H. B., 1997, "State and Society in Nepal" in *Nationalism and Ethnicity in a Hindu Kingdom: Politics of Culture in Contemporary Nepal*, edited by D. N. Gellner et al., Harwood Academic, Amsterdam.

Hofer, A., 2004, *The Caste Hierarchy and The State in Nepal: A Study of the Maluki Ain of 1854*, Himal Books Classics 4, Lalitpur, Nepal.

Koirala, B. P., 2001, *Atmabritanta: Late Life Reflections*, translated by K. M. Dixit, Himal Books, Jagdamba Prakashan, Lalitpur, Nepal.

Koirala, M. P., 2008, *A Role on Revolution*, Jagdamba Prakashan, Lalitpur, Nepal.

Patterson, G. N., 1963, *Peking Versus Delhi*, Faber & Faber, London.

Renu, F. N., 1977, *Nepali Kranti Katha* (in Nepali: Story of Nepalese Revolution in Hindi), Rajkamal Prakashan, New Delhi and Patna.

Rose, L. E., 1971, *Nepal: Strategy for Survival*, Oxford University Press, New Delhi.

Shrivastava, K. P., 1955, *Nepal Ki Kahani* (in Nepali: Story of Nepal in Hindi), Atmaram & Sons, New Delhi.

Thapa, B. K., 2017, *Migration, Development and Citizenship: An Ethnographic Study of Bhojpur VDC in Eastern Hills of Nepal*, PhD Thesis, Kathmandu University, Kathmandu.

7

BHUTAN STATE CONGRESS

A premature democratic experiment

Patterson, (1963: 216–17) wrote a column while stationed for years at Kalimpong. He had intimate knowledge of the Himalayan affairs in the mid-20th century.

> The former Maharaja (the Second Wangchuk ruler of Bhutan (Jigme Wangchuk: b. 1905, r. 1926–1952)) had a reputation of being a tyrant and had used his reign to perpetuate the feudal administration he had inherited, the big landlords receiving bulk of the state's income and residue trickling into the "Government's coffers to pay for the unenthusiastic administration . . .". While the Maharaja's power in Bhutan was absolute, there were many of the hereditary feuds which had always obtained in Bhutan . . . Because the Government was so scattered and isolated, administration was limited to a few officials. Like his father, Raja (Sonam Tobgyel) Dorji, Jigmie Dorji, (the Prime Minister of the country) spent most of his time in India; other **Penlops** (regional Governors) and Jongpens (administrators of the Forts) remained in their own districts, the 'capital' moved with the Maharaja and nobody bothered a great deal about anything. The hospitals and dispensaries were oftener than not without medicine. Schools were unattended because teachers were not paid and had to find other means to supplement their income . . . Forming political parties is forbidden and criticism of the Government is not only discouraged, but suppressed; but outlawed party, Bhutan State Congress, is very active clandestinely in the country, particularly in the south and west. In these areas live the bulk of the Nepali inhabitants of Bhutan. Estimates of their number vary; the Bhutanese Prime Minister claims that they only form 25 percent of the population of Bhutan, while the

> Bhutan State Congress and the (All India) Gorkha League of Darjeeling claim that they number 64 percent of the 700,000. Whether 25 percent or 64 percent, or somewhere in between, this is a very discontented group in Bhutan, for they are not represented in the Bhutan Government . . . This discontent makes them easy target of the Bhutan State Congress whose programme is abolition of this discrimination against the Nepalis, liberation from the "autocratic and arbitrary rule" by the Maharaja, and introduction of a popular government.

Traditional social structure of Bhutan

The state of Bhutan was created by a theocrat, Ngawang Namgyal, as a church state in 17th century. The political system bore strong resemblance in certain critical respects to the political system headed by the Dalai Lama, which emerged stronger in Tibet at approximately the same time. Incidentally, that was the only familiar system of state formation with which he was conversant. The office of the theocrat was passed to next one to an incarnate boy, duly to be discovered and trained by the qualified and legitimately authorized monks. Ideally, the secular head of the state known as the Druk or Deb Desi was selected for a period of three years by the monks, Jongpens and Penlops, but many of them held of office for better than a decade. On the other hand, there were occasions, when there was more than one Druk Desi, ruling their respective domains at the same time at the biddings of their regional patrons (Aris, 1979). There were half a dozen incarnate theocrats (Dharam Rajas or Zhabdrungs) in all after the demise of the first one and the last one, when he expired in 1903. Similarly, there were about four and a half dozen Deb Desis altogether when the last one remitted his office in 1905. In reality, there were regional Jongpens and Penlops, who controlled the both the offices and it was this oligarchy, which in reality controlled the destiny of the country. Ugyen Wangchuk (b. 1860, r. 1907–26), the Tongsa Penlop, emerged as the most charismatic personality in Bhutan by the first decade of the 20th century. He effectively controlled the both the above offices in the first quarter of the 19th century. He helped the British colonial power India in an appreciable way in their expedition to Lhasa in 1903–4 and for that he was duly rewarded, as the British were instrumental in getting him crowned as the first Druk-Gyalpo (king of Bhutan) on December 17, 1907 (White, 1972).

During the time of the first two Wangchuk kings (1907–52), apart from the estates of the royal family, the regional feudal chiefs controlled a huge chunk of land. Then there were monasteries, which had estates for the maintenance of the huge resident monk bodies and nunneries. Land revenue was paid in kind; taxes were heavy and were paid for a variety of reasons and slavery was prevalent in the country. The country continued barter economy till 1960s. There were no markets for selling goods and services and similarly there were no urban centres for that purpose. The king resided mostly at Tongas *dZong* (fort) in the central Bhutan and in reality, wherever the king was, the 'capital' would shift. It was a simple and personalized system, which had little of details of statecraft known elsewhere. Bhutan had no surface transport system and wheel transportation remained unknown in the country till 1962. Similarly, there were no schools, no health centres or hospitals for the treatment of the sick persons as it is understood normally. In such a situation, there was hardly a possibility of the subjects organizing a democratic movement for some or other real or imaginary demands against the power to be. As late as April, 1962, J. K. Galbraith, US ambassador to India, described Bhutanese administration as something like a "correspondence-school administration". He noted that Bhutan was "devoid of cities (largest has only one or two shops), telephones, electricity, newspapers, public opinion, sanitation or any of the other encumbrances of modern civilization". Further, it

> does not even have a capital. The P[rime] M[inister] functions mostly from Calcutta and Kalimpong [in India] . . . The Maharja moves from one to another of seven Dzongs – half fortresses, half monasteries – and wherever he resides is the capital.
>
> (Galbraith, 1969: 319)

Situation in the Duars in the south was different; the Nepalese immigrants were settled in the western part of the Duars, who were granted forest land to clear and develop into agricultural fields. They had to pay house tax and land revenue in cash to the Bhutan Agent Ugyen Dorji and his family. This experiment was copied in Bhutan at the instance of the British from their experience of Sikkim, where immigrant Nepalese had turned south and west Sikkim into thriving agricultural economy. Slowly and slowly, Nepalese population increased considerably within five decades. In the absence of a formal administrative structure, they organized themselves in large villages and followed the provisions of the Maluki Ain prevalent in Nepal. As the immigrants had to pay house tax for constructing a 'house', they tend to have huge joint families as an economy drive. They could walk across the hills to the Indian plains for commercial exchange in the markets. They specially dealt in orange and other monsoon fruits during the season. Thus, unlike the thinly inhabited interior parts of the country, immigrant settled Duars gave the impression of prosperity and autonomy. Not for nothing that the king was worried of their loyalty within three decades of their settlement in 1917.

Nepalese (Lhotshampas: the 'Southerners') immigration to Bhutan

Chronologically speaking, the Drukpa kingdom of Bhutan was last to experiment with the democratic dispensation among the three Himalayan kingdoms. A point to be kept in mind is that unlike other two kingdoms, Bhutan was neither south oriented, nor were its rulers and their locations easily linked with the south, which may mean its Nepalese-settled southern foothills or the adjoining Indian plains were isolated from the seat of authorities. Furthermore, the Lhotshampas (Southerners in Zongkha, which refers to Nepalese immigrants in Bhutan; a nomenclature given to them by the third king of Bhutan in 1975) were not permitted to settle down north of an imaginary line drawn from east to west just north of the Duars. No doubt, Raja Sonam Tobgyel Dorji, the Bhutanese external face with some opaque titles and the controller of the affairs of southern Nepalese settlements, resided at Kalimpong in the district of Darjeeling. It is presumed that the Bhutan Duars are thickly inhabited mainly by Nepali immigrants. As there was no state-sponsored health, education and even formal administrative arrangements, the settlers were left to their own device for such amenities. They had organized themselves in relatively big villages with their shrines and ritual performances at hand. They gave the impression of being hard-working rustic folk, who would pay land rent and house tax in cash on time and demand nothing from the establishment. It was a typical lord and vassal mediaeval feudal relationship in which even minor offences resulted in harsh punishments. Thus, it will be instructive first to inform the readers about Nepalese settlements in Bhutan.

In spite of the historical claims of some Nepalese scholars that Nepalese had been in Bhutan since time of the first Zhabdrung (the Dharamjara, an incarnation of the holy spirit addressed by the Nepalese), there is no concrete evidence of Nepalese settlements prior to 1865. It was possibly because of the fact that Bhutan was least attractive prior to that date for the simple reason that there was no attraction for anyone to stake one's life for gaining nothing in return.

Bhutan was perennially in turmoil and elsewhere in the neighbourhood such as Sikkim, Darjeeling and Assam were more rewarding as potential settlements, as they had increasing demand for inexpensive labour with security. At the most, some Nepalese ran to the Bhutan Duars (foothills) for some days and collect natural rubber juice and lime from the forests in the winter season. Situation was so wild that nobody thought of settling down in those densely forested, malarial and inhospitable land. However, after the Sinchula Treaty in 1865, situation began to change as tea planters began their activities in neighbouring Jalpaiguri and Darjeeling districts in the adjoining districts of southern Bhutan. Furthermore, the Bhutanese herdsmen learnt of visiting the Darjeeling market for selling their surplus milk, cheese and other products and return with clothing, salt, thread and other household articles. Jungta Kazi Ugyen Dorji, an ally and relative of the Tongsa Penlop, was one such person, who was farsighted enough to understand the significance of inexpensive Nepalese labour for developing Bhutanese resources. It appears that inspired by J. C. White, Ugyen Dorji persuaded regional strong man, Paro Penlop, to grant a land deed to father and son, Dalchand and Garajman Gurungs. They were small-time local gang leaders (*sardars*) working on lime mines, supplying bamboos and timber to the tea planters. These two came to be known as the Gurung of Chamurchi, who owned the Samchi estate in 1887 (Dhakal and Strawn, 1994: 602–3). Similarly, Moti Chand Pradhan, the former chief magistrate of Sikkim and the grandson of Laxmi Das Pradhan of Darjeeling and the famous lessee of Sikkim, informed the political officer that Dzongpen of Wangdiphodrang, under the authority, wrote to Laxmi Das Pradhan in 1891 offering lower Sibsu estate excluding Sambe Dzong for an annual rent of Rs. 20,000. Pradhans did not want the area offered and tried to negotiate for some regions higher up in the hills, but it was not given to them. Later on, Sibsu area was integrated with Samchi and descendants of Dal Bahadur Gurung secured it (Prasad, B).

Samchi estate of the Gurungs stayed under the overall control of the Paro Penlop up to 1947, when Raja S. T. Dorji prevailed upon the Maharaja to give it under his care. It is alleged that Garajman Gurung went to pay the annual land revenue to the Paro Penlop sometimes possibly in the 1920s and did not return. Michael Hutt records the various sets of myths around his personae among the remnants of the Bhutan State Congress and the dissenters residing in the refugee camps in Jhapa district of Nepal in 2003 (Hutt, 2003: 47–57). It is said that he had become so powerful and rich in cashless Bhutan that he managed to build a huge palace with 52 doors on a hilltop near Samchi known as Saurseni Palace; and he had risen so much extraordinary in stature in Nepalese estimate that the Paro Penlop had him murdered out of envy. The Gurungs were granted express permission to settle the estate for "making the land fertile, not to leave it barren and encourage habitation" in a well-defined area. And for that they visited their village in Illam district of Nepal for recruiting potential settlers and bring them to Bhutan. In course of time, Samchi turned out to be an example of thriving Nepali settlement with paddy fields, orange orchards and cardamom plants in place of the dense tropical forests. They would collect the house tax from the settlers; land revenue from the cultivators and taxes for the fruit trees and travel to Paro Dzong once a year to deposit the proceeds in cash. Dewan Dalchand's son, Garajman had three sons: Hemraj, Jasraj and Motiraj. C. J. Morris, who had visited Samchi district in company of the eldest one, 'Dewan Hemraj' in 1932, found them squandering their wealth in frivolous luxuries and did not refer to any imposing palace as their residence (Morris, 1934).

Morris prepared *A Report on the Gurkha Immigration in Bhutan* in 1933 with a view to exploring the possibility of Gurkha recruitment for the Gurkha regiments of the British Indian Army. It is said that when Dalchand began bringing settlers from eastern Nepal, the Government of Nepal took a serious view of it and ordered him to appear before the prime minister. The old man managed to dodge the summons for some time and waited for an opportune time when the prime minister was in Calcutta. He was able to impress the prime minister of Nepal with his spirit of enterprise and instead of blames; he received commendations and a letter of authority to bring in more immigrants to Bhutan. Unlike enterprising and hardworking Dalchand, his grandsons began squandering their wealth in luxuries. Seeing many of their weaknesses, Raja S. T. Dorji began gradually to take over control of areas under Samchi district.

There were allegations that the Raja had confiscated their privileges and properties. Especially hard heating was confiscation of orange orchards depriving them of cash income from the sale of the fruits, on the plea that they were planted on forests, which were under the control of the Raja. Devoid of such income plus their extravagance, the Gurungs began defaulting on the payment of the land revenue collected from the tenets. Thus, they were obliged to mortgage with the Raja Dorji shares of the value of some lakhs of rupees, which they had held in a tea estate on the Indian side of the border. Meanwhile the unfair method they had adopted to raise money from whatever resources they could still command, caused much ill will against them among the tenets around. The complaints reached to the doors of the

Raja against the Gurungs and through him to Maharaja, who dismissed them from their services and the administration was taken over. Three of the grandsons were awarded annual pensions of Rs. 4,000 each on the condition that they would reside in Bhutan and their duties were entrusted to the Bhutan officials under the control of the Bhutan agent. Among them, Hemraj began residing in Siliguri, forfeiting the pension; Motiraj was of unsound mind and lived at Chamurchi in Jalpaiguri district adjoining Samchi and Jasraj remained at Sibsu earning due rewards from the Bhutan agent as an obedient subject. Garajman's grandson, Dal Bahadur (D. B. Gurung), would become president of Bhutan State Congress in 1952 and would continue to file anti-Bhutan or mainly anti-Dorji resolutions passed by the party to the passing dignitaries and the regional Press.

Appasahab Pant, the political officer in Sikkim and Bhutan in a visit to the central district of Chirang in 1958, found it thickly inhabited by the immigrant Nepalese, who were brought under the care of Ugyen Dorji around 1900. He found at least one among the earliest settlers still alive. He was known as Nepal Mandal, 78 years of age, residing at the village Lapse Bhote and who was still going strong. He was "over 6 feet tall, massively built, a specimen of good health and manhood, having over ten children and hundred or so grand-children" (Pant, 1958). Pant came across another first generation immigrant to Bhutan, Dasho Jhulendra Bahadur Pradhan (J. B. Pradhan: 1895–1975), the commissioner of Southern Bhutan at Jaigaog, an officer of the old vintage and (who) knew his job of "keeping the King's peace well". Pradhan's was an unusual story: born in 1895, he managed to get some education at Kalimpong to the extent that the Bhutan contingent to Delhi Durbar hired him as a member in 1911 at the age of 16. Since then, he never looked back, being given some or other administrative charge in the "South" under the Dorjis, which he accomplished with diligence and loyalty. We shall meet him again in 1954, when he had ordered firing at the Bhutan State Congress demonstrators at Sarbhang. It was he, who had to make arrangements for labour, ration and provision during the road construction programme from the Indian borders to the interior in 1960s. Again, when Bhutan decided to colonize the south-eastern most corner of Bhutan, it was Dasho J. B. Pradhan, who commanded the settlers from thickly inhabited Chirang and Dagana districts to Samdruk Jongkhar. After Jigmie Dorji's assassination in 1964, the king had so much faith in him that he was entrusted with the administration of Southern Bhutan as the Commissioner. He had four wives and four families at four different locations, which he would frequent. He had commanded his children to marry among the Dukpas, a prescription, which was followed by one and all of his children. And most prominent among them is that of Om Pradhan, one of the few Lhatshampas, who raised high in official hierarchy in Dukpa administration even during the worst days of anti-Lhotshampa drive. Pradhan senior remained faithful to his king all through his life and breathed his last at the age of 80 with all privileges of the office of the commissioner.

Beginning of democratic stirrings

The Lhotshampas lived rather an isolated and deprived life of their own, as their habitations were not linked to the world outside through any form of transportation and communication. The only occasion they chanced to meet anybody from outside, when they frequented the *haats* (rural markets) across the borders in the adjoining Jalpaiguri or Goalpara districts in India. These markets were play grounds for various political for agitating for independence of India or others representing/demanding for varied political interests. Among such institutions, the All India Gorkha League (AIGL) was one, which had agitated for the cause of the Indian Nepalese. The Gorkha League demanded for creation of a separate political unit in British India known as Uttarakhand as their homeland, with southern Bhutan as one of its constituent units. Unlike other political fora, it is the Gorkha League which canvassed its objectives through the medium of Nepali, and thus it is obvious that Bhutanese visitors from across the borders found it of some interests to them. There was another aspect of the Gorkha League, which attracted the ordinary Nepalese including the Bhutanese Nepalese to it; and that was its leadership consisting of ex-soldiers. Many of them were war veterans, who had fought for the British and were decorated for their bravery in the battlefields. Possibly, the League leaders would end their public address with slogan of 'Jai Gorkha' (victory to the Gorkhas), shouted in chorus by the assembled populace at the end of their public address.

Among the earliest account of political activities on the part of Nepalese in Bhutan was reported from the village Lamidera, Chirang district, central Bhutan. Pashupati Adhikari, the Mandal of the village, protested against the exorbitant rates of the land tax charged from the Nepalese settlers in cash. For that he was beaten up and expelled from Bhutan by the Bhutan Agent, Raja S. T. Dorji, and his property was confiscated by the government. Some of his descendants still lived in the village Jharbari in Kokrajhar sub-division of Goalpara district of Assam in 1950s. Govind Adhikari, a relative of Pashupati, informed Christopher Strawn that the family got back about five acres of land at Chuwa Bari village in Sarbhang district in 1970, when amnesty was granted to the Nepalese dissenters. Further, their ancestral house had already been allotted to some Dukpas (Dhakal and Strawn, 1994: 135, 575). We had noted elsewhere Col Weir, political officer of Sikkim, informing the Government of India in 1929 about increasing the 'Gurkha menace', a population which did not owe allegiance to the Bhutanese king (Sinha, 1991: 171).

By then, Bhutan House at Kalimpong, where the offices of the Bhutan Agent and Assistant Political Officer Ha Thrungpa were located. These offices were manned by first Ugyen, then his son, Sonam Tobgyel (1897–1952), and at last his grandson, Jigmie Palden (1919–64). The Dorjis turned out to be the external eyes of the Bhutan Maharajas from 1907 to 1964 in the absence of a ministry of foreign affairs. As they were the authorities through whom Bhutan Duars were largely settled, they had substantial cash income in old world economy of the country. And it was this family which had the last words in the affairs of Bhutan up to 1960s. However, this idyllic, stable Bhutanese world was disturbed by one Satbir Rai, a claimed activist of the All Indian Gorkha League (AIGL), who came to the Nepali settlements in Bhutan foothills looking for subscription and recruits for the party. It is alleged that he inspired some settlers to agitate for political reforms and even tried to open a branch of the AIGL. Once the Raja came to know of that, he sent a contingent of the Bhutanese militia to the site and malcontents were not only rounded up and but they were also chased away. Their houses were knocked down and properties were confiscated. By this act, the Raja had bought peace for a couple of years, no doubt.

It is alleged that the trouble started in Southern Bhutan either early or towards the middle of 1948, when Satbir Rai entered Bhutan and started enrolling members to the League and he began collecting money for the same party from the Nepali settlers. Raja S. T. Dorji ejected the League leaders, but Satbir and his associates managed to get a foothold in Dagapela and Burgaon in the Chirang district and began working up an anti-government movement among the Nepalese. Raja Dorji sent a body of militia and got several of the agitators arrested from village Emiray. Naturally, most of the leaders of the League left Bhutan as a result and took shelters in neighbouring tea estates in Assam or West Bengal. It appears that the representatives of these 'refugees' approached the Government of Nepal for help through Colonel Daman Shamsher, the Nepalese consul-general in Calcutta. Some of them even reached Major-General Bijaya Shamsher, the director general of the Department of Foreign Affairs, Government of Nepal. The major-general wrote some letters to the political officer in Sikkim, Harishwar Dayal, urging him to look into the grievances of the Gorkha community in Bhutan. The political officer had some informal talks with Raja Dorji, who assured him that the Nepalese, who had left Bhutan in 1948, could return provided they stood trial in Bhutan. The Rana prime minister sent relief funds to 'the affected victims' through his Calcutta-based trade agent, who visited Siliguri, Kalimpong, Darjeeling and Gangtok to meet the victims and the Raja with the request to permit them to return. Calcutta-based Nepalese representative Kaisher Bahadur KC noted how the prime minister's monetary assistance was swindled by unscrupulous alleged refugees. He did contact the political officer in Sikkim against the alleged Bhutanese eviction, who then reached Raja S. T. Dorji, the Bhutan agent in India, for the purpose. The Raja promised to allow them to re-enter Bhutan on the condition that they would stand trial for the "crimes committed by them in the country" (Pant, 1958).

Dhakal and Hutt inform almost universal story ('martyrology') of Mahasur, Masur or Mansur Chhetri in their interviews from the refugee residents of the camps in eastern Nepal. It appears that he was a peon in some office and thus he was exposed to going on at certain level of authority. It is also said that he was possibly "involved in efforts to establish a Bhutanese branch of the All India Gorkha League during the early 1940s" (Hutt, 2003: 116–117). It is claimed that 'Mahasur Chhetri' of village Suntoley (block Lapsibhote, district Chirang) had sought support possibly in 1951 from Matrika Prasad Koirala for organizing a political party in Bhutan in view of the brutal crackdown on the activists of the Jai Gorkha movement. He had also provided some details of ill-treatment of the Bhutanese Nepalese by the officials of the Royal Government of Bhutan to the Nepalese prime minister. Jigmie Palden Dorji, the Ha Drungpa, got him arrested in a wild-goose hunt; held a make belief court; charged him for the treason at his discretion and awarded him death penalty for the alleged crimes. It is believed that he was tied alive in a raw leather bag and thrown into the flooded river Sankos at village Majigoan, block Lamidera, district Chirang.

Birth of Bhutan State Congress

Dhakal informs that Ganesh Prasad Sharma Parsai, who was known to Mahsur; possibly was an accomplish in his anti- Bhutanese efforts and a witness to his execution, felt threatened in Bhutan and decided to cross over to India. Again, there are enough hints that he knew D. B. Gurung, a scion of Dalchand Gurung of Samchi estate residing in Siliguri. D. B. Gurung appeared to be educated, resourceful and willing to plunge in

Bhutan politics. Moreover, he was possibly associated with activities of Jai Gorkha and All India Gorkha League not as a leader, but possibly as a sympathizer and active supporter. Thus, G. P. Sharma's proposal to form a political party found ready acceptance of D. B. Gurung. They consulted other local leaders and after some discussion assembled a Patgaon, district Goalpara, Assam in November 1952 to form a political party of the Bhutanese Nepalese: the Bhutan State Congress (BSC). The meeting chose the following functionaries of the party: D. B. Gurung, president; D. B. Chhetri and Til Bahadur Gurung, vice presidents; Ganesh Prasad Sharma Parsai, general secretary; and Dalmardan Raye, Nandlal Sharma and Dambar Singh Sunuwar as the members of the central co-ordination committee. The Congress was instituted to introduce human rights and democracy in Bhutan and redress the grievances of the Nepali Bhutanese farmers (Dhakal and Strawn, 1994: 136–43, appx. C: 598–601). It is not clear why did they choose Chirang in Bhutan instead of Samchi, the oldest Nepali settlement in Bhutan and D. B. Gurung's ancestral district, across which they held their first formal meeting to establish the Bhutan State Congress. Incidentally, that region would also be the locale from where they would be launching their first and only public agitation for the cause of the Bhutanese immigrants. We learnt that the party chose the Indian National Congress flag with a *dorjie* (a symbolic thunderbolt used as a ritual instrument in the Mahayan Buddhist rites), replacing the spinning wheel of the original Congress flag (Sinha, 1991: 180). It looks some of their leaders travelled to Delhi to meet Congress leaders in general and the prime minister in particular. What resulted out of those meetings is not clear. But possibly they confabulated with the AIGL leaders available around their place in the region and with whom they were more familiar with and added more weighty demands such as political reforms. Leo Rose suggests that political reforms inside Bhutan and closer association of the kingdom with India were extension to the original agenda (Rose, 1977: 110). Among such demands two may possibly be added: abolition of zamindari (they failed to inform what type of zamindari Bhutan had). It was possibly a carbon copy of Sikkim State Congress demands and their frequent appeal to the Indian political leaders to intervene in their favour without realizing the external implications of it.

Hutt rightly records the atmosphere prevailing on the eve of the formation of the Bhutan State Congress:

> The impression one gains as one attempts to form a picture of the period is that a small number of relatively educated Lhotshampas moved out of Bhutan around the time of Indian

> independence, in believe that the Indian Congress government would support their political agenda and come to their aid.
> (Hutt, 2003: 121)

Delhi advised them to resort to peaceful civil disobedience (satyagraha) and broaden their political and organizational base, possibly inside Bhutan, which was never tried for obvious reasons. As the situation in newly independent India was shaping up, Bhutan State Congress leaders appealed for membership enrolment to everybody: Bhutanese, Indians, Nepalese and Sikkimese. But by and large, they got ready response from among the regionally floating population of Nepalese, as it had happened earlier in case of the Sikkim State Congress. It appears that the impatient Bhutan State Congress leadership did not properly understand and analyse the outcome of the populist movements launched by the Sikkim State Congress in Sikkim and the Nepali Congress in Nepal and failed to draw lessons from them before launching their movement. In their efforts to launch a mass movement for redress of various obnoxious exploitative practices in Bhutan, they got inspired by agrarian movements in Sikkim and Nepal. But they forgot to take a note of the Bhutanese reality of non-availability of effective surface transportation and media communication, as there were no roads and no wheel transportation even for the royalty, and there were no newspapers – not even state gazettes to keep the significant state decisions on record.

Civil disobedience by the Bhutan State Congress

It looks they were more than eager to launch a satyagraha in Bhutan in spite of the fact that their petitions were either ignored or they did not reach the power to be. It is a fact that the leadership of the Bhutan State Congress never reached the main power centres of Bhutan: the king or the Bhutan agent. However, determined in their resolve to launch the Satyagraha, they got in touch with the Gorkha League in Darjeeling and Secretary General Parsai travelled to Nepal to solicit the support of the Nepali Congress. It is not clear whether they solicited support from any Indian political party in power or in opposition active in their neighbourhood in the Indian provinces. Similarly, there is no evidence whether they had contacted leadership of the Sikkim State Congress for that matter. It is reported that the Nepali Congress did depute the young firebrand labour leader, Girija Prasad Koirala, and an active and experienced leader, Pasang Sherpa, from among its ranks. Perhaps assured of ethnic support from the Gorkha league and Nepali Congress at hand, the Bhutan State Congress leadership went ahead with their Satyagraha and 'jail *bharo andolan*' (fill the Jails movement) in imitation to Indian National Congress in spite of the fact Bhutan neither had the police force nor the jails as institutions known elsewhere. The Satyagrahis or civil disobedience volunteers in a body assemble at Bilasipara in Goalpara district in Assam and marched to Sarbhang gate (in south-central Bhutan) to offer their civil disobedience in Bhutan. Buddhist Pasang Sherpas was purposely selected to hand over the charter of demands to the "Sarkar" (the government) or its appropriate authorities, in case somebody comes forward to meet the body of the volunteers, an eventuality, which never arose. However, there was no mention of another high-profile Nepalese participant, Girija Prasad Koirala, if he participated in the movement, what was his role? We are also informed that with a view to maintaining the tempo of the movement, the Bhutan Congress volunteers were to be sent to front in a body of a hundred, one after another, but that situation never arose. Out of inexperience or nervousness, the highest authority on the spot, Dasho J. B. Pradhan, the Commissioner of the Southern Bhutan, ordered to open fire. Dhakal informs that "when the shooting was over, 25 (persons) lay dead and 17 wounded. Several protesters were also caught and imprisoned, including Pasang Sherpa" (Dhakal and Strawn, 1994: 140).

The jailed protesters were reportedly not being treated well to the extent that they were denied adequate food and medicine. They kept on chanting anti-J. B. Pradhan slogans and shouting for long life of the king (J. B. Pradhan: Murbabad: Down with J. B. Pradhan; 5 sarkar zindabad: Long live Druk gyalpo). Again one has to learn from D.N.S. Dhakal as to what happened next:

> Pasang Sherpa was kept with other protester in prison for 21 days. On the 21st day, King Jigme Dorji (or Wangchuk?) came to the prison. First he asked Sherpa why he had marched in the protest and admonished him for disturbing peace in the country. The King called a meeting in the nearby villagers and asked the people present: "What problem do you have (with us in Bhutan)? These people come from Nepal and claim that you have problems". Facing the silent crowd, Sherpa felt betrayed and humiliated. The King then ordered separation of the Bhutanese citizens from other. Dalmardan Raye, who was a resident of Chirang, was given life imprisonment. But those from India or Nepal, including Pasnag Sherpa, were set free at the border, and (Pasnag) Sherpa retuned to Nepal.
>
> (Dhakal and Strawn, 1994: 140)

Bhutan Agent Jigmie Dorji took up the issue of the Bhutan State Congress launching its movement from the Indian Territory with the Government of India through the political officer, Gangtok. He drew the attention of the Government of India that Indian agitators including the Congress men along with the Gorkha League and a number of Nepalese political activists had instigated the Bhutanese 'Nepalese' for the 'trouble'. Mr Dorji especially referred to the use of the Indian Territory for anti-Bhutan agitation, in which the Nepalese were permitted to connive with the agitators. The Government of India instructed the concerned administration to forbid such as activities in its territory. Not only that, Prime Minister Nehru also wrote on March 23, 1954, to Mr Matrika Prasad Koirala, the prime minister of Nepal, on the issue and drew his attention towards undesirability of such a move. In his own words:

> A number of Nepali organizations are organizing Satyagraha in Bhutan. They have made their base in Indian Territory. I have just received news that there was conflict between them and presumably Bhutan troops. This is exceedingly embarrassing to us as it must be to your Government. Bhutan is your neighbour(ing) country and you would, no doubt, like to have friendly relations with Bhutan. I am aware that there are difficulties in Bhutan for Nepali residents there and the policy of the Bhutan Government has not been very favourable to the Nepalese. I would welcome progress in Bhutan in various ways. But we cannot encourage Indian Territory to be made the base of operations. I am sure that your Government also cannot approve of this method. Governments do not function in this way. I hope, therefore, that you will discourage, in so far as you can, these aggressive activities. I know that many people who are indulging in them are probably not amenable to your influence and represent your opposition groups (a hint to M. P. Koirala's, step brothers, especially Girija Prasad and Bishweshwar Prasad of Nepali Congress). Nevertheless, it seems important to me that your government should take up a clear attitude in this matter.
>
> (Koirala, 2008: 286)

That was the highest landmark of political activities of the Bhutan State Congress, though the party did try to launch some mild agitations at different places on the borders, but with no success. Having no active agenda, inactive cadre of the party outside Bhutan were lost to the organization; the leaders began bickering among themselves and President D. B. Gurung kept on the BSC flag fluttering for years by issuing handbills informing the visiting political dignitaries and journalists to the region. We are in possession of a copy of the proceedings of the meeting of the Central Committee of the Bhutan State Congress, which contains five resolutions passed on August 27, 1965 under the president ship of Sri D. B. Gurung. First resolution takes a serious view of attempt on life of His Majesty the King of Bhutan and expresses its unflinching loyalty to him and the second one expresses its sense of relief that the His Majesty escaped unhurt. The third one is an interesting resolution, which possibly drawing inspiration from King Mahendra's introduction of Panchayati Raj in Nepal, pleads for introduction of the *panchayati* system in Bhutan and extends support of the Party provided H. M. extends recognition to it. Last two resolutions of the proceedings were on practice of *jharlangay* or forced labour in Bhutan and condemning Pakistan for aggressive design on India (Bhutan State Congress: Proceedings of the Central Committee, August 27, 1965: Siliguri). At last, the Druk-Gyapo helped the surviving leadership to bury the once alive Bhutan State Congress in 1969, when a general amnesty was announced. Gurung, Chhetri and Sunuwar accepted the offer of amnesty returned to Bhutan and were rehabilitated and they formally closed the office of the Bhutan State Congress for good.

Factors behind the failure of the Bhutan State Congress

The 15-year life of the Bhutan State Congress remains a sad saga of premature political experiment in the eastern Himalayan political landscape of the mid-20th century (Sinha, 1991 (1998), 2001), which requires to be retold below. First, Bhutan was ruled in the 1950s on the pattern of feudal despotism, in which civil and political rights were simply not recognized and unheard of, as the kingdom had subjects who were not treated as citizens. Moreover, Nepalese settlers' status in Bhutan was not clear: how Bhutanese were they? Second, in the absence of an effective medium of transportation and communication such as roads, wheeled transport, newspapers, radio and so forth and prevalence of universal illiteracy, it was an uphill task to educate the masses politically. Third, neither did the Bhutan State Congress extend its activities among the Dukpas, nor did the latter recognize the former as their organization. Consequently, the Bhutan State Congress remained an out-and-out Lhotshampas' party on the southern fringe of Bhutan. As the Dukpas were reluctant to accord a national status to the immigrants, it was not considered respectable to be associated with the real or imaginary cause of an irritant population. Fourth, it appears that even the Lhotshampas did not identify themselves with the cause of the Congress at large. It was mainly because of their threatened and insecure existence in Bhutan and internal social division among them. Furthermore, there were individuals like Neoli Babu or Jeet Bahadur Pradhan, Commissioner of Southern Bhutan, who was more than committed to the cause of Wangchuk ruler. Fifth, though Congress demands were vague, but whatever the party demanded such as abolition of zamindari or introduction of civil rights fall flat on the Bhutanese at large. However, in words of Leo Rose, they were simply strange ideas to the Bhutanese: "it was not that most of Bhutanese were resistant to modern political concepts; they had never heard of them" (Rose, 1977: 109). Furthermore, on the confused intents of the Bhutan State Congress, look at Damber Singh Sunuwar's answer to question on demands of the BSC, the last surviving founder member of the Bhutan State Congress on December 9, 1999, at Kundanbari refugee camp in Nepal: "We just said (demanded?) there was nothing in Bhutan. There should be weekly markets, there should be offices (regular administration in the region), there should be television".

Television (in 1954)? (interviewer's query remained unanswered).

> Papers should go all around to other countries, there should be a postal service, there should be roads, there should be irrigation schemes, there should be Pathshalas, there should be some development of education.
>
> (Hutt, 2003: 124)

Sixth, the Congress committed a blunder by soliciting support from and identifying itself with the Indian National Congress (INC) and the Nepali Congress, which were considered disruptive by the Bhutanese in terms of their national interests. Moreover, they were already suspect of being in league with All India Gorkha League, a political forum, supported by the Ranas from Nepal. Seventh, the Government of India under INC was itself not sure how much control it could have on Bhutan in early 1950s. Same was the case of the Nepali Congress led the Royal Government of Nepal, which did not have a clear vision as to its relations with the Lhotshampas or the Sikkimese Nepalese. Thus, attitudes of the Indian National Congress and the Nepali Congress to the Bhutan State Congress were ambivalent to say the least. However, the Indian government was interested in stability of Bhutan, which was realized in continuation of the Wangchuk rule.

Furthermore, the Bhutan State Congress' hobnobbing with a suspect forum such as All India Gorkha League was a danger signal to the Government of India. Lastly, Bhutan was making all possible efforts to express and guard its autonomy distinct from India as a strategy to claim full sovereignty in near future. The efforts made by the Bhutan State Congress were contrary to the above Bhutanese policy and thus, the Bhutanese establishment was opposed to all moves of the Bhutan State Congress and suppressed its activities by tooth and nail.

On the positive side of the Bhutan State Congress, one may venture that it made the Bhutanese strategic elite to think afresh in the second half of 1950s on the issue of presence of the Nepalese in Bhutan. Naturally, the stage of development of the Bhutanese kingdom required an inexpensive, hard-working, cash-generating Nepalese labour force at the time. Ignoring them completely was easier but perhaps more dangerous than finding a way to accommodate them in the system legally. Thus, the Drukyul passed the National Law of Bhutan (1958) with the provision to award citizenship to those of the Nepalese born in Bhutan, residing in the country for more than 10 years and even the foreign-born wives of the citizens could be naturalized as citizen. Benefits of the provision were soon forthcoming, as the Nepalese provided much needed labour, once Bhutan decided to open its doors southwards by establishing regular administrative structure, constructing all weather roads and social infrastructures like health centres and primary schools. This led to a phase of honeymoon period between Dukpa administration and Lhotshampas for the next three decades, when the Bhutan followed an active policy of incorporating the Lhotshampas in the national fold and even tried to absorb them in the national social system through the provision of inter-ethnic marriages (Sinha, 1991). What went wrong with that policy in 1980s is an issue beyond the scope of the present exercise.

It appears that neither the Bhutan State Congress nor the Kingdom of Bhutan was ready for political party-based politics in 1950s. It was a premature demand made by the naive activists of the Bhutan Congress. The socio-political conditions of the kingdom were so theocratic and archaically feudal that public participation in the affairs of the state was simply an impossible and implausible preposition in 1950s. The leadership of the Bhutan State Congress failed to reach the king, or the most important state functionary next to the king, the Bhutan agent and the royal brother-in-law, Jigmie Dorji, in person with their charter of demands. Instead of being innovative in their style of functioning, the leadership of the party appeared to be imitative in nature in terms of their programmes and style of agitation for their achievement. They launched a civil disobedience movement in Bhutan and kept on running to Delhi for seeking advice and support from the Indian leadership in imitation to the Sikkim State Congress, forgetting the fact that Sikkim and Bhutan were at two different footings as far as New Delhi was concerned and the stages of development in the two principalities were so dissimilar. In Bhutan, where there was dynastic rule on feudal pattern free from institutionalized administration, the very talk of 'popular government' was preposterous. Similarly, one wonders the far sightedness of the leadership of the Bhutan State Congress in keeping themselves away from the dominant Dukpa population completely from their reformist political agenda and lack of their efforts to extend their activities inside Bhutan among the Dukpas in spite of the difficulties. Neither there is evidence that BSC had a Dukpa as its member, nor had it ever operated from inside Bhutan. After all, it is they who had decided to launch the movement for reforming political system in Bhutan and any reform without the support from the Dukpas in Bhutan was doomed to be a failure. In this way, seeds of failures of the Bhutan State Congress were sown right in its inception and it was certainly a premature political exercise in waging the democratic struggle in the politically barren soil of Bhutan in the eastern Himalayas.

Apparently, the Bhutan State Congress was under the strong influence of Darjeeling-based All Indian Gorkha League, which was a suspect organization so far the authorities in India, Sikkim and Bhutan were concerned. The regional leadership of various Nepalese political fora did encourage the Bhutanese dissenters to launch a political party and the Lhotshampas did so on the imitation of Sikkim State Congress. But when their civil disobedience movement failed, none of them were in a position to show the light and guide them to even survive organizationally. Similarly, it was intriguing that there was participation of the Nepali Congress in the civil disobedience in 1954 side by side with the Bhutan State Congress, but their support appears to have vanished in the thin air, when that movement failed miserably. The Nepalese leadership would similarly support the Lhotshampa dissenters initially in 1990s in their struggles against the Dukpa atrocities and even accommodate them in refugee camps in eastern Nepal, but leave them to fend for themselves once the Bhutanese establishment stoutly refused to readmit the Lhotshampas back to Bhutan. Moral of the story is clear: Lhotshampas looked westwards to their ethnic fraternity right from 1950s for instant support in their hours of needs instead of relying on themselves, only to repent.

Bibliography

Aris, M., 1979, *Bhutan: The Early History of a Himalayan Kingdom*, Vikas Publishing House, New Delhi.

Bhutan State Congress, 1965, *Proceedings of the Minutes of the Central Committee of Bhutan State Congress*, held on August 27th 1965, Kamal Kutir, Sevak Road, Siliguri.

Dhakal, D.N.S. and C. Strawn, 1994, *Bhutan: A Movement in Exile*, Nirala, Jaipur.

Galbraith, J. K., 1969, *Ambassador's Journal: A Personal Account of the Kennedy Years*, New American Library, New York.

Hutt, M., 2003, *Unbecoming Citizens: Culture, Nationhood, and the Flight of Refugees From Bhutan*, Oxford University Press, New Delhi.

Koirala, M. P., 2008, *M P Koirala: A Role in Revolution*, Jagdamba Prakashan, Lalitpur, Nepal.

Morris, C. J., 1934, "A Report on Gurkha Immigration in Bhutan" in A. C. Sinha, 2001, pp. 144–61.

Pant, A. B., 1958, *Southern Bhutan, Tour Notes of Apa B Pant, February–March, 1958, Secret, Private Papers of Baleshwar Prasad*, Nehru Memorial Museum and Library, Teen Murti House, New Delhi.

Patterson, G. N., 1963, *Peking Versus Delhi*, Faber & Faber, London.

Prasad, B., *Private Paper*, Nehru Memorial Museum and Library, Teen Muti House, New Delhi, Sub File No. 16.

Rose, L. E., 1977, *The Politics of Bhutan*, Cornell University Press, Ithaca and London.

Sinha, A. C., 1991, *Bhutan: Ethnic Identity and National Dilemma*, Reliance Publishing House, New Delhi. Second edition 1998.

Sinha, A. C., 2001, *Himalayan Kingdom Bhutan: Tradition, Transition and Transformation*, Indus, New Delhi.

White, J. C., 1972, *Sikkim and Bhutan: Twenty-One Years in North-East Frontiers*, Vivek Publishing House, New Delhi.

8

DEMOCRATIC EXPERIMENTS AND REASSERTION OF THE FEUDAL ORDER

The dawn and fall of the democratic movements in the eastern Himalayan kingdoms within an eventful span of less than two decades were significant developments for the region. These setbacks to the cause of democracy continue to haunt the travail of participative democracy in the eastern Himalayan states, and it will be worthwhile to examine the fault lines and draw appropriate lessons for the future. In the final analysis, the dawn and fall of the democratic movement in the eastern Himalayas was almost entirely a Nepalese affair. It was they who had initiated it for themselves and others; it was they who led it and had suffered for that; and again it was they who failed to deliver on the promises they had made to themselves. The failure of the democratic movements in three Himalayan kingdoms in 1950s led to the emergence of the three kings much stronger than before in the second half, rather in the third quarter of the 20th century and the democratic parties had to wait for decades thereafter for their turn to come up. This wait was shortest in case of Sikkim, which had to wait for about two decades for arrival of democratic dispensation. In case of Nepal, it took three decades from 1960 to 1990 and in case of Bhutan, it was the longest wait even for a limited and skewed democracy – it was almost six decades. And that too, was after exclusion of vocal and articulate Lhotshampas, the Nepalese elements from among the Bhutanese.

It will be worthwhile to understand the salient features of the eastern Himalayan principalities prior to the democratic movements, which browbeat them and lessons to be learnt from the failure of the movement almost entirely initiated and executed by the Nepalese commonwealth. We hasten to add that Darjeeling happened to be the nursery for incubation of political leadership of populist movements in the three principalities. And it is also a fact that their most of the successful adversaries were also educated in more than one sense in Darjeeling:

Palden Thondup Namgyal, Jigmie Dorji/Jigmi Wangchuk, ultimately, King Birendra and the last, Gyanendra.

Objective conditions in the principalities under the shadow of the empire

The principalities, by and large, were British creation in the sense that if the British colonial power had decided to take them over as parts of the British Indian empire, they would have done so easily, as they did in case of Nainital, Almora, Shimla and Darjeeling. But they did not do so simply because of the fact that their security interests were taken care of by these principalities at no cost to the British. The British did not have any investment to make to develop those topographically difficult terrains. It goes without saying that the British had created the three eastern Himalayan principalities as the units of the internal buffer states on the northern border of the British Indian empire and the rulers were happy to play the role of the pliant collaborators to the British design. More than once, they were paraded in Delhi Dubar like any other rulers of the Indian princely households. So much so that Sikkim and Bhutan requested Political Officer Basil Gould to reach the king emperor on their behalf to maintain their relations with the British as before even after the British departure from her Indian empire. Gould informed them that was not possible and advised them to reach Delhi with their memorandum of expectations to meet the Cabinet Mission, sent by the British government. And the British had assured them of their continued support even after their departure from India and they proved true to their promise till last as they had left an advisory note to the successor Indian Union to maintain status quo in the region on August 10, 1946, which we noted earlier.

The principalities were closed, repressive and autocratic social systems run by the Kazis in Sikkim, Ranas in Nepal and monastic cum feudal lords of Bhutan, lorded over by the British resident and political officer. It was a fact that the feudal system was so contrived that the "sovereign rulers" role in administration was invisible and actual decisions were usurped by others, the feudal landed gentry, at the cost of the rulers. Thus, there was an absence of accountability in the administration. While feudal chiefs such as the Kazis, Ranas and Dorjis were naturally reluctant to surrender their privileges, the rulers were also opposed to sharing power with commoners and unwilling to incorporate even sincere, honest and efficient commoners in bureaucracy to run administration with the changing time.

It is the fact that the Nepalese literati, ex-Gurkha soldiers, disinherited Ranas, students and political activists were the first to become politicized and make demands for reforms to be introduced in the administrative systems. In this context, role played by the activists of the AIGL cannot be wished away. It goes without saying that subsequently the ethnic Nepalese were in the forefront to organize an invigorated AIGL, SSC, NC and BSC. And naturally, it was they who were more articulate in the matters of organizing public fora. The role of the Nepali Congress leadership, especially Bishweshwar Prasad and Girija Prasad Koiralas, in attending sessions of democratic movements in Nepal, Sikkim and Bhutan as pan-Nepalese democratic leaders across the political boundaries have been noted above. Was their reach-out to Sikkim and Bhutan a casual expediency or was it under a thought-out strategy to explore possibilities of pan-Nepalese solidarity?

Similarly, role of the INA (Indian National Army under late Subhash Chandra Bose during the Second World War) or the ex-soldiers of the British Indian army in Mukti-Bahini was equally salutary. However, the political parties had weak social base and thus, political socialization of the masses was a major problem among all the political parties in the principalities. They could collect the crowd of the deprived, suppressed and agitated peasantry, but they failed to politically educate them for concerted actions, as many a time these new leaders were drawn from the same landed gentry: L. D. Kazi, Kashiraj Pradhan, the Koiralas and D. B. Gurung for illustration. The political leadership was invariably vulnerable to financial mismanagement, as they had no experience of handling public fund. There were innumerable instances, when the political parties became factionalized in hours of their glory and/or crisis, as every politically ambitious person desired to be the leader without much experience of public organization. Similarly, charges of financial misappropriations were numerous. Once the feudal ruling class manoeuvred the political parties out of power, it was easy for them to enlist socially ambitious, politically ill-trained and financially vulnerable elements from the political parties to incorporate in administration run by the same discredited feudal element, as it happened in Sikkim and Nepal.

Ideological moorings and organizational base of the parties

It appears that the political parties in these kingdoms were organized as an instrument to solve certain problems created by the feudal dispensation. In this way, these organizations were reacting to the then prevailing situations in these princely states. We have shown above that the founding leadership of the parties were subjected to maltreatment at the hands of the feudal dispensation. Indian independence turned out to be an instant reference point for the deprived masses of the principalities to seize upon. It is pertinent to note that leadership of the Sikkim State Congress deserves credit to organize their first meeting for founding the SSC in the heart of the state capital, Gangtok, in an open public gathering. This stands favourably when we note that Nepali Congress was organized in Calcutta far away from Nepal and Bhutan State Congress was similarly founded in a rural ambience outside Bhutan in Assam. All three political fora with the possible exception of Nepali Congress, which occasionally did refer to socialism, did not have any abstract ideology to bind the cadre and which could give them a vision to the future. Another point worth noting is the fact that none of the parties took the Indian National Congress, the ruling party in independent India, in confidence about their programme of actions, but they expected the latter to rescue them, when they ran in problems with the rulers. We find them sending their delegations to New Delhi with their charter of demands once they had launched their movements and expected instant support for their cause. Interestingly, with exception of Nepali Congress to some extent, they had little contact with the leaders of the Indian National Congress from the neighbouring states, who had ears to New Delhi leadership and would have been an asset on time of crisis.

Another significant point is that of their failure to make a distinction between crowd/mob and the organized cadre/membership of the organization. This becomes clear as most of the leaders had no experience of politically organized institutions with the possible exception of Nepali Congress. It was natural for them as they were drawn from armed forces or feudal background. The leaders such as Subarn Shamshere, Mahabir Shamshere, M. P., B. P., and G. P. Koirala, Kashiraj Pradhan, L. D. Kazi, D. B. Gurung and many others took advantage of the democratic upsurge and appeared to be mass leaders, but in the heart of hearts, they did not stand for Madhesis in Nepal and Deswalis in Sikkim. Thus, it is not surprising that, though his massive support base was derived from the Nepal Terai, but even an avowedly socialist leader such as B. P. Koirala identified Nepal with its Bahun-Chhetri-Newar core at the cost of Madhesis and that became his undoing. The popular support base he had all along in Nepal, he mistook it as a blank cheque in his favour in all the eventualities. Thus, the traditional feudal base of Nepal found it convenient to prefer King Mahendra to a doubtful claimant such as B. P. Koirala. Had he introduced land reforms in the country and identified himself with cause of the suppressed toiling masses instead of burnishing his image at international fora, the story of Nepal possibly would have been a different flavour today.

It is a fact that the Indian freedom struggle in general, and the Indian National Congress, the All India Gorkha League, the Communist Party of India and the Congress Socialist Party in particular worked as the reference points and inspiration for these eastern Himalayan communities for getting themselves organized politically. It may be noted that these Indian political parties played significant roles in the political movements in these principalities in pre-1950 phase in a haphazard way. But soon after that, there appears to be an end of former informality in the matters of party politics of the principalities on the part of the Indian National Congress. The most frustrating role was that of the Darjeeling-based Gorkha League. Once their demand for creation of Darjeeling as a state in the Indian Union was turned down, they appeared on the scene as the mercenaries instead of working hard among the people, as many of the worthy functionaries of the AIGL were enrolled as the foot soldiers of King Mahendra in his anti-India and anti-Nepali Congress snippets disturbing the age-old order of the region (Sinha, 2014). In this context, we are reminded of the advisory note left behind by the British administration on August 10, 1946, to the successor Indian state and the regional principalities, which may throw some light to uncover the ambiguity, which was in the knowledge of the rulers of three principalities and the Indian Union, but possibly unknown to the populist leaders of the principalities.

Reassertion of the crumbling feudal order

We have noted how successfully had the Sikkim State Congress and the Nepali Congress been in their democratic struggles against the feudal oppression in their respective states by 1950. Incidentally, rulers of both principalities, Sikkim and Nepal, took shelter under the Indian dispensation: with the political officer in Gangtok and the other with that of the Indian ambassador in Kathmandu. And New Delhi did help them to re-establishment against their own subjects, who had waged anti-feudal war through popular upsurge against the aristocratic autocracy. Why did such developments take place? What were the compulsive reasons to bolster the already uprooted 'rulers' against the struggling multitude? There must be some plausible explanation for that.

India had not turned anti-democratic all of a sudden; she must have her own understanding of the geopolitics of region in the changing world. It so happened that by then, two significant developments had taken place in the neighbourhood of these principalities, which forced the Indian establishment to think afresh on their policy vis-à-vis the eastern Himalayan region. And they were: first, the Communist takeover of China on October 1, 1949, with an aggressive propaganda that they would follow an expansionist policy around (to liberate various Himalayan principalities); and second, their impending threat to 'liberate Tibet', a serious design affecting the Himalayan region, where India had her vital interests at stake. George Patterson (1963) notes in this context:

> A written ultimatum was delivered to the Kham leader, Topgyay Pangdatsh, in January 1950, by the Batang magistrate, who rode into the (eastern Tibetan Kham) mountains personally to deliver it. It stated Communist China's intentions of taking over whole of Tibet, and after that, Nepal, Sikkim and Bhutan, and the necessity for the Kham Tibetans to co-operate in this or be annihilated. The Kham leaders made attempts to get help from Lhasa (theoretically under His Holiness the Dalai Lama, who was a minor young boy of about 15 years at the time) and outside powers, India, Britain and USA, in March 1950, to fight against the Chinese, but this was refused.

A new China from Siberia to Indo-China and from the Pacific to the Pamir had come into being with the Communist takeover, which had a vision of a strong and centralized government and a mission to reclaim its imagined land from the alleged usurpers. And there was another factor of the Western propaganda that the democratic movement launched by the political parties in the principalities were at the instance of the New Delhi with a view to merging them in India, which was far from true (Koirala, 2001).

In this way, the contents in the British imperial note of August 10, 1946, to the successor Indian Union possibly began haunting the New Delhi, which was itself fighting a war of aggression on its northwestern frontiers in Jammu and Kashmir with Pakistan. Moreover, many of the recalcitrant princely states like Hyderabad, Travancore-Cochin, Junagarh and others were yet to be integrated in the Indian Union. India, unlike Communist China, had promised itself to be a democratic federal political system, for which it was busy in drafting a constitution. It was not only that, but India had also inherited a war ravaged and divided country with disrupted communication network. Unlike the battle-hardened communist leadership of China,

Indian leadership, especially Prime Minister Nehru, was liberal, humane and an idealistic consensus builder. It perhaps appeared to the Indian leadership that the eastern Himalayan region was relatively much less problematic at the time, that is the early 1950s. Thus, perhaps it was convenient to the Indian leadership to be guided by their British trained bureaucrats to maintain the status quo in the eastern Himalayan region to a great extent. In this way, it seems the old feudal elements were preferred as lesser evil than the untested leaders of the populist democratic movements. Thus, the Government of India signed standstill treaties with all three princely states and bound them in relationship with new friendship treaties on the same old British imperial lines by 1950. One of the cardinal points of these treaties had been the promise of non-interference by the Indian Union in the internal administration of the eastern Himalayan feudatories, a concession, prized by the rulers of the principalities as something like a precursor to their sovereignty. The provision of non-intervention in the internal matter of the principalities was used on occasions by the rulers in their favour against their own people, at times to deny their rightful due.

Perhaps those were the considerations on which the democratic Indian government acted something like a mediating broker between the crown prince of Sikkim and the Sikkim State Congress instead of playing a partisan role in support of the democratic movement. And that is how the controversial 'understanding' on the notorious 'parity system' was arrived in 1953, a concession from the recalcitrant Maharaj Kumar for agreeing to accept immigrant Nepalese in Sikkim as his subjects. And similarly Pandit Nehru did the same between King Tribhuwan, the Ranas and the Nepali Congress, still engaged in armed insurrection in Nepal Terai, in 1951 by hammering out the controversial Delhi Agreement. And that paved the way for formation of a joint government headed by Rana Mohan Shamsher and the Nepali Congress much against wishes of the party cadre of Nepali Congress still fighting on the battle front.

In the process, while the democratic Nepali Congress got derailed from its avowed 'liberation struggle', the king, who was a prisoner in his palace, emerged as the most important institution in Nepal with help of the discredited elements from the notorious Rana stock. Of course, we have noted above another reason for the Indian consideration to take steps in its interest. It was the connivance between unpredictable crown prince of Sikkim, his cousin from Bhutan, Jigmie Dorji, the Bhutanese prime minister and the Druk-Gyalpo's brother-in-law, and a significant Tibetan functionary, their uncle, to confabulate on a possible creation of the Himalayan federation of Tibet, Sikkim and Bhutan. Incidentally, King Mahendra would seriously toy with the idea of a revised blueprint of a potential federation of the Himalayan kingdoms consisting of Nepal, Sikkim and Bhutan in 1960s with a view to embarrassing the Indian Union during its hours of crisis, to which even socialist B. P. Koirala would subscribe (Sinha, 2014) in the 1960s, possibly unwittingly. All these antiques led to the retarded growth of democratic movement in the eastern Himalayan region from which it has yet to recover completely.

Some significant issues still to be sorted out

Our study is mainly based on secondary data, and we have tried to uncover the common threads among the three democratic parties and their movements. At the end of the day, the geographically smallest among them, Sikkim, lost its existence at the cost of the Sikkim Congress (a successor to the Sikkim State Congress) by merging into the Indian Union in 1975; Nepal saw the ascendency of a more ruthless monarchy for three decades to come only to register demise of dynastic rule within five decades of King Mahendra's takeover in 1960. At the end, politically isolated archaic Bhutan emerged as a much stable and stronger monarchy at the cost of the democratic movement launched by their politically immature Nepalese immigrants, the Lhotshampas of Bhutan. These complex developments deserve in-depth analysis and better understanding of the political processes in these former kingdoms and we hope the scholars will take up the challenge. And for that purpose we pose some issues to be probed further:

As there was an open border between the three principalities and the Indian Union, what type of communication, if any, did they receive from the Indian National Congress and Indian democratic movements for their organization, programmes, movements and resolutions of their claimed objectives?

How innovative were the above three political fora in their style of functioning? Did they adopt/modify or reject the easily available model of the Indian National Congress of mass agitation for their purpose? Why did the Indian National Congress, which appeared to have inspired the three political parties in early 1940s, did not support the democratic cause and movements after 1950, when it was the ruling party in the Indian Union?

Why did the functionaries of the Nepali Congress, who had reached their eastern brethren during their struggles initially, could not sustain their momentum of support in 1950s, when they were much better off in Nepal and such a support was urgently needed for their guidance/sustenance in the case of the Sikkim State Congress and the Bhutan State Congress? In other words, was the Nepalese leaders' reach-out to Sikkim and Bhutan a casual expediency or a considered strategy for the betterment of the toiling Nepalese immigrants? Or was it simply out of curiosity that went to the eastern extension of the Nepalese over-reach?

Is it possible for the deprived and toiling Nepalese social and cultural commonwealth in the former Himalayan principalities to come together to initiate/launch a coordinated democratic movement in the region for the betterment of their lot in near future?

We have noted how intellectual input came from to the Nepali-speaking social commonwealth from the traditional intellectual base in India, Banaras. The early scholars tried to model their creativity on the pattern available as per Indian standards. Second, Darjeeling emerged as the centre of the Nepalese renaissance, initiated by a new class of pioneering Nepalese professionals. They created standards for modern Nepali language, literature and indirectly inspired social reforms, which was being done in other parts of India. Third, the role of Darjeeling in general and Indian Nepalis or Indian expatriates in particular in moulding the much larger mother country of Nepal in every walk of life was simply immeasurable. They did not only provide much required intellectual input, but also the trained and duly qualified personnel to man the positions in course of time. Fourth, there has always been a very thin line to separate among the Nepalese from the Sikkimese, Bhutanese and Indian speakers of the Nepali language. The existence of open borders even after Indian independence has further facilitated the opaque existence of Nepalese nationality in the eastern Himalayas. And lastly, we have noted how Nepalese, Sikkimese, Bhutanese and Indians collectively worked on anti-feudal anachronism in late 1940s and in early 1950s and played decisive roles in the destiny of the three Himalayan principalities. Incidentally, Nepalese ethnic expansion beyond Nepal in the eastern Himalayan foothills also facilitated a move on the part of some wildly imaginative operators, who dreamt of creating a 'Federation of the Himalayan Kingdoms' – a sterile proposition in the past.

From dawn to downfall of the democratic parties and their valuation

We shall end this chapter with an evaluation of the Nepalese potential by one of its all-time political icons: Bishweshwar Prasad Koirala. In his assessment, the Nepalese will leave India and other nations far behind, both economically and politically, provided they get an opportunity. It was because of the fact that they were very receptive to new ideas and not bound by the traditions. In his own words to Bhola Chatterji, an Indian academic and a socialist comrade in arms to B. P.:

> I will tell you why our traditional roots are not very deep. We have only one community that is deeply tradition-bound, Newar. They are not so eagerly receptive to change and they are comparatively immobile. But the Paharis, they are very mobile, they are very adaptable people. Second, and fortunately, there are a large number of men who are with an army background. One who has been in the army is always exposed to new ideas. Besides, he also acquires certain social qualities, discipline, aptitude to work and a collective attitude. These are some of the qualities that are certainly of inestimable value in building up a nation. We can build up very strong democratic institutions in and (that we may accomplish that) very fast too.
>
> (Chatterji, 1980: 115)

B. P. Koirala's optimism for his country remains a pipe dream even decades after his demise. But his adversary, King Mahendra, took steps to cash in on the presence of a politically conscious Nepali speaking population in the eastern Himalayan region. Prominent among them to his antiques, was the role played by certain elements from among the most strategically located Darjeeling district. And for that, the ambitious and scheming monarch tried hard to build on, where populist politicians such as Kashiraj Pradhan of Sikkim, B. P. Koirala in Nepal and D. B. Gurung of Bhutan had left the scene wide open by the end of the 1950s. And King Mahendra tried to achieve what B. P. prophesied after the dramatic takeover of the administration by imprisoning his charismatic and duly elected prime minister. As he did not believe in reigning, but ruling over his kingdom, he decided to widen the scope of his operation by involving operatives from other two kingdoms in a clandestine way on his eastern frontiers. But unfortunately for him, nothing worked in his way not for lack of trying, but in spite of hard sale of the idea, because nothing will happen in the Himalayan region at the cost of either India or China. And neither had any interest in such efforts of impossibility by disturbing the status quo.

Bibliography

Chatterji, B., 1980, *Palace, People and Politics: Nepal in Perspective*, Ankur Publishing House, New Delhi.

Koirala, B. P., 2001, *Atmbritanta* (in Nepali: Late Life Reflections), translated by K. M. Dixit, Himal Books, Lalitpur, Nepal.

Patterson, G. N., 1963, *Peking Versus Delhi*, Faber & Faber, London.

Sinha, A. C., 2014, *State Formation and the Issues of the Greater Nepal in the Eastern Himalayan Kingdoms National Fellowship Report*, Nehru Memorial Museum and Library, Teen Murti House, New Delhi, MSS.

INDEX

NAME INDEX